Body of Wisdom

Women's Spiritual Power
and How it Serves

Body of
Wisdom

Women's Spiritual Power
and How it Serves

Hilary Hart

BOOKS

Winchester, UK
Washington, USA

First published by O-Books, 2012
O-Books is an imprint of John Hunt Publishing Ltd., Laurel House, Station Approach,
Alresford, Hants, SO24 9JH, UK
office1@jhpbooks.net
www.johnhuntpublishing.com

For distributor details and how to order please visit the 'Ordering' section on our website.

Text copyright: Hilary Hart 2012

ISBN: 978 1 78099 696 7

A CIP catalogue record for this book is available from the British Library.

Author photograph: Dorie Hagler (doriehagler.com)

Design: Stuart Davies

Printed and bound by CPI Group (UK) Ltd, Croydon, CR0 4YY

We operate a distinctive and ethical publishing philosophy in all
areas of our business, from our global network of authors to
production and worldwide distribution.

CONTENTS

Thank You

I am so grateful to all the contributors who offered their time and wisdom for this book, to Sara who was there at the beginning with good ideas and good company, and to Nan, my dear friend and excellent editor, who was always there when I needed her.

Introduction

Women's spiritual power is a missing piece in a world out of balance. Human health, the vitality and regeneration of the earth, the maturity of our worldly systems so they can serve the needs of the whole and not just the few, and our collective spiritual evolution all depend on women living their power as women. Women are not, collectively, doing this yet. In part because so many of us simply don't understand how our power works – how it's different from men's power, how it's activated and strengthened, and how it serves life.

And women who do have a sense of it still often don't trust it. Women's power is so at odds with the workings of our patriarchal world that to live it means going against almost everything that is modeled and expressed and valued outwardly, and internalized as 'good,' 'important' and even 'spiritual.' Many women feel hesitant to live as we are. But there are times when forces are in our favor – like now – to help us discover and create an entirely new territory of power and possibilities.

To enter this new territory, women will need to reclaim aspects of our own nature that lie hidden in our psyches and bodies, which have been denied and desecrated by the society most of us live in. These 'powers' include longing, beauty, our synchronization with the earth, and our capacities to receive, nourish, purify, recognize life's sacredness, know all life as community, and work with the mystery of creative space. These aspects of women's nature may not seem like powers, but the more we live them consciously the more we come to know that they are tremendous forces of sustenance and change. And we will come to see how the world we live in now, which denies these powers, is like a shrinking shadow of what is possible.

How do we reclaim and honor what is natural to us in a world that continually throws up distractions and substitutes? We can trust that just as life needs us to contribute to life as we are, it will show us how. For many women, it is happening already. We feel an unrest and unease with life around us and with how we, as individuals, are living. We feel an emerging and undeniable longing for something radically different. We long for lives that feel more natural.

Women's longing itself is tremendously powerful and will draw to each woman her own opportunities to wake up to what is real and shed what is false. Often, this happens through dreams with their capacity for revelation beyond the restrictions of the intellect or cultural conditioning. And many women are drawn to meet with other women – in circle and in ceremony – where they can feel something deep and true reflected back into their being.

Regardless of how it is happening, this surge of remembrance in women forces an honest reckoning and a removal from the structures – social, spiritual, psychological – that have restricted us from living as ourselves. It includes recognizing that we are part of a dominant cultural paradigm that enshrines primarily masculine values like will power and self-focus as means of achievement, and fails to honor the tremendously powerful aspects of our collective feminine nature, like our attunement to relationships, longing, honoring the earth, and a natural capacity to nourish, all of which serve the community of life more than our personal goals. It shines light on the patriarchal aspects of our spiritual heritage and how our major world religions have been designed by and for men's spiritual development. This heritage includes an emphasis on effort, ascension beyond the earth, mastering of the body and its needs, and exaltation of physical suffering. This approach is generally antithetical to women's natural spirituality, as women do not need to master our bodies, but to explore and honor our bodies and how they serve the whole of life. Women focusing on ascending to transcendent realms risk abandoning the perhaps more important descent into the creative darkness of earth. One of women's greatest spiritual gifts is how we sustain in an ongoing way – not gain knowledge about – the sanctity of life. We do this through love, care and attention, and even sacrifice, not through knowledge or effort.

It takes so much courage to live true to one's nature when one has been denigrated by society for so many centuries. Even when we catch a glimpse, usually in the simplest of moments, we look around and see no place for our experience, no reflection of it and no reverence for it. For women, life so often seems at odds with life – with survival, success, and simply being seen. It's so easy to forget and to compromise ourselves. And at the same time, it's so heartbreaking and destructive.

Contemporary spiritual teachings have emphasized that our 'beingness' is where women's power is. But how can we value our being when the world continuously directs our attention elsewhere? And how do we come to understand that women's being is transformative and creative, not sedentary, constricting, or homebound as patriarchal images might suggest? We need to find the power of our being and honor it as a force of change in our modern world. This takes courage and perseverance – and wisdom.

It is not just the patriarchal structures of our world that keep us veiled; so much of women's nature is essentially hidden. Our light has its roots in the darkness of the unknown. But women can recognize the small glimmers of ourselves that are flashing out of the mystery like fireflies in the night, here one moment and gone the next. And we can do so without losing the darkness that is home – not just a backdrop – to that light. This is a paradox we have to live with as we emerge more and more into the outer world that tends to rely on clarity and direct light to function. It is our challenge to honor a hidden depth that is central to our nature as we step into a spotlight of the currently patriarchal world.

This book is a way for women to gain support and confidence

in what we see and know. It includes information from spiritual teachers, visionaries, and healers about women's esoteric bodies that has not generally been available before, but the heart of this book is women's experiences and dreams. Here we depend most on what rings true in our hearts and our bodies, regardless of any 'information' we glean. This book hopes to be like a circle of women, reflecting and affirming what is real within us.

There is something very powerful in women coming together to honor our nature. Just as when we use our power against ourselves and each other we feel a special violation, so too when we use our power to support each other we create a special harmony. As Sobonfu Somé, elder in the Dagara tribe of West Africa, says: 'The best support for another woman is another woman. But the enemy of a woman is another woman when she doesn't know the value of sisterhood.'

Women's Spiritual Power

The powers described in this book are natural to women. This means they are integrated into our bodies and energy systems, and coordinated with our minds and hearts both. They are how we instinctually live in the world – how we relate, how we trust, how we love, and how we serve. They are not how most women actually live, as most of us have curtailed what is natural in order to survive or thrive in patriarchal society. But because they are natural, they are always with us, like an invitation that is never withdrawn. These powers are not owned exclusively by women. Men can work with beauty; men can know life's sacredness. But women are uniquely connected to them, awake and open to them, and needed by them.

The book focuses on nine particular powers, but there could be more or less. They could be called by other names (and probably have been!). You'll see that they are often inter-changeable and all work together. Can we live our longing disso-ciated from the earth? No, because our longing resides in the cells

4

of our bodies and serves the earth beyond our own individual needs. Can we know real beauty and not know our spiritual nature? No, because beauty is an expression of the divine and speaks to our own divinity. Can we recognize life's sacredness and avoid nourishing others? No. Our conscious awareness of life's sacredness *is* nourishment. Women used to know this to be true. But in this modern world that emphasizes separation and individualism we have forgotten the deeper truth that everything is connected and interdependent; all aspects of life can be seen as a reflection of everything else as well as the whole. This natural sense of oneness and wholeness is a key element in women's wisdom.

Some women will identify with one or two powers and not have a sense of the others. For some, longing might be as natural as breathing. Others might not get it, but will so easily relate to animals and plant spirits that their intuitive ability to care for the earth is always accessible. Another woman will instinctively know the power of her beauty, how it opens life to her and transmits love. Another will understand the power of nourishment, and sense how those around her can flourish through the glow of her being. We all have our divine qualities and our unique gifts.

In this book, these powers are identified as 'spiritual' because they serve important functions spiritually, in a dimension that is embodied in the physical but largely unseen. When a woman lives her power consciously, she finds her place beyond an isolated sense of self in an expanding multidimensional whole. This 'whole' is bigger than you and me and serves more than the needs of any individual, or even humanity alone. It serves the great mystery. It serves the unfolding of life from life. It serves the process of divine revelation – how the depths and expanse of spiritual energies are born into creation in a never-ending evolutionary process.

The possibility for a woman to live in a way that draws her

attention beyond a very restricted sense of 'me' and orients her towards and within an incomprehensible vastness where she can actually *live* is what is here referred to as 'spiritual.' But there are few rules and no dogma in this lived spirituality, just the opportunity for expanding awareness and increased possibilities to live as we are in a world that makes sense to us as women. Because the more we become ourselves, the more all aspects of the world will change. We are that powerful.

Women's spiritual power serves the whole in ways that are distinct from men's. Just as women's bodies serve the continuance of life differently than men's bodies, so does our spiritual nature. As Dr. Guan-Cheng Sun, researcher, Taoist, and Chi Gong teacher, says so clearly: 'Women's bodies are alive! Women's bodies are wise because they are alive in ways men are not!' This simple and totally mysterious fact – that our bodies are unique – points to an important distinction between women and men's spiritual responsibilities within life's systems.

This will sound surprising to some, especially to those whose spiritual orientation focuses them away from the body towards a general, universal, non-gendered reality. But it is a primary theme repeated again and again by the contributors of this book – women provide a distinct spiritual function in life. Llewellyn Vaughan-Lee, Sufi teacher, emphasizes women's ability to 'regenerate the light cells of the earth' – a task men simply cannot do, he says. Aleut elder Ilarion Merculieff explains that women must come together in ceremony or 'nothing new can be born in the world.' Men's job at this time, he says, 'is to support and protect women while they do this work.'

It is time to consider that women's spirituality is distinct. In part, this is because it is time to honor the body. To deny the relevance of our gendered body in spiritual life is part of a worldview that sees the physical and spiritual as separate, and the physical as an illusory shadow of something much more real. For those women who instinctively understand the utter holiness of what our bodies are capable of, this separation – and diminishment – makes no sense.

How could it when what is natural to women has much to do with seeing and working with an indescribable magic that threads through all life regardless of labels like 'physical' or 'spiritual,' or 'ordinary' and 'extraordinary'? This is one of our spiritual gifts – the wholeness that is our nature lived outwardly in life. Women often cannot bear the split between ordinary and spiritual or physical and spiritual because in the smallest little hand or smile we find the entire universe – on a daily basis. We can't sustain a turning away from 'ordinary' life, because we feel how many people depend on us. We know love is not separate from the earth, because when we gestate and breastfeed our children we are both – *at the same time* – love and food. Physical survival is intermixed with spiritual nourishment in an extraordinary oneness that is present in women like a gift.

Many of women's powers are activated naturally and in the body. They are gifts that life gives itself. We purify when we menstruate so we can bear a child, but as this physical purification happens, so too does an energetic clearing. We receive spiritual light into our physical bodies in order that a soul can be born into this world. Our bodies become love and food – the only nourishment needed – for a child in order that he or she may thrive. So many of our powers are so natural that we don't see them as powers. Certainly the world doesn't.

Not only are they not valued as spiritual at the time they are active (who would think that menstruation is a spiritual power?) but women ourselves do not even recognize them as such. These are ordinary functions of our bodies, after all. But spiritual experiences often work in this way – they are given freely and wholly and unconditionally, but it is up to us to catch them with our consciousness, see them for what they are, and lure them into our lives again and again because we love them, long for them, and need to share them. And because those around us need them as well.

Women can understand that our powers and insights are evolutionary requirements, not just in a physical sense, but in a spiritual sense. They are powers that we can reclaim and re-engage for a purpose in an arena beyond the safety of home-life where sometimes they are honored. Too many women understand the power of longing in our personal lives, but fail to stay true to this power in the world of business or politics. Too many mothers remain lost after childrearing, uncertain how to live the power of creative space or nourishment – so present and accessible in birth and childrearing – in a vaster context of world culture, as though there were no place for them in the structures of society.

And there usually isn't. To succeed at work all too often we leave love and care at home. We forgo the power of receptivity and listening in order to express ourselves; we forget wholeness and its power to harmonize in an attempt to break away and get ahead. We objectify the earth – and our own bodies – because most men in our culture do, and we want to be loved and respected by men. Rather than using our natural power to create a new world, we let it go in hopes of finding a safe place in the old.

Much of this is unconscious. We have all too easily internalized patriarchal assumptions and values. We believe that our power to love, to nourish, to purify, and create is best kept in a private sphere of family and friends, inappropriate in politics or business. We have been convinced that our longing is a degraded shadow of some kind of psycho-spiritual detachment and thus a continual impediment to genuine spiritual experience. We do not admit it, but too often we have believed that our bodies – like the earth itself – have little purpose other than to be used for man's needs and projects.

If we didn't believe these aberrations, would we allow the degradation that has gone on for so long and taken us to the brink of ecological disaster? Would we allow our government to value war over health care? Would we allow the crazy greed for money to eclipse so many other opportunities for cultural and human development? Even if we don't fully subscribe to patriarchal ideals, we generally hold what is true and real close to us, unable or unwilling to step out with them, imbued by them, honoring them, enlivening them in all areas of our lives. In either case, we all have suffered from women's complacency.

Women have forgotten that we have access to a tremendous spiritual power, and that what comes so naturally to us is of great spiritual relevance in the world.

The need – and the opportunity – is for women to reclaim and remember that our experience as women *is spiritual*. To live who we are with an increased understanding of how we serve the whole. To trust that our power – when activated – will do most of the work creating opportunities for increased engagement and great change.

This means tapping into those powers themselves with humility from a place of deep need, following them as they reorient us and our collective culture toward serving – not destroying – life. All our powers at work at home and hearth have a place in the world. All our powers that serve physical life have a role in spiritual renewal.

It's not easy to traverse the abyss between personal and impersonal, between local and global, between living what is given and creating new ways to live our gifts. But luckily we have the template inside us for stepping up to this challenge – we just need to activate it.

Women and 'the Feminine'

This book has been written for women who long to uncover their power as women and live in a world that makes sense to them. This longing is taking many forms from irritation and rage at how our governments cannot protect human life to deep despair at the loss of entire species and ecosystems. It manifests in confusion around individual spiritual possibilities that have not been realized despite great efforts, and grief over feeling powerless despite so many gains in socio-political freedoms and opportunities. It is arising through tears of loss, but at the same time if we attune to something subtle and deep we can feel a joy and sweetness – promises of a new world and an intimacy and harmony with life.

The powers described here could be called 'feminine' since by definition the word refers to characteristics of women. But generally this book is about women living the power that is natural to us. It is not about the feminine energies – psychological, archetypal or divine – that are available to everyone regardless of gender. This emphasis on 'women' is intentional. Because while the challenge of knowing and honoring both masculine and feminine qualities is important, it also has a subtle way of keeping men and women both from honoring women.

This is a strange and subtle phenomenon that has to do with a patriarchal power drive that unconsciously strives to abstract qualities and power away from earthly embodiments. The abstraction of 'feminine' power out of actual, living, breathing women easily perpetuates the oppression of women. Historically, this phenomenon was at work during the Middle Ages when the Cult of Mary and the reverence for ideals of feminine spiritual purity gained in popularity, just as the persecution of actual, living women for heresy was at an all-time high.

More subtly, we see this dynamic played out in a psychological context when a man projects his inner feminine nature (anima, according to Carl Jung) onto a woman and in doing so denies the real woman a chance to be known as she is. Any expression of the real woman challenges the anima ideal. This can cause disappointment and then hostility for the man, and in the woman creates confusion, frustration, and often withdrawal. Marilyn Monroe was a cultural target of a collective anima ideal, and she shrunk under its smothering shroud.

The tendency to admire spiritual 'feminine' qualities and forget about actual living, breathing women is also at work in our modern spiritual milieu and its renewed interest in 'the feminine.' We think and believe that 'feminine' power is equally available to men and women both. Today, this trend is in part sustained by an American idealism that emphasizes equal access to all power, which we know in a socio-political context is not actually true. It is a trend supported by a variety of assumptions that are masculine in nature and pervasive in a patriarchal culture – the most obvious being that the body is largely irrelevant or illusory when it comes to spiritual energies.

If we truly acknowledged that the body is relevant spiritually then we must also acknowledge that men and women's bodies – so different from each other – are home to distinct spiritual powers and possibilities.

'It seems like embodiment – a full return to naturalness – is almost here, individually and collectively,' says Pamela Wilson of the non-dual Advaita Vedanta tradition. And so it is. Spiritually, we have been focused on heaven for centuries, largely ignoring the wonders and powers embedded in earth. Coming back down into the earthly body is a stage in development – a stage many of us are approaching tentatively. As we receive awareness of our own embodiment, many of the internalized values of our modern world will dissolve in the new understanding of who we are. New worlds will open to us. New energies both in the earth and in our individual bodies will stir and become active, just as everything that is newly attended to reveals itself anew.

As we descend and awaken into embodiment, doesn't it make sense to explore the possibility that just as our physical bodies are different, so too is our spiritual nature?

This book is such an exploration. It is written for women, many of whom – since we live in a patriarchal culture – have consciously and unconsciously absorbed tools for living our masculine qualities, all the while distancing ourselves from our own nature. 'Know the masculine but stick to the feminine' is the advice of the *Tao Te Ching*. But women know the masculine and its patriarchal aberrations all too well and still lose our footing in the shifting mystery of our own being.

This book was not written for men who long to understand and relate to feminine energy and archetypes, though I think some men might enjoy it. For men, the task of knowing and honoring the many aspects of the feminine is distinct. I believe men who have made that journey to their inner feminine need to guide other men on that same strange and frightening route, and establish for themselves the right relation to the feminine and to women in their own lives. As a woman, I can hardly be a guide in that endeavor.

The delineation between men and women in a spiritual context and the focus here on women should not be understood as a rejection of men or men's power. Dorothy Atalla, who experienced a visitation by the energy beings who call themselves 'the Grandmothers,' delivered just such a message:

> Our emphasis is not to exclude men, but rather it is on the connection that women have with the lineage of the Mother as representatives of her power. Men are here on earth to serve in a different capacity: they embody a different aspect of life on earth, a different quality of energy. But the point we want to stay focused on in this whole commentary is women's embodiment – not men's.

Just as men mustn't feel excluded by this focus on women, women mustn't feel that men are irrelevant. The contributors in this book with the most detailed esoteric information about women's spiritual nature are men. One, Aleut elder Larry (Ilarion) Merculieff, explained that in the patriarchy it will be men who 'open the door' for women to discover and live their power. And this makes sense. In the world they created, men will have to create a doorway out. But it is women who must step through and work to create the world beyond.

Why Now?

For the last thousands of years men have dominated, leading the way (with women's support) in developing most of the aspects of our global culture with masculine ideals, goals, hopes, and values. While this has allowed for great leaps forward in politics and science and technology especially, it has also created a world in which many of our living systems – our own mental and physical health, the health of the earth – have been degraded, compromised, and destroyed. We have lost far too many species, far too many cells in our own brains and bodies, far too many community members, far too many forests. Our water and our food are toxic and of course it follows that our bodies have become toxic too. We have reached a crisis point. The whole of life now needs regeneration and renewal. It needs nourishment and love.

This is largely women's work. We all have to participate, but women's physical bodies, our esoteric bodies and our psyches are especially attuned to healing and regeneration. We live this capacity when we bear children or when we love uncondi-tionally. We live it whenever we are awake to ourselves. We become a way for life to nourish itself. This nourishment includes the physical dimension in ways that are unavailable to men. Just as men cannot gestate a child, they cannot be a vessel for spiritual energy in the way women can.

As women come to recognize and value the powers described in this book, the powers themselves become activated. Longing pulls into creation the love we all need. As we value our need for nourishing relationships, our circle of community widens, creating pathways of love and care that benefit more and more of life around us. Our vision of life's sacredness ignites the sacred essence within life so the cells of the earth can glow with new vibrancy. As we understand how our purifying systems take in and transmute energy, they can be used for greater and greater transmutation. And so on...

These are not theories or concepts, but real possibilities supported by esoteric understanding and women's genuine, lived experience.

There is so much that can happen when women know and honor ourselves and each other. Our world needs this so much – men and women both need it. There can be a balancing and harmony between men and women that has never been realized, a way of working together that heals and supports our collective evolution.

We need to acknowledge that new times call for new attitudes and approaches. This is true in regard to women and our power. In the past, women stayed in the background. We worked behind the scenes. But now something else is called for. We will each wake up to this new call in our own way, but there will be similarities and trends, emphasizing something different from what we are used to. A mother from California had this dream recently as she went back to work as a kindergarten teacher when her own son was old enough for school:

I am starting a new project, and need funds from a bank. I must answer a question – and the question is about how to grow tomato plants. I answer, 'Turn the tomatoes toward the sun and feed them a little.'

But this is not the right answer. Suddenly, it occurs to me to say something about how much pollution there now is. I understand that growing things is harder with this pollution.

Things have changed. What used to help life grow no longer works. Women must readjust as we contribute to what's needed now. What is needed? How do we help? The world we have known has few answers to offer. But we can acknowledge that things are different, and we can step into the unknown. And we can recognize the pollution that is present – a modern impediment that has changed how things grow. For the dreamer, it is important that she consciously acknowledge that things have changed. This is a first step to discovering how to serve life now.

So much is undetermined. But in this, women have a great deal to offer. We have a living instinct to be at home in the darkness and to work with mystery. We can remember how it was long, long ago, before a patriarchal imbalance dominated, and use that remembrance to create the future. We can bear the longing and the unknowing, share our hints and our dreams, create a space where something can be revealed and come together honoring our need to see and be seen.

The time is now.

Chapter 1

Wholeness

The cries of the deer
Joined by the bell's sound
Inquire about my tears
As the sky brightens with dawn.
Lady Nijo[1]

The various aspects of women's power described in this book are like spokes or arms of a wheel, reaching out and drawing in at the same time. When the arms are activated with our attention and reverence, we are given access to our center, that mystical circle whose center is everywhere.

Wholeness is the foundation of women's power. This wholeness embraces the physical ground of our being and does not lose this ground as we expand into infinity through love, creativity or spiritual awareness. When we live our natural power, we are taken into this wholeness at the center of our being where our own heart meets the heart of life.

Wholeness is not unique to women, but it is lived uniquely. Just as women tend toward rootedness in a home, using a home as a base for expansion and as a way to invite others in, and just as women relate through connectedness and value relationships in a psychological context, so too are women attuned to a wholeness that emphasizes connection between others and between our spiritual nature and the earth. We live this wholeness as we give birth, receiving the light of a once-distant soul into the nearness of our bodies, feeding a child from our physical breasts, loving our family as it expands and grows from its home base in our heart, and knowing all life as family.

The more confidence we have in our power as women, the

more we will allow our consciousness to be at ease in wholeness, so it is not fractured at every turn of a reasonable mind. Why is this important? Because our power works with energies and experiences that are whole. As we become more attuned to the wholeness within, we access powers that connect, harmonize, and bring peace.

All the powers of this book spring from wholeness and empower wholeness itself. Individually, they can repair a psyche that is fractured by loneliness and restore relationships with trust and love; lived outwardly they can repair societies destroyed by conflict and empower the earth–human relationship.

A woman's wholeness is reflected in so many ways. In our brains, neurologically, it is seen in how many parts of the brain can be active at once, while in men's brains activity tends to be compartmentalized. In our lives, it can be seen in how we wear so many hats – mother, lawyer, mediator, volunteer, spiritual seeker – without feeling at odds with ourself. Our wholeness is in how we are taken to the brink of death while bearing a child's new life, and here so often find infinite love so close to home.

Psychologically we live wholeness through our ongoing sense of connection and relationship, the foundation of community. In Carol Gilligan's groundbreaking research, presented in her 1982 book *In a Different Voice*, she noted a specific difference between boys and girls in terms of moral and psychological development. Boys develop along a trajectory of autonomy and independence, she found, while girls develop along lines of relationship and care. Early feminist theorists pointed to the importance of same-gender care-giving as a source for women's sense of connection. Being cared for by a woman – the mother – it was suggested, accounted for a girl's sense of sameness and a boy's sense of otherness. But there is more to this nurturing and connectedness of women than conditioning. There is a deep and natural power in women having to do with our spiritual responsibilities in sustaining life, how we stay connected to life in an ongoing way through longing, love, and care.

In a spiritual context, our wholeness is experienced and expressed through the ways we integrate the spiritual search into daily life. One Zen student explained: 'As a mother of four boys, I could not go to retreats. So, I meditated when I could, like in the car after driving with my children. Driving would lull them asleep, and upon arriving at my destination I would sit quietly in the front seat sometimes for ten or twenty minutes before getting everyone out.' And a busy Sufi woman says: 'I can't always meditate, but I have come to see most things in the day as my practice.' These are testimonies of wholeness from women whose lives do not support endless hours alone in seclusion.

As natural as it can be to feel and know the intermingling of spirituality and ordinary life, recount these stories above to a 25-year-old woman just starting a spiritual search and likely she will feel this approach to be not nearly as enticing as a lengthy retreat she wants to sign up for. Most 50-year-old female spiritual seekers understand the patriarchal delusions that this younger woman will have to face in herself. If she does not unravel these ideas that spiritual life is primarily a life of retreat, she will lose connection with her genuine spiritual nature, which so often simply cannot flourish under that sense of compartmentalization or separation.

Women's sense of relatedness and connection is born from a source much deeper than social conditioning. When we feel empathy, when we gravitate toward harmony and cooperation, when we know the embrace of love – this is wholeness coming into our awareness. By definition, wholeness itself has its own agenda beyond our brains and our society. It is a part of life's holiness, alive in all of us, right here with those who can join it, feed the birds with it, plant the garden with it, love another person with it, love the infinite with it. As we honor our connectedness and the many ways wholeness reveals itself to us, we become more conscious with it. This happens in as many ways as there are moments of the day. It emerges in small moments at the computer or during mystical experiences. A woman writes from New York:

> I was getting emails from someone and they were disorganized emails – sort of unclear. I found myself irritated and annoyed. But then, I suddenly realized what a strange miracle it is that this person so far away is sharing something with me, connecting with me, giving something to me. It was sort of a shock. I could be irritated, or I could be in awe of this connection. With that choice – well, suddenly I was aware of this whole other reality of being with her. And it was so subtle but beautiful. I had the feeling I could make this choice in so many ways, to be with or to be distanced. And being with seemed mysterious and new…

Another woman from Connecticut writes:

> One night I was lying in bed when my consciousness seemed to gently leave my head and descend into my body. Suddenly, there was not a focused consciousness (not the normal thinking process at all). But instead, it was like my awareness was sort of pulsating in the body as a whole, and at the same time, there was no limit to me. It was dark and undulating and soothing. It was my being, and yet it was not me. It was all.

Women's attunement to wholeness is critical to how much power we can access. It is a doorway and it is the room we enter, and the hallway we pass through. We generally will not be able to access our individual power or the power within life if we do not accept the invitations we are given into this inner and outer world of connectedness. Once honored, it is present and limitless.

A Woman's Path

This affinity with living wholeness has significant ramifications on our spiritual path. It means a woman does not generally need to focus on formal spiritual practices. She does not have to master her body. Everything she needs is with her and inter-woven with life. She needs to live as herself and help her sense of wholeness grow.

A woman's path is one of expansion, of letting go when things are old or no longer useful. This is largely a matter of trust, perseverance, and surrender, not striving. This expansion of our world to include more, even as we let go of what is no longer useful, happens in many ways. It can happen when children grow up and a woman must orient herself to a very different world beyond the home. It can happen as a love affair ends, or when a job becomes rote and a new way of participating is needed. It happens in any situation of great change. A Sufi mother of two daughters experienced a time of great change during which she had this dream:

> I am standing on my deck, which is normally surrounded by a large redwood forest. Now, however, as far as the eye can see, every single tree has been cut down, from the trees in the forest all the way to the ocean fifteen miles away. It is a devas-tating picture. However, I realize that until this happened, I had been unable to see the ocean because of the trees. Somehow, I can adapt to this shocking situation.

As a woman's circle of life expands, it includes death and destruction. There is so much to let go of. For this woman, the task was endurance and surrender, devotion to her family, teacher and path, and waiting. She had a second dream months later:

> I am with a friend of mine who has a new home. She lives in

Louisiana, and I had spent time in her old home, which was gracious and elegant, just like her. I stand on her deck and see that a tree outside her home has been cut down. What remains is a massive trunk, about one hundred feet in diameter, larger than any tree I have ever seen. The round pieces of the tree have been placed as stepping stones that lead like a path to her new house. I tell her what a wonderful idea it was, to use this ancient tree to create a pathway to her home.

Then I am outside, looking underneath the house because I notice that it doesn't quite touch the ground. Instead, the foundation is raised a few inches, firmly attached to thick steel girders that go deep into the earth. This is a solid house! I then see that the house moves ever so slightly along steel rails, so that it can absorb any shocks from the earth. It can slide only 2–3 inches along this rail, but it is enough to absorb an earthquake or tremor. I say to her, 'You must feel so secure with this new foundation.'

There are paradoxes in this dream that echo how a woman grows and transforms. The tree has been cut down, but it lives on as a pathway to a new home – a new way of living. The new home is detached from the ground, suggesting a new space and independence, but at the same time firmly attached through new girders into the earth – indicating solidity and connection. The new home moves – it can roll with the tremors of the earth – but it's more solid than the last.

For many women, loss and the separation that comes with it can be extremely hard to bear. As birthers and nurturers, our powers to sustain life are right here with us, and we tend toward holding connection and resisting separation. But as in this dream, for a woman attuned to wholeness, life's dying is part of the new expression of life. This is a hard lesson for women but it is key as we grow and serve. We need to learn to let go. In these dreams, the devastation of loss has opened up to new life; the destruction of the forest has opened up to a view of a vast ocean, a new and unimagined vista that was, nonetheless, always present but hidden. The venerable tree that had been felled has become the stepping stones to a new, more flexible way of living.

Healing and Wholeness

Our wholeness is rarely harmed or destroyed, but a psyche fractured from trauma or abuse can repeat patterns of cutting itself off from wholeness through an excessive reliance on reason and rationality, which have a strong linear quality that distracts us from unity. Extreme competition can undermine the feeling quality of wholeness as well. But wholeness is always here. Our collective history of violence and neglect has not harmed our wholeness, but it does mean we have something to heal. We have wounds that keep us from knowing ourselves as whole and trusting our connections within life.

Healing wounds is a requirement for many women. But living our power takes this into account. The more empowered we become, the more is healed. And our healing is the world's healing.

One barrier to living our wholeness is our belief that we are not ready – that we are too wounded to fully contribute or to live our power, that before we can do anything important we must first heal. But this is not how wholeness works. One of its mysteries is that our wholeness is here with us even as we attend to trauma or loss. The idea that we must wait and first be healed before feeling and knowing wholeness is one of the biggest impediments toward living our power.

We need our wholeness to heal. If we think wholeness comes later, nothing happens now.

The 'me first' attitude of our western culture works very effectively with women's general low self-esteem to keep our focus on our own problems and inadequacies, restricting our time and attention to the therapist's office or the next workshop, so that we never step onto a bigger stage where we can live our true relationship to the whole and make a genuine contribution. But usually that bigger stage is right here with us, just waiting. A young pregnant woman from Seattle shared this dream during a university class on the Divine Feminine:

> I believed my niece had been kidnapped, so I broke through a window into the house where I believed she was being held. I could not find her, but her young friend was there, and she was fine. The first room I came upon was beautiful and full of gold coins. They were everywhere, hanging from the walls and the ceiling. I took a handful and threw them out the window so I could use them later. They landed in the mud, sank, and disappeared. Then I began my search in earnest. With each empty room I became more and more angry. The house was like a maze. When I finally came upon the couple I thought had kidnapped my niece, I began to cut them with knives while screaming at them. By the end of my dream, I knew my niece wasn't there, but it wasn't about her anymore; it was about my own rage.

Like many modern women, this dreamer is on a search for a missing girl, for an innocent, feminine aspect of herself that has been kidnapped – hijacked. This search compels her to break into her own psyche – imaged by the house – which contains both her feminine nature and the destructive violence that has been so much a part of her life. She finds a young girl, though not the one she thought she was looking for, and of course she finds a pile of gold coins, symbolizing the purity, value, and wholeness of her true Self.

In order to not distract herself from her search, she throws the coins out the window, thinking she can save them 'for later.' The way the dream ends suggests that perhaps she has not made the best choice. The violence ramps up in desperate rage; meanwhile, the pile of coins has disappeared, and the young girl is left behind.

This is a common theme in women's dreams and it reflects a common reality for many women. Often, the most important step towards healing is the simple turning toward ourself. 'Take one step toward me, and I will take ten toward you' is a Sufi description of God's power similar to the quote in Matthew 7: 'Ask and ye shall receive.' We often do not have as much 'work' to do as we think. But we are so caught in dynamics of inadequacy, searching, revenge, and self-destruction that it is actually more difficult or challenging to simply acknowledge what is *already available to us*.

The gold coins in this dream could have been received, held, and used. They had a purpose, a need they could meet, and a potential. As we activate the powers that are truly essential within us, they come alive and serve our healing and serve the need of the moment. As Elizabeth Frediani, a healer and energy worker who contributed to this book, explains, 'As you move into an expression of power, things that need to be healed will arise.'

The dream above illustrates how our power becomes available *as we need it*. Our own nature is present to us as soon as we turn to it. Everything is contained and given as it is needed. And yet, our psyches do not notice, and the power disappears. Why do we choose to live out patterns and dynamics of rage and revenge instead of living as we truly are?

This is a question all of us need to answer ourselves. But it can be helpful to understand that healing is part of wholeness and vice versa. Healing is served by wholeness and it serves wholeness. All these words – *whole, heal, health,* and *holy* – stem from the Indo-European root *kailo*. Our need to heal draws us into our power and activates it. But these deep powers will not serve revenge. Just as the dream shows, the dreamer who chooses her own agenda over the wholeness that is given loses access to that wholeness.

Women are so in sync with life and love that what serves women serves life. What is authentic to us is authentic to life. But we always have the choice to give ourselves to what is real – or turn from it.

No Journey

Rather than strive to become perfect in order to be of service, a woman's path is more about coming to see and value the ways in which we already serve. This is a constant expansion of consciousness, a remembering of what comes naturally and an honoring of that nature despite all the ways the world degrades it.

Two ancient myths of feminine transformation – the Greek myth of Persephone and the ancient Sumerian myth of Inanna and Erishkegal – help describe the wholeness that is women's nature and our birthright and our way of serving. These myths speak of the dangers of isolation, the meaning of connection, the price of becoming wise, and the expanding wholeness that synchronizes a mature woman with the powers of life on earth.

Many of the powers described in the upcoming chapters are wrapped in these two stories: women's connection to the earth, the creative interdependence of death and life, the role of connection and empathy, and the ability to include darkness and unknowing even as we live in a world of light.

In the myth of Persephone, a young woman leaves the company of other maidens playing in a meadow and, wandering off on her own, becomes fascinated with a narcissus flower. Her isolation and absorption in the flower make her suddenly vulnerable to Hades, who sweeps her down into the underworld to be his bride. Her mother, Demeter, goddess of fertility, is left in great grief and despair, to the degree that she refuses to tend to the earth, so the earth is stricken with drought. In some versions of the myth, it is Hecate, goddess of magic and the crossroads who roams at night flanked by dogs, whose sympathy is responsible for bringing Persephone home. In other tellings, it is the fallow earth (and resulting lack of offerings from people) that finally convinces Zeus to allow Persephone to return. But as many of us know, journeys below never result in a total forgetting of that world, and Persephone – having eaten the fruits of the underworld – is destined to live half the time above and half below. As a result, the world remains infertile for half the year.

In the older Sumerian myth of Inanna, Queen of Heaven and Earth, Inanna, out of respect for the grief of her sister Erishkegal whose husband has died, braves a journey to the underworld over which Erishkegal presides, to attend his funeral rites. But once she is there Erishkegal strips Inanna of all her outer raiments and jewels, hangs her sister on a meat hook and forgets about her. In this myth, it is the empathy of two wailing creatures who had been sent in case Inanna did not return that moves Erishkegal to release her and free her to return to her world above. Here, again, Inanna is not entirely released, but like Persephone must herself return for half the year or find a replacement. Demons from the underworld suggest a number of replacements, all of whom Inanna refuses, because they had mourned her disappearance. It is her husband who is then taken, as he did not mourn Inanna. Then it is her own mourning for her absent husband that leaves the world infertile for half the year. In some versions of this myth, her husband's sister goes in his place, releasing this obligation.

These myths are perhaps two of the oldest and most complex descriptions of female transformation we have available to us and have been interpreted over and over throughout the centuries. They contain mysteries whose meanings are best guessed at. But both describe the depth and reality of a woman's power, her connection to the earth and fertility, and her role as connector between the above and the below. And while the myths emerged from different times and cultures, they describe universal patterns – most notably perhaps the ultimate potential of wholeness that resides in women, which serves to hold together all the seemingly disparate aspects of ourselves, as well as death and life, dark and light, and all that transpires in the above and the below.

The wholeness that is lived in the end of these myths is not easily realized. There is loss, violation, despair, humiliation, and death/unconsciousness to endure. And once realized, the picture is not all sunny, as the cost is half of the year spent in the darkness of the underworld, which leaves the earth barren. Such a journey as theirs, which is the potential journey of every woman, expands one's experience from the familiar world of everyday appearances into the depths of the dark unknown, the world of death, upon which all life is predicated. Once one is initiated into those depths, the greater wholeness is revealed and its life-essence released and life can never be the same. After such a journey, one never returns completely to upper-world normalcy. Seemingly back home, we are strangers amongst those who believe in appearances, belonging more to life itself than to any person, role, work, or dream.

The expansion into the underworld and the integration of that experience into daily life is available to those who are willing to experience the realities of life's losses – deeply – and to allow the ocean of suffering to wash us onto new shores.

This is the ongoing opportunity of our lives. Of course we are taken into this opportunity reluctantly, pushed by events far beyond our control. After years of treatment for stage-four breast cancer a 45-year-old photographer from San Francisco had the following dream:

I was in the hospital being treated for a post breast-surgery infection. I was waking up and in that state between sleep and waking. I heard a woman's voice from my right side say: 'Now are you going to turn towards my secret?'

I turned to her. I then knew that my tumor had not come from outside of me, but I had made it from the inside, and it was made with love.

After years of suffering the ravages her illness has inflicted on her body and her psyche, the dreamer is invited into the bigger meaning of her experience, the wholeness out of which it comes to her and in which she has a part to play. This is one aspect of the 'secret' to which women have natural access – the ground of our power.

In the pain of loss, in the darkest moments of life when we are forgotten by anything we know as 'good' or 'just,' when death reminds us of our utter aloneness and the reality that life as we know it is disappearing, we open to the secrets of feminine power – that nothing comes from the 'outside' for there is no 'outside' in the great round of nature. Life, including suffering and death, emerges from the center. And the center is not other than ourselves, the dream says, and it is not other than love. We are invited in this center more and more deeply as we live the realities of our lives.

Long after this day in the hospital the dreamer says:

After many more years, I had a deeper understanding of the experience I went through. In a very short period and without much recovery time between, I lost everything – job, money, apartment, security, boyfriend, dignity, and friends. Each time something else went, there was the shock of loss and the deepest despair, but eventually I could feel something else inside of me. I found myself resting more solidly in a place that I've come to understand as stillness. When there was nothing, there was still 'me,' not relying on anything outside myself – my one true source of strength.

Then at some point the waves of destruction were over and

it was time to live again. Life is still hard, but now I have a new place to live from. And remarkably, this place of stillness is not just stillness; it is the source of creative life-force and pure joy. This place is the celebration that is at the heart of life. The joy of creation. The place where everything real comes from and my participation is part of this joy.

Out of nothing comes everything. And the only way to the experience is to lose everything that this 'nothing' isn't.

Experiences of loss, death, and great suffering have the potential to open us to this measureless dimension of life's wholeness at the center of our being, and wake us up to joy and humility as we become aware of our smallness in a vast universe of mystery. At the same time that we see how small we are, we wake up to how central we are – literally – at the center of life that is everywhere. How much we matter and how little we matter both. From this strange paradox we can live our lives more authentically and more freely, gaining access to powers that are only available when we allow this strange balance point of humility and full responsibility.

These myths and dreams are not an 'American dream' version of spiritual accomplishment, but stories of how we become human and wake up to ourselves.

Chapter 2

Nourishment

The greatest strength of women lies in their innate motherhood, in
their creative, life-giving power.
And this power can help women to bring about a far more significant
change in society than men could ever accomplish.
Amma[2]

Women give. We care. We nourish. We give on so many levels, consciously and unconsciously. It's so much a part of our nature that we, and others, take it for granted. And as with other qualities so close to us, we often don't understand how nourishment is a spiritual power.

Powers that are natural to women are often so simple and so much a part of life that we don't honor them, and nourishment is no exception. We forget that, like food, it is utterly foundational. But we do know what happens without nourishment. Life falls apart – physically as well as emotionally and spiritually. If we don't take in the nourishment of the earth through food, we die. When we are not nourished emotionally and psychologically, we do not develop as human beings. When we do not receive spiritual nourishment, we cannot expand our capacity to see clearly, to be present or to love. Nourishment sustains life, is needed for life to continue, and it exists on every level of existence.

Women often understand the power of nourishment through withholding. We manipulate others through withholding love, attention, or care – things we know that others need from us. And we withhold nourishment from ourselves in order to create a sense of power and control, as through eating disorders and other forms of self-defense. A woman's power to withhold nourishment is a dark shadow in her personality, effective only for a feeling of instant empowerment but never serving genuine growth.

The power to refuse and withhold is sometimes all the power we think we have in difficult situations, but in part this is because we don't truly connect to and use the capacity to nourish consciously, which can require a great deal of maturity and vulnerability and often depends more on the security of inner trust than on outer circumstances.

As we expand our awareness of nourishment as a power and accept it as a gift and a responsibility, we will also see how nourishment works with other powers like the power of knowing life's sacredness. The expanded vision of life as sacred is nourishing – to us and to those around us, as it changes both how we feel and how we give. We do not withhold from what is sacred; as we start to know life's sacredness, we naturally want to give of ourselves.

Or when we deepen our conscious connectedness to the earth, we uncover our power to nourish and heal – and be healed by – nature. When we value our natural instinct toward community, we help create social systems – from friendships and neighborhood groups to hospitals and schools – that support life, not destroy it. When we live the power to nourish in harmony with our longing, our heart finds its way toward situations where what we truly need and what is needed from us are often synchronized.

This is not wishful thinking or spiritual illusions, but simply how our power works with and depends on other powers within life. But to live this power, we need to move beyond psychological dynamics and step into a deeper wholeness where we participate in life sustaining itself.

With women's power, we are pointed back to this wholeness in life, and nourishment is no exception. The more we understand how the power of nourishment works, the more we can feel nourished and the more we can nourish others. There is a way of balance that does not contribute to the depletion so many women feel as they give and give to others and in so many directions. And it is a way that grounds us in our bodies, as in this wholeness there is no separation between spirit and physical life.

We can touch into this wholeness so that when we give we do not deplete. Life is not a battery that gets drained; it is a forest that takes rain and births plants and absorbs sun and gives oxygen and on and on... This cyclical, rhythmical, re-birthing quality of nature is so essential to women's nature. And the continual inflow and outflow of sustaining power is a key part of it.

Women are blessed in that all of us have the template for this power of nourishment in our bodies – not just our physical but our esoteric, energetic bodies. And this template is naturally activated in particular times of our lives, giving us direct access to a very deep experience and the possibility of conscious awareness of who we really are and how we can live. Most notably, we feel this exceptional capacity to nourish when we gestate a child and breastfeed, when our bodies so mysteriously become food for another, and not just physical food, but spiritual as well.

Sadly, women often move past a stage of early childrearing and breastfeeding as though the gifts of that time were lost forever. But something in this incredible moment of time can still be active later in life – dependent on our awareness and our willingness to see our bodies as the miraculous spiritual vehicles that they are.

The Nourishing Breast

Women's bodies are designed to create and nourish life, and perhaps nowhere is this power so visible as during the gestation and breastfeeding of a child. In our world that has so degraded women and feminine wisdom, it is no wonder that what is so common and so much a part of the physical dimension as giving birth and breastfeeding has never been recognized as spiritually powerful.

But mothers know there is a hidden spiritual aspect to these functions. We know it through immense feelings of love and oneness that overtake us during these times. These experiences are not reflected in religious canon or practice, so they are held as deeply personal experiences without awareness of how they could fit in to a bigger sense of the divine or revelation. A new mother from Seattle described this deeply spiritual and personal aspect of breastfeeding:

I grew up in a fairly religious but not particularly spiritual home. We had a strong sense of our religious identity and morals, but no true connection with G*d or higher power. When I had my first child, however, I was overwhelmed by the bond I felt with my daughter during breastfeeding. It wasn't just the physical connection. Giving life and nourishment to her, and watching her grow over the weeks and months, was miraculous. But what threw me was the emotional response. It was joy, wonder, devotion, and hope rolled into a connection shared only by the two of us.

As with so many mystical experiences, most women have little esoteric knowledge to support the spiritual feeling of these ordinary experiences, and thus keep them close to the chest, unaware of wider implications. But this knowledge does exist, as some people who see into the energy systems of human beings can describe what is happening during these times.

Dr. Guan-Cheng Sun, Chi Gong practitioner, researcher, and founder of Seattle's Institute of Qigong & Internal Alternative Medicine, explains how an energy point in a woman's chest works with the breast to provide spiritual nourishment to a child:

Breastfeeding naturally activates a chakra, an energy point, near a woman's breast, which allows energy to flow with the breast milk to the child. This helps the child grow just as much as the milk itself. This chakra works with the heart. It sustains the child and it also protects the child. It can have a strong purple color, which indicates the energy of the lymphatic system and the spleen. It enhances the lymphatic system of the child.

Breastfeeding is not solely a physical function. It has a spiritual component. The energy from this chakra is spiritual sustenance and light given through the mother to nourish the child. It is this spiritual energy that contributes to the mother/child bond that most women experience as extraordinary and deeply nourishing. The spiritual aspect of this fundamental relationship is usually so great it can overshadow a mother's utter exhaustion and depletion on the physical level.

We can honor this experience and see that it has critical spiritual lessons to teach us about life beyond those early childrearing years. This was the experience of a new mother from northern California:

My experience of breastfeeding showed me something so important. It was like an imprint about how much love and connection there can be when you don't put yourself first – when you're not the center of the world. I never had a picture of myself as a sacrificing person, and it's not really accurate to call it that; it's more that you are just in it.

Breastfeeding is like a template of how women's spiritual power can work. It happens naturally, in service to life. It includes the body completely. It awakens us to oneness and connection and evokes a natural sense of sacrifice and service. All with very little effort (but sometimes a great deal of pain), we are mostly just asked to be present and respond and not withhold.

Sadly, often after a woman has weaned her children she leaves this profound experience behind, as if it has no place beyond the intimacy of childrearing. The grief of the weaning process can be immense, as the very conscious and deeply instinctual experience of unity between mother, child, and creative life-force transitions into a sometimes painful awareness of separation and individuation.

But the capacity of every woman – mother or not – to transmit love through this same chakra in the breast is always present. The chakra can be dormant and unused, or it can be activated. And Dr. Sun assures us that even those with mastectomies or breast augmentation have this potential. 'Sometimes cutting something makes it more sensitive,' he says. 'The body remembers... and this memory is easily activated.'

The activation of this chakra will never be the same experience as nursing a child, but most women do not comprehend that something of this early experience can be part of life after early childrearing. And even fewer understand that it must be.

The Inner Sun

If this chakra is active, a woman constantly emits nourishing light through the breast. This experience does not have to be limited to breastfeeding, Dr. Sun explains:

> If a woman is really vibrant or healthy she has a special light coming from this chakra in the breast. It is a pink light – like a sunrise radiating from the chest. This is not in the heart, but close to it. It is connected to the blood of the heart and to the breast. Heart energy is really red. So, the red combined with this pink can become a beautiful purple. In a healthy woman, it is pure and bright and warm, like the inside of the sun.
>
> In my experience, men's chest energy looks more silvery and white. This is why they are attracted to the sun. They

bring energy in from the head to be drawn into the inner white or moon-like energy.

People think that men are the sun and women are the moon, but it's the opposite!

Often when we think of the nature of feminine power, we focus on the inward and receptive aspects of women's nature. But there is an expressive nourishing spiritual power – creating, giving, sustaining. Just as women receive, reflect, and live hidden in a vast night, we can also nourish like an eternal stream of daylight. This aspect is imaged through the magnificent ancient solar goddesses linked with the sun, like Isis or Sekhmet, the lion-headed goddess in Egypt or the Greek Hestia whose sustaining hearth was not just aflame in private homes but also in the city center, or the Celtic fire goddess, Brigit, who contained 'a lasting goodness that was not hidden.'

Many women know when this light is on – it might not be visible to our ordinary eyes, but we certainly feel it. We know when it is on and when it is off, and those around us do too. We turn it off intentionally, sometimes as a habit of control. We feel it naturally turn on during early childrearing and also lovemaking, when we give ourselves completely to another human being in a wholeness that includes love, spirit, and the physical body all in the same experience.

Becoming more aware of our esoteric energy systems is important, as our awareness can provide a strong basis of trust in our experience. We know we can turn on like the sun, and we can recognize what contributes to our turning off.

Spiritual Bodies

The need for women to sense and trust our bodies as unique vehicles for spiritual energies can't be overstated. We are not just life-givers on a physical level whose job is over once a child is grown. Rather, we are mothers of all life with an ongoing spiritual capacity – *and responsibility* – to nourish life as long as we are capable.

The power to nourish is activated as we honor our bodies as spiritual vehicles. This challenge alone can seem immense. We live in a world that has abused the body in all its forms – human, animal, plant, mineral – and misused and objectified it. Women's bodies are no exception. And our spiritual nature, so intertwined with the body, has similarly been degraded and then forgotten, even by us.

This challenge of reclaiming the spiritual nature of our bodies and the spiritual nature of our most instinctual and natural functions – like breastfeeding – can feel overwhelming. Where do we start? Dr. Sun's information can be a ground, reminding us of what we already know, that how we nourish our children is utterly sacred and that our bodies are uniquely designed to spiritually sustain life. The biggest challenge is simply to stay true to what we know despite how little reflection there is for this wisdom.

The sexualization and objectification of our bodies and particularly our breasts is like a veil that covers our spiritual power. Breastfeeding wakes us up to something else – the miracle of how our spiritual nourishment is absolutely intertwined with our instinctual nature and our bodies. Of course, this primal experience is not honored by our patriarchal society. Breastfeeding is so often seen – especially in American culture – as an embarrassing behavior that should be restricted to private homes. The 2011 outcry over Michelle Obama's support of breastfeeding (children who are breastfed are less likely to be obese) illustrates both our culture's disdain for this mysterious experience as well as breastfeeding's power. For if it were not – subconsciously at least – felt as powerful, why would there be such an outcry?

But it is up to us to not believe what the world reflects back to us and to trust an inner knowing and live this knowing fearlessly.

For most of us, this depends on repairing the split in our psyches between the world of matter and the body and the world of spirit, to reclaim and honor our own bodies and their sacred processes, to see them for what they are – spiritual gifts that can be lived in so many arenas.

A Sufi and mother of three from Switzerland explains her own process of unraveling her capacity to nourish from the psychological dynamics that kept her from living it fully:

I had a lot of spiritual conditioning that told me my feminine nature was worthless, that as a woman I did not really deserve spiritual life – even though my teacher reassured me that it was not true. I slowly became more and more aware of these feelings of being inadequate... I became more aware that I was living out of this deep shame about being a woman and not being worth anything. I saw that I gave to people out of a need to resolve this inner inadequacy. I gave attention to people to feel less ashamed and more worthy. To be and feel confirmed. So I looked after other people. But really, that mother dynamic just kept people feeling childish.

Her insecurity was deep – an ingrained worthlessness perhaps from lifetimes of internal and external prejudice against the earthly realm and the closeness of a woman to the earth. As a mother of three, her life and her path were very much tied to the home and to the physical world, while her teacher lived a life largely of retreat. She had to come to terms with her own way of loving the divine, which unfolded within her own life as a mother and also as a manager at a big corporation. At one point, she had this dream:

I am in a very beautiful, light, archetypal landscape with other beautiful women. It was a very, very long time ago, and it is so beautiful. I am walking with a long-haired woman who looks Native American, but isn't that... and we see a man. He has been a guest in this landscape. He is a genius, an intellectual.

I see that he thinks he is in love with this woman I'm with. But really he wants her sexually. She thinks he loves her clear mind, her clear seeing, and she wants to be with him to show him that she is intellectual too. So she gives him her attention and her body.

I see this mismatch and tell her to let him leave. I'm not sure she really believes me, but he leaves. We remain, discussing this dynamic.

Then I am alone. I have to go through a tunnel in the earth. It is like birth. I really don't like this feeling of the space getting tighter and tighter, but I don't panic. I come up into a space of light. But it is still as though in the ground, like a cave. I had left this place behind thousands of years ago. It is a healing place. It has all these beautiful stones that contain healing essences. The finest essences. I am in awe of how this beautiful fine essence could be held in these rocks – the densest kind of earth. It is so mysterious, so beautiful. This space has been closed under the earth through centuries of warfare and fighting. Closed so nobody would see it. But it is the same space as before.

In the next scene I am with a young woman with a child. Now, the access to this place is open. Now it is available.

This woman's mysterious dream highlights the importance of honoring one's feminine nature, of not letting it be misused by masculine dynamics – inner or outer.

And as this work is done, the dreamer finds herself in a process like birth; she is born deep into a light within the earth. This inner light, a fine essence within stone, is now available and known to her. It is available in her daily life – in the most ordinary situations, as illustrated in the final scene of a mother and child. This is the healing place for her as a woman, the dream says, not in the heavens or some transcendent realm, but in the body of the earth, our own bodies, the matter of our lives. It is as though a split that kept spiritual light out of the densest earthly matter is now gone, and no separation of earth and spirit remains in the woman's psyche or in her being.

This dream came at a time when the dreamer's deep insecurity about being a woman felt resolved. She found a more direct connection to her inner nature, one that honored and valued who she was as a woman. She explains:

> For me, it's about – who are you serving? Now, the way I nurture is different – it does not come from this place of solving my own worthlessness. I am not the mother of the others – I feel responsible for something else. Now, it is more that situations arise and I have to be very conscious and attentive to understand what is being asked of me at that moment.
>
> I can just reflect back to people their own value, as I experience it. For example, there is a woman at work who has her doubts about herself. It is because she is a woman. I can just confirm that she has value – that her ideas are good, that her contributions are good. But this is very natural. I do not feel that I am 'serving' or 'helping.' I am just being myself.
>
> Now, it's not their needs or my needs – it has more to do with what is needed.

Every woman finds her own way to consciously reclaim and restore to her own body and the body of the earth its inherent sacredness, and to free it from psychological dynamics. When the split between the sacred and the physical is healed, a woman understands and honors her body and the body of the earth as a spiritual vehicle. Her love, care, and compassion – 'spiritual' energies – flow into life through her physical presence, and flow into her own consciousness from the web of life.

Within this wholeness women receive tremendous knowing – intuition – directly from the earth, the body of life, uninhibited by detached rationality or doubt. This knowing is free from psychological dynamics, insecurities or personal agendas and serves the cycle of give-and-take modeled in nature.

This is how nourishment and love become free, and are freely given. Released from psychological deficit and the resulting fruitless attempts at self-protection, the power of a woman's breast is activated beyond childrearing. The outpouring of energy from the breast is imaged in so many ancient goddesses of fertility, and particularly in the great sculpture of Astarte, the early Aphrodite, whose breasts pour milk into a bowl to be served to life. This beautiful image reflects the mature, developed and even transpersonal process of breastfeeding beyond the nuclear family. The breasts are activated in service to community, to life, to a living wholeness.

Sitting in the presence of a woman who has repaired the split between spirit and body and whose spiritual consciousness is integrated into her body can be an extraordinary and befuddling experience. Love is felt, but no words are spoken. Nourishment is absorbed, but how? This transmission of energy is often experienced in great saints and teachers of both genders, and yet there can be a distinct quality present in the female teachers that includes the physical, as the great Amma, the hugging saint from India, enacts through her actual hugs.

We know when we are in the presence of this power; we *feel* and *absorb* what is given in a way that includes the body. We are the child at the breast of a divine mother, who loves all her children throughout their entire lives.

Self-nourishment

Women's power is so tied to our bodies that to deny the body its spiritual nature means cutting ourselves off from our power.

Repairing this split by surrendering into and honoring our bodies and our instincts is key. Another important piece is that we take responsibility for nourishing ourselves, thereby maintaining our capacity to nourish others. This is like the maintenance of any kind of system. All systems – living and mechanical – need maintenance and attention. At times we need to use discipline and discrimination to work in ways that help us receive nourishment, fine-tune our nourishing systems, and facilitate our giving.

Many women today are so lost to nourishment – to what really nourishes us and what nourishes others – that we have to start from scratch. This means using our nourishing systems to nourish ourselves and to be honest about what truly sustains and what is just passing pleasure.

For many women, the practice of including ourselves is a stumbling block. Women are conditioned to give, in part because we are recognized as nourishers and thus it is a safe role to play, in part because we are so attuned to the needs of others in our community. But any conditioning inhibits our real power, just as the previously discussed Swiss woman's need to give and give in order to affirm her own worth actually inhibited something deeper.

Dr. Sun sees the prevalence of diseases like multiple sclerosis, fibromyalgia, lupus, and other auto-immune disorders more common to women than men as a sign of how women deplete themselves by giving without including themselves. He notes breast cancer's prevalence as an indicator of our lack of awareness of the power of the breast. The challenge for women, according to Dr. Sun, is to learn to activate our power to nourish – both inwardly and outwardly. And as he says, we have a 'special body' designed just for this purpose.

Women give so much; the depletion can be extreme. But women have a special body – its nature is to nourish a child from the breast. This body structure can also be used to nourish the self and the soul. The revolution is to really bring women to self-empowerment, self-love. Then the nourishment of others never depletes.

In Dr. Sun's Taoist tradition, the key to self-nourishment for women is the use of our reproductive organs for something beyond giving birth to a child: for creating and generating new inner spiritual energy. All aspects of our reproductive system include spiritual power.

The reproductive system has the nature of immortality. For the ordinary human body, the cells and organs, the liver, the heart – everything – work hard to support the reproductive system. The Taoist masters observed that this reproductive energy is amazing.

When a woman gets pregnant, what has been a loss of energy through her menstruation now is reversed. This means she is no longer losing energy. Suddenly, energy is there. When a woman gets pregnant, energy comes in from outer to inward. The uterus shifts from working closely with the large intestine and lung and starts working more with the small intestine and the heart, which helps bring nutrition and energy to the inside of the body. This is done to nourish the child, which is an inner process.

But when childrearing is over, it's possible to use this reproductive energy for internal cultivation. This energy is about creation and synthesis – synthesis and creation. One can do practices and use this immortality, this creative energy, this never-die kind of energy from the reproductive system. Then the body and soul can get regenerated! Refreshed!

If you are not pregnant or if you don't do energetic practices, the energy is available but doing nothing.

Dr. Sun explains that in Taoist thinking and practice, human beings have a duty to procreate. When that responsibility is complete, an individual then can use the body for the cultivation of spirit. A woman, whether she has had children or not, has a unique vehicle for this cultivation, centering on her uterus and her breasts, which work together to nourish both inwardly and outwardly.

The uterus is an internal field and a powerful assembly of energies – they are proactive, creative, and pure. When a female practitioner is able to work successfully with the uterus, it is like the body has a memory of pregnancy and the creative process happens. The physical body starts to shift. The internal organs change quality. Spiritual energy grows and influences the physical.

A woman's body is so beautifully designed. The uterus brings in energy, just like the oceans of the earth. The breasts emit energy outward, just like mountains of the earth. This is a cycle unique to women.

Energy practices in the Taoist tradition honor the organs and their spiritual purpose. Health and vitality are consequences of practice, but the point is to create spiritual energy that can serve.

It is not just about bringing energy in, but about bringing energy in for spiritual purpose – to let it work to cultivate more energy to flow out. For example, the uterus color and breasts color is different. If you bring these two energies together, you create a golden color. This golden light is for body and for spirit. It affects the individual and everyone around.

And within the breast is the capacity to bring the spiritual energy of nourishment from inner to outer, where it can affect 'everyone around.' As Dr. Sun says,

> The function of nourishment is to bring the nourishing consciousness out. The breast is a tool to project milk out to feed a child. After breastfeeding, energetically, it's still the tool to nourish the collective energy field. The breast still serves this function to nourish, but it is now beyond just the child into the collective field.

As a Taoist and Chi Gong teacher, Dr. Sun is trained in Chi Gong as a method to cultivate energy for spiritual purpose. But he acknowledges that there are so many ways available. All religions have spiritual methods from prayer and meditation to selfless service.

But Dr. Sun warns that if the method is too focused on the mind it will miss a key component. Including the body is very important for the development of spiritual energy that can serve human and earth-based life.

> Every religion has its wisdom. But when people don't have the knowledge about the body and how it participates, then the process will not be so effective. To develop your energy system you need the right intention; you need conscious direction. If you think that the important part is the mind, and you don't include the body, then this kind of replenishing and creative energy work does not take place. It just depends on intention and consciousness engineering. The body responds to the direction and the intent.

Energy Exchange

At the heart of the power to nourish is the power of energy exchange. We bring energy in; we give energy out. Like our breath, life enters us and moves through us. We are part of an expansive multidimensional system of energy exchange. The more energy, love, light, or other forms of power we can receive into ourselves, the more we can offer out.

If we move through life unaware of the reality of interdependence and energy exchange, we often do not take care of ourselves the way we should. Dr. Sun sees the effects of this lack of awareness.

Gray light in the chest means a woman is exhausted or polluted. This happens when she spends time with unhealthy people or eats junk food. Even a young healthy woman if she has sex with the wrong person, this chest aura changes immediately. When there is gray energy in the chest, it means unhealthy energy has blended with her own, and her energy is becoming weak. Of course this influences the energy she can emit back into life.

Becoming conscious of energy exchange means we become more responsible for nourishing ourselves not just through formal spiritual practice but through the most basic aspects of life, like maintaining healthy relationships. This sense of relationship includes everything in life from who we make love to, to what we eat and where we spend our time. Spending hours in a bar, for example, can compromise one's energy, as the unguarded darkness – anger, sexual need, despair – that often thrives in bars can be absorbed into our systems. Similarly, the devotion and prayers held by the walls of a church or a temple can also be absorbed.

As we develop our nourishing systems, Dr. Sun recommends becoming more attuned to the environment and also spending more time in nature, which can be very balancing for women.

Because the woman is so receptive and intuitive she can directly relate to nature and in doing so exchange energy with nature. This can be very nourishing to your energy system. If you love your garden, the harmonious life energy there can influence yours. If you tune in to animals, and you relate to a healthy animal with a developed energy system, you can exchange energy and benefit. I see this often in women with strong relationships to animals or nature in general.

The awareness of energy exchange is a critical piece in self-care and honoring the power to nourish. When she became pregnant, the young mother from California shifted her willingness to care for herself. She says, 'It took knowing that what I put in my body was going to have a real effect on another human being to start nourishing myself.'

This is not an uncommon experience. Often we wake up to the critical aspect of self-care only when we see how our own self-care impacts others.

Slowing down can help us become more aware of energy exchange. A young woman who had suffered from eating disorders for years was at a silent meditation retreat that included a formal Zen style of serving and eating food. The slow pace of the food service allowed her to really see what was in her bowl one morning:

I was just holding this small bowl of nine-grain cereal when I could almost see how these grains were part of the earth. The grains were so earthy in my bowl – they looked like plants and I could visualize them in a big, beautiful field. I also under- stood that they would enter my body and I would become them! I would become that same field of grains through bringing these plants inside me. It was such a clear and simple insight. But it changed so much. For many years after, before I ate any food I would repeat 'From the earth, of the earth' as a reminder of how connected I was, and how grateful I was.

One of the most powerful spiritual practices women can engage has to do with food – with eating healthy food and with preparing food with love and reconnecting to how food is grown. The energy of the earth comes into us through eating, and that same energy flows through us to others and to the earth. If we engage with food with more awareness, as in the story of the young Buddhist woman above, we empower our entire nourishing systems.

It is not a coincidence that in a culture dominated by patriarchal values, a Twinkie, which sounds more like a toy than something to eat, is more affordable and easily accessed for most people than organic carrots. It might not be fair to say that women suffer more than men do in a culture of unhealthy food, as we all become sick in such a culture. But the patriarchy, by definition, is always at odds with women's power and in so many ways undermines it. And food systems in a patriarchal society are no exception.

The sense of food as a gateway to spiritual nourishment has been part of the worldview of many cultures, especially indigenous peoples who have not overemphasized the transcendent aspect of the divine but stress the intrinsic sacredness in creation. We hear this divine recognition ringing out from the nearly 3,000-year-old Vedic tradition of the Indian Upanishads, for example, which honored the divine feminine. From the Taittiriya Upanishads:

O wonderful! I am food!
I am a food eater!
I am a fame-maker!
I am the first-born of the world-order,
Earlier than the gods, in the navel of immortality!
Who gives me away, he indeed has aided me!
I, who am food, eat the eater of food!
I have overcome the whole world!
He who knows this, has a brilliantly shining light.

Such is the mystic doctrine.[3]

Hildegard of Bingen, the great 12th-century Benedictine abbess who was not always in favor with church authorities, was also aware of the power of food, as an aspect of the sacred power of nature, which she understood in a way that contemporary spirituality might describe as 'shamanic.' She explains that through eating, the stomach

> ... claims the powers of the creatures it absorbs and then expels so that it can derive nourishment from their juices. God has decreed this to be the way of nature. For there are concealed in all nature – in the animals, birds, and fishes as well as in the plants, flowers and trees – certain hidden mysteries of God which no human being and no other creature can know or feel unless this is granted by God.[4]

For women, a healthy, spiritual relationship to food can be critical. It is a direct link to wholeness, and to the utter sacredness of our most simple, daily needs and gifts. It can unite us with nature, with others, and with the divine. It is a way to be nourished and to nourish, and to embody the truth that these are essentially the same.

The reality of energy exchange compels us to wake up to everything we allow into our bodies as well as to what might be absorbed through our daily habits. Changing how we eat, how and where we spend time, who we make love to, and who we hold close emotionally are all foundational requirements to self-care. If we are not responsible enough to care for ourselves, how can we expect to serve life?

Nourishment and Other Powers

With nourishment, we see how integral women's powers really are to one other. Without the power to receive, the power to nourish cannot exist. We simply cannot give if we don't take in. And the deeper and greater the nourishment we receive, the greater and more sustaining is what we offer.

And we see how women's connection to the earth contributes to our capacity to nourish and be nourished within the earth's life-systems. We find nourishment through eating healthy food, and women have always been the servers of food in the family system. And of course women's physical bodies become food for our newborns.

At its most profound, nourishment is spiritual and the spiritual is nourishment. But this is not a spiritual essence dissociated from life; rather it is found somehow, mysteriously, within even the densest parts of life, as the Swiss dreamer found light in stone.

As we come to know this sacredness in all aspects of life, our capacity to nourish deepens. We do not just serve food, but we serve food with love, and awe at how the earth provides. We play a role in how sacredness itself nourishes life, using women as a vehicle and a thread between the worlds.

We hear this sense of divine sacredness in the poetry and prayers of many women spiritual leaders or those – men and women – with a strong sense of the feminine side of the divine. This is again from Hildegard of Bingen:

Flowing in and out like the breath
The marrow of the hip sweats its essence,
Carrying and strengthening the person.
In just such a manner
The vitality of earth's elements come from the strength of the
    Creator.
It is this vigor that hugs the world:
Warming, moistening, firming, greening.
This is so that all creatures
Might germinate and grow.[5]

The 'vigor that hugs the world' is both divine and fully earthly. This is women's natural understanding. It is within us waiting to be acknowledged. It's at the tip of our memory. It is a vast and unending source of sustenance meant to be inhaled, digested, expressed.

Mother Teresa could love and care for the destitute and diseased of Calcutta because in each human being she saw the divine. 'The dying, the crippled, the mentally ill, the unwanted, the unloved – they are Jesus in disguise,' she said in a 1989 interview.[6] Partaking of the divine love in each encounter, she was able to give tirelessly till the end of her life.

The deep experience of connection and of sharing a sacred essence is integral to the power of nourishment. The more free we become of our prejudices and the inner splits within us that limit our love or keep physical nourishment separate from spiritual renewal, the more we are able to give in to the heart of life, and trust that heartbeat to spread nourishment through the body of life where it is needed.

There are aspects of nourishment – love, peace and joy for example – that are present and alive when we activate the power of community and honor how interdependent all life is. Just as the love we feel for another human being is amplified when we live together and nurture the relationship itself, not just the other person, or as the joy we feel in life is amplified in a relationship to nature, or a loved one, the power of nourishment grows as we grow in relationship to the community around us.

We can see how nourishment works with the power of beauty – how our soul has a place that can only be touched and moved and fed by things that are beautiful. We can sacrifice a great deal for beauty, as many women know, giving up so much in order to find this particular form of sustenance.

One of the most important powers needed to activate and empower nourishment is longing. Longing draws to us what is needed and keeps our heart open and available. When we honor our longing for nourishment – our need to feel loved, our need to give to others and to know where we belong – we open ourselves more and more deeply to the energies within life that can bring us this nourishment and bring us into the depths where meaning waits for us.

For women, our longing to belong and to give and receive nourishment has a role to play in the restructuring of our outer world. We need to feel part of a world that makes sense to us, to live in a way that is in accord with our nature. So much of the patriarchal world goes against our nature. The nourishment we want and need is not readily available – it does not flow through the structures of society in the way that money or material goods do. That doesn't mean it can't.

Women's longing to live in a world in which care, love, healthy food, the honoring of life's sacredness and the beauty of the earth are consciously acknowledged and valued is a force for change. As we wake up to our longing, listen to it, honor it and make the changes it calls on us to make, the world itself changes.

Nourishing the World

Many women do not understand how needed we are. We know how much we are needed in a demanding daily sense by our children and partners and jobs, but sometimes this ongoing demand veils us from a deep reality in the same way that psychological or physical needs can veil present but hidden spiritual needs.

Beyond the often exhausting daily demands put on women, and beyond our defenses against those demands, lies a level of life that needs a kind of nourishment that only women can give, just as only a woman can breastfeed a child. This outflow is activated when we are ourselves, consciously touching into our deepest nature and trusting how it serves the earth and others.

But to give at this level means opening ourselves in the deepest ways. It includes remembering the power of our vulnerability, how a tender heart is more receptive and more available than a heart guarded by anger or defense.

For women, to enter this deeper level of nourishment often includes forgiving men the harm they have done to us – to our bodies and to our shared body of the earth. Each woman faces the task of honestly looking at how we love and nourish and how we withhold. Doing this might include psychological counseling or spiritual practice, but more often it depends on our longing, which splits us open and does away with protective measures very effectively.

There is no rulebook for this challenge. There are just the ongoing yearning to connect more and more deeply to life and the honesty that is required to assess when we are trapped in patterns of withholding. Withholding is not just a defensive posture; it is an act of violence, and we need to acknowledge that when we withhold, we are doing great harm.

Gandhi recognized this truth: 'The principle of ahimsa is hurt by every evil thought, by undue haste, by lying, by hatred, by wishing ill to anybody. It is also violated by our holding on to what the world needs.'[7]

This is so important now, as the world is heaving under the collapse of so many patriarchal systems, and renewal and regeneration depend so much on women's willingness to see where we hold back our power.

A mother of two boys, living in Milan, Italy had the following dream:

This morning I had a vision about women: there were these angry, vindictive women here on earth carrying out revenge scenarios, and then a huge circle of women formed across the planet and the message was that all these centuries women have been the custodians of love, women know love, have love in their hearts and know how to use love, so all these women began unlocking and unleashing love everywhere, in hidden places in nature, the earth, trees, men's hearts, the sky, each other's hearts, and all this anger was coming out of these women like dark smoke and they were remembering their gift.

The world is hungry. It is starving for something that historically has not been given. It is up to every woman to honestly acknowledge what we truly need and what is truly needed from us. When we are honest in this way, we will be able to live our power with trust and with courage, just as Dr. Sun's insights can reassure us of what we sensed all along – women are uniquely created to nourish, life needs our nourishment, and nothing holds us back but ourselves.

Chapter 3

Earth

Friend, this body is a great ocean,
Concealing reefs and sea vaults heaped up with jewels.
Enter its secret rooms and light your own lamp.
Within the body are gardens, rare orchards, peacocks,
the inner Music.
Within the body a lake; in its cool waters, white
swans take their joy.
And within the body, a vast market –
Go there and trade, sell yourself for a profit you can't
spend.
Mira says, her Lord's beauty cannot be measured.
She wants only to live near his feet.
Mirabai[8]

'Women's heart communicates with the heart of the earth,' says Dr. Sun, 'which is our planet's seat of consciousness.' How many of us understand that our hearts are connected to the earth's heart? And that through this connection women speak to the earth in a special language with special meaning?

There are so many ways people describe women's connection to the earth. Dr. Sun's perceptions come from a lifelong Chi Gong practice, which started when he was nine years old in China, and his more than thirty years' experience working with energy and healing in men and women both.

Dr. Sun's observations about women echo what has been expressed throughout the centuries. Sky gods, transcendent gods, deities from 'above' are more often than not masculine and imaged by male names as in the Judeo-Christian tradition (God the Father, who art in Heaven...) or the Lakota (Grandfather

Sky); whereas earth deities tend to be goddesses – goddesses of fertility, nature, and earth (Greek Goddess Gaia, and Grandmother Earth, in Lakota). From the early Sumerian Goddess Inanna to the Zulu Mbaba Mwana Waresa, civilizations throughout the millennia have indicated that the earth resonates more closely with the female form than the male.

Perhaps nothing more clearly indicates our intuitive understanding of the feminine nature of our planet than our tendency to call her 'Mother Nature' or 'Mother Earth.' And the Latin root for 'matter' is the same as for 'mother': *mater*.

These generalities about earth and gender are not absolute. Some men identify more with earth elements, while some women might orient toward the heavenly realms. And yet at the root of many generalities about women's connection to the earth we find specific realities related to our physical and spiritual bodies. Our bodies are in sync with the physical world in ways that men's are not. For example, men do not menstruate. For a woman, menstruation is an undeniable attunement with the planet, which has specific cycles related to a universe of other forces. As we menstruate monthly, women *are earth* in relation to the moon; we are tidal with other earth-elements, like water. How conscious a woman becomes of this attunement, and whether or not she finds meaning in it, does not change the fact of it.

Similarly, while it is not true that every woman is a mother or homemaker, it is the case that women – not men – give birth and are created with physical and esoteric systems designed to feed and attend to children. We not only create a home for children, like the earth; we *are* that home in our bodies and our being. Like the earth, we do not only provide nourishment; we *are* that nourishment. Men cannot breastfeed. There is a deep spiritual and psychological dimension to the physical relevance of this embodied reality.

Women's bodies and the esoteric systems profoundly and inexorably tie us into this physical plane in ways men's don't. Dr.

Sun's observations, for example, that 'women's blood has more iron in it than men's, and the core of the earth is iron,' reflects a connection between women and the physical earth that reverberates through our whole being, both physical and spiritual, for iron is not just a mineral, but a mineral with its own energy and purpose influencing our hidden realm of spirit.

The challenge is to honor the unique features of women's bodies that mimic, accentuate, or create intimate relationships to the body of earth and be curious about their meaning. Historically, most cultures have yet to even look at the material world with the kind of attention needed for this to happen. But some spiritual traditions – including the Taoist tradition of Dr. Sun – hold the mystery of the body in such a way as to reveal the spiritual meaning that is also present.

Women's deep attunement with earth – the synchronization referred to by Dr. Sun – is a potential source of great power in all women. Women's closeness with earth gives us a unique advantage in working with all the energies that come from and are generated by the earth. Witches, who work with the spiritual nature of plants and animals, are traditionally women. 'Women are by nature shamans' is a proverb from the Chuckee people of northeast Asia, reflecting this earth-based power available to women. And in his community, Larry Merculieff, Aleut elder, says 'all the shamans were trained by women.'

In order for women to discover our power, we must honor the earth and our own bodies, which are the earth. The earth's forces come through our bodies. If we fail to see and know that our own bodies are the microcosm of the entire earth, we cut our consciousness off from this vaster power. To work with the earth, we work with our bodies, and working with our bodies is the same as working with earth. This inseparability, this incredibly beautiful oneness, is right here with us. So close, it is in our cells and in our blood.

This living power of earth, flowing through our veins, is

described by a group of beings called the 'Grandmothers,' whose wisdom reminds us of women's natural intimacy with the magic of earth.

Women and the Lineage of the Mother

'The Grandmothers serve the Divine Mother,' explains Dorothy Atalla, author of *Conversations with the Goddess: Encounter at Petra, Place of Power*, a book describing several years of dialog between Dorothy and the Divine Mother whom she refers to as 'the Presence.' When asked to gather new insights for *Body of Wisdom*, Dorothy journeyed through meditation for information about women's power, and she was answered by the Grandmothers, who were willing to contribute to this book.

'The Grandmothers' intention is to serve the planet by restoring the balance of yin and yang,' Dorothy says. 'I'm sure that in these momentous times of change on earth I have not been the first person to communicate with them, and I will not be the last.'

The contribution from the Grandmothers offers a complete re-conceptualization of spiritual power, one that emphasizes the full embodiment of women's power and women's closeness with earth. They describe all women as 'representatives of the lineage of the Mother.' All women – by nature of being women – carry a direct ancestral connection to the divine feminine. They speak to us of a new way of understanding who we are and the power available to us:

We are the Grandmothers. We serve the Divine Mother and the planet at this time in order to bring back the great yin, the Divine Feminine. We wish to plant some seeds in women's consciousness across the world by talking about lineage, bloodlines, and ancestors.

You wonder why we even broach this topic when for most people the idea of lineage, bloodlines, and ancestors seems outdated, elitist and confining. We would agree that the way that lineage, bloodlines, and ancestors have come to be understood is restrictive. And we want to show that this way of understanding is exactly how it should not be.

We speak of women in connection with the lineage of the Mother because women have so long thought of themselves as being in the lineage of the father, by which we mean the lineage of males that their fathers belong to. Even in these modern times girl children are given their father's name as identification of their ancestral heritage. We wish to challenge that old idea of lineage because so many have been born into the lineage of the father and do not even realize the extent to which it has dominated their consciousness.

We are emphasizing the need for woman to discover her yin power, because it is only women who can step forward to challenge and rebalance the excessive power of yang energies on the planet. But women must first discover the power of yin within themselves before they can take on a different kind of mantle of power.

Our emphasis is not to exclude men, but rather it is on the connection that women have with the lineage of the Mother as representatives of her power. Now, do we mean by our reframing of lineage to imply that men should not or will not have power? No, we do not mean that. Let us say briefly that men are here on earth to serve in a different capacity: they embody a different aspect of life on earth, a different quality of energy. But the point we want to stay focused on in this whole commentary is women's embodiment – not men's. We focus on the idea of the lineage of the Mother and women as representatives of her power because we want women to rethink the whole idea of lineage.

The message of the Grandmothers about the nature of women's power begins with an emphasis on the ordinary and the simplest and most embodied aspects of women's life. They start with women's capacity to gestate a child:

> To begin with, we invite you to consider a fact of human life, one that is so much a part of your everyday world that it seems very ordinary: a mother's body is a home for her unborn child: her bloodlines, her own circulatory system, literally feed the child in the womb. Every human on the planet has been literally connected with and sustained in the womb by the bloodlines of a mother.
>
> We are talking about women across the entire world. Women might think of themselves as having the power to give birth to a child, but they do not think of themselves as connected with the Mother's lineage, or as having her power, or as understanding what that power is.

As the Grandmothers tell us, the power of the Mother's lineage is so much a part of women that it is alive in our own blood. This emphasis on real 'blood' undermines the traditional patriarchal understanding of heredity and ancestry as a historical connection taking place through time, and emphasizes the utter and essential presence and availability of the Mother's power as manifesting through life on earth and with earth:

> For many centuries bloodlines were believed to be a carrier of heredity – in particular, heredity from a male ancestral line. In contrast we would submit that the bloodlines of a mother are important because her blood is a carrier of spirit. What do we mean by spirit? We will explain at length. You see the mother's blood carries more than oxygen and nutrients to the unborn child. Blood carries the lineage of the Mother to whom the child belongs – we refer to the Mother who is the primordial mother of all.
>
> You have also heard the phrase 'power of the blood'? This

is more than just a metaphor, for blood carries life-giving nourishment. This is a fact that people take for granted yet without the bloodline of the human mother no one can receive life.

Now what is this life-giving nourishment that a mother's blood carries? It comes from the veins of mother earth. The life-force energy that flows within earth's body is carried by earth's veins. Earth has an energy system that is a giant circulatory system, and it provides nourishment that feeds the whole planet. Every living thing is plugged into this bloodline of the primordial Mother and could not exist without it.

To your eyes blood is a 'physical' substance. Yet there is really no separation between 'physical' and 'non-physical' except in how your eyes see and how your brain interprets what your eyes see. The blood that your eyes see as a physical substance is not separate from the invisible life-force that flows through living things. Your circulatory system and the blood that flows through it are simply an outward expression of your energy system. There is no separation between these visible and invisible systems that are part of you.

Now when we say a mother's blood carries spirit and carries the lineage of the Mother we mean that the human mother's blood flow is at one with the life-force energy flow of the mother body of earth. Blood flow and earth's life-force energy flow are not separate.

We would note also that a mother embodies earth's energy flow in a particular way, because the human female embodies the earth's generative power, the power to give birth to living things. Woman replicates the mysterious female nature of earth's generative power within her own person.

The 'power within her own person,' which is not just in sync with but is *one with* the power of the earth, is a woman's natural power, say the Grandmothers. It is the power to create and sustain life. It is so essential that it is nearly invisible. Yet without this fundamental power, all life would cease. This power arises naturally in girls around the world through their interest in dolls and in the play of mothering, say the Grandmothers.

We wish to talk about girl children who play with their dolls. We would speak to that because we want to stick with everyday life's happenings. Little girls who play mother to their dolls all across the planet are playing out the magic of being female.

A girl's interest in 'making a baby' comes from her pure recognition of magic when she sees it, and from her wish to own that magic. She will see herself as female like her mother and therefore able to have babies, a power she wants to have.

We are pointing to what seems obvious. This is because we want what we are saying to be understood in relation to 'ordinary' life, so that the true dimensions of the Feminine can be seen as it exists in everyday life. And we wish to speak of all of this in relation to what we mean by the ancestors. By ancestors we do not mean godlike beings or goddess-like beings nor do we mean ancestral spirits as they are known and honored in some societies, but rather how from an early age the impulse of the ancestors is at work in a girl child as she becomes aware that her mother gave birth to her and that her own mother also had a mother who gave birth to her, and so on back into the past.

What we are talking about here is the magic that the girl child recognizes in all of this, for we wish to honor her insight that the power to bring forth life is a magical power that is ancestral. As the child recognizes this, her feminine psyche plays out those impulses within her that move toward the birth and nourishment of life, a magic that she sees is part of her very own self, her own natural equipment.

We are talking about a lineage that the girl child has inherited from the primordial Mother. Notice that we are staying with our subject of lineage, bloodlines, and the ancestors of human females in connection with the primordial Mother, for when we talk about the ancestors we mean those 'ordinary' women who are part of the girl child's own family tree.

The Grandmothers link the absence of awareness around women's connection to the lineage of the Mother with humanity's general sense of feeling unnourished, tying together in their own way these two essential powers – connection to earth and nourishment – emphasized in this book:

We are not intending to introduce the idea of a matrilineal succession. What we are wanting to do here is to challenge old ideas about lineage, bloodlines, ancestors, and to reframe them so as to look at these concepts in a different way. Why? Because human beings are cut off from their connection with the lineage of the Mother and they do not honor it, nor do they honor its representatives, ordinary women, flesh and blood women, who embody the Mother's generative power.

Right now humanity feels a great need to be pacified. We do not mean that humanity is behaving like an infant, but rather that there is a great craving for nourishment among people because they are disconnected from their mother earth. Their disconnection robs them of the vitality of lineage, bloodline, and the ancestors, which would feed them.

You see, we have an incarnational problem – for though human beings are born from the Mother, they feel motherless. They do not have a feeling of being connected with their Source. But there is more to this. In the way that your human world, or civilization, has been designed, there is a literal dissociation from Mother Earth. That is why many people 'act crazy' by overconsumption, acquiring things, and by dominating people and nature. These behaviors are not, to use a common phrase, 'natural to human nature' when humanity rests content within its maternal home, within its connection to its maternal home.

Why do we say that human beings are cut off from their connection with the lineage of the Mother and then contradictorily state that women are representatives of the Mother's lineage? We mean that both women and men are cut off from their connection with the lineage of the Mother. We say this because it is not only men but also women who live within these thought-forms – and since these thought-forms exist in dissociation from the primordial Mother, they do not serve either of the sexes. Yet at the same time that women exist within a cultural thought-form, which cuts them off from realization of their connection with the Mother's lineage, they are naturally in that lineage to the extent that they embody her yin power.

The Grandmothers articulate a paradox of women's power – that in this world, which seems so devoid of the feminine, women are still absolutely and completely connected to the Mother. It is rather our forgetting that undermines the manifestation of this yin power through our consciousness and throughout the world. Women are one with the Mother and one with the earth. Women's power is the power of the earth, which is the power of the Mother, regardless of how we honor or live it. The need is not for women to become powerful, but to wake up to the nature of our power.

Esoteric Underpinnings
Dr. Sun echoes the Grandmothers' assertion that women are needed to restore balance to an imbalanced world. The need for more yin energy to balance a yang or patriarchal world is the

need for feminine power in general, but also the need for more women living their power. Collectively, we all can learn to honor the yin aspects in life, but a woman becomes a vehicle for yin in a unique way. Dr. Sun explains: 'A healthy woman becomes like a yin machine. Her energy system continually gives forth universal yin energy. It nourishes, it purifies, it receives. This is the beautiful elegant nature of a healthy woman.'

It is important to note that a 'yin machine', as Dr. Sun calls a healthy woman, is also fully balanced. Her inner balance of yin and yang (feminine and masculine energy) contributes to her work as a transmitter of yin energy. Being a 'yin machine' is not an out-of-balance state of being, but a balanced state that allows a woman to live her essential nature, which, because she is a woman, is feminine. She cannot become a yin machine without exploring, developing and integrating her yang energy. But when this balance is found, she lives as a woman.

This understanding of women as potential 'yin machines' is important to consider. It goes against a western spiritual ethos that suggests – or hopes – that men and women as they become more evolved actually become more and more alike. This often unconscious prejudice for sameness – for equal access to yin and yang energy, for equal power, for equal responsibilities and ways to contribute – is part of a western spiritual mindset that insists that all people have access to all the same resources.

Spiritually, this myth is alive in our western collective beneath many of our assumptions that men and women have equal parts masculine and feminine energy or power. A man cringes when a woman suggests that she has more feminine power, just as a woman protests if a man suggests he has more masculine power. We all have a primal hope for equal access to resources – physically and spiritually.

But beneath this resistance there is something to think about. Women have access to different physical experiences than men. Why not spiritual? In Dr. Sun's Taoism, men and women's creativity works on the physical as well as spiritual levels. A woman therefore accesses and embodies energies and powers that are distinct from a man's.

And many of these powers that are naturally available to and in sync with women are in the earth.

Like the Grandmothers, Dr. Sun sees a woman's connection to the earth as part of her very nature, a nature that is visible to him due to decades of spiritual practice and healing work. Dr. Sun articulates this connection from a variety of viewpoints:

Consider the uterus and the breasts. This is a whole system of receiving through the uterus and emitting through the breasts. This is so much like the earth – like the earth's oceans and mountains. Oceans are great purifiers. What comes into the ocean is made clean (of course, we are becoming out of balance now, and this might not be true for long). The mountains of the earth emit tremendous energies – volcanoes but also ordinary mountains. This system is also women's system. The uterus absorbs energy into the human being, this energy is purified, and the breasts will transmit energy. It's very beautiful.

I also see how women's feet absorb energy from the earth. Energy rises from the earth into a woman through her feet and circulates back down to the earth. For men, it often enters down through and stays in the area of the head. Men are electrical, like the sky. Their energy systems are more electrical – their thoughts more linear, moving linearly as electricity moves along a line. Men's energy fields often reflect this. Lines of thought emanate out of the head area. The brain – the way a man's brain works – creates these lines. The field is ordered, and in front of the head.

For women, her magnetic field is usually less linear. Her field is concentrated at her chest area, or sometimes behind the head. It is magnetized, and working with the magnetism of the heart, and the magnetism of earth. Her field is like dreams. It's not linear. Some women – like Hilary Clinton for example – who have very developed rational aspects also have much yang (masculine) energy, and they have clear ordered lines around the head. But still they do have more magnetic aspects. And some male artists for example will have a more fluid field. But in general, women have less linear consciousness and more fluid non-linear magnetic field.

Dr. Sun understands that women can ignore, undermine, or even degrade their feminine nature. But as women return to themselves, allow and honor what is natural, the yin power returns. This yin nature always includes connection with and awareness of earth, both the earth outside themselves and the earth that is within them. He continues:

When I work with women, I see how easily they are able to sense what is happening in their organs. In Chi Gong, we pay a lot of attention to the organs. The body is the seat of the soul, and the soul is in various organs. At the same time, the organs are the earth. We feel into the organs to know how they are and to heal and bring balance. I see how this is easy for women. They feel their organs quickly, because they are attuned to the earth – the body. For men in Chi Gong, they are more easily attuned to the space in the body – to the energy or the chakras. They don't often feel their organs or hear what the organs are telling them. It takes much more work for men to become synchronized with the earth.

Simple observations from a practiced healer and energy worker ground what the Grandmothers say and echo what many of us intuitively feel, that women's consciousness works differently from men's and one of its principal differences is the way it can communicate and consciously know nearness with the earth.

The collective challenge of bringing a patriarchal world in balance for a healthy future cannot be accomplished without empowered women. As 'yin machines' women empower the universal yin, and provide an embodied vehicle for universal yin in this world.

In other words, women have a particular responsibility to honor and live our connection to the earth as part of a universal balancing process. Men will have their own ways and responsibilities, but women, as potential yin machines, will play a unique role in the rising of yin energy.

As with so many powers, an important task is to sift through the shadowy delusions and behavioral habits that block what is otherwise a natural exchange of energy and intelligence.

The Earth in Shadow

In a patriarchal world, the earth plays second fiddle to the heavens. We see this all around us, from a collective religious focus on heaven after death and the corresponding degradation of the earth, which we feel free to exploit to serve man's purposes, to our government's budgets that fund faraway wars and ignore basic on-the-ground needs like health care, public education, or the support of a healthy food industry. Even the advances in technology that allow us to continually expand and increase connections through the ethers often work to subtly discourage genuinely deep and embodied relationships.

In a world that values heaven and the abstractions it fosters, connection to the earth has kept women in a back seat. In a secular context, this continual conscious and unconscious devaluation has supported the abuse of women's bodies as a subcategory of the abuse of the earth's resources. The objectification of all things earthly contributes to the objectification and sexualization and the use and abuse of women. And women's internalization of these attitudes continually puts us in conflict with our own health and stability – and with our deepest wisdom. We are at war with our bodies and our embodied wisdom on a daily basis, rarely experiencing our true beauty and power and so often experiencing how inadequate we are by patriarchal measures.

Interestingly, we are often struggling to have less body – to be thinner and lighter, as though our very substance itself were fundamentally problematic.

Western medicine has been very slow in recognizing that women's bodies are worthy of special attention. Until very recently our standard medical practice has been based primarily on studies done by men on the male body, ignoring the fact that women's bodies have their own unique systems and that women's health might require different approaches. Fortunately that has begun to change now as the field of women's health continues to grow.

But as a western culture we still have little space for women's wisdom and few ways to honor it. We cannot imagine the power and energy that are lost in this forgetting, the potentials that are continually denied, derailed, or re-directed. The effect of this lack of recognition, which amounts to a profound collective denial, reaches beyond our relationship to our bodies; it goes deep into the energetic systems that connect body and soul, matter and spirit. It affects everything in life, as all life is dependent upon earth as home.

Sadly, as women gain ground in a patriarchal world, we too often lose the ground of ourselves. We create more and more distance between our consciousness and what is natural; we cut the umbilical line between our individual consciousness and its embodied seat in the mystery of planetary life. These themes of elevation and its counterpart – longing to descend and connect – are evident in the dream of a mother from Cape Town:

I am driving a car on a narrow track of shallow water between sand dunes. I arrive at a pristine beach – here, it is not clear where the sand ends and the ocean begins. I have come to find the animals. I get out and lie on the dunes on my stomach. There are wild animals around. They sense our presence and immediately they are gone from the ground and up on a balcony overlooking the sea. It feels like a strange empty building – like a façade. Two bears wave us away. They want nothing to do with us.

Then I am standing on the sand next to a large stainless-steel pole that holds up a platform. A creature walks toward me from where the animals are. This creature is not really an animal – it's a being of some sort. But it's not human. As it approaches, I try to climb the platform, but can't. The being communicates to me that if I want to connect with the animals, the platform has to go, and I have to be completely naked. I see a suitcase on the sand and I understand I have to put all my clothes in it.

In this dream, the animals – the instinctual earth energy she hopes to see and connect with – want nothing to do with her. As she steps toward them, they are suddenly high on a balcony in a strange building. Their retreat likely suggests that somewhere she creates ideas or concepts about these 'animals' and what they offer that end up distancing her from the grounded reality she truly wants. This is extremely easy to do when we try to connect to or find something that has been distant for a long time. We relate to ideas and expectations instead of a living reality.

The dreamer's proximity to a stainless-steel platform is another sign that she resists being on the ground – and grounded – with the animals. But she is given important guidance from a creature that is neither quite human nor animal. We all have within us a place where human and animal connect – a place where animal instinct and unique human consciousness work together. From this part of herself she is given guidance having to do with her own nakedness, her humility, and perhaps also her own body, unclothed and unhidden – finally recognizable to herself. She explains:

> If I want to build a relationship to my instinctual wisdom and to the earth I have to dismantle something hard, cold, and unnatural in myself that elevates me above and takes me up – I sense this has to do with the masculine mind, so over-developed in me through 'higher' education. I need to be truly humble. And I have to be completely vulnerable, let go of all self-protection and conditioning...

This dream takes place in a strange land where the sea meets the shore, a potent juncture, perhaps representing the place in a woman's consciousness where she can be aware of the all-absorbing darkness of instinctual power while remaining awake and grounded enough to guide energies and experiences in and out of this dark realm.

A woman who has uncovered and honors her intimacy with the earth through developing a relationship with nature or through the power within her own body carries a wisdom of infinite mystery and potential. She moves through life with one foot in that ocean, one on the solid land of her ordinary life. This is not just an idea, but a way to live.

But for many of us, as with the dreamer, this way of living is a distant possibility. Three aspects of this dream are critical in the process of remembering and reconnecting to it – the longing to be with the animals, the presence of a guide that knows just what's needed, and a call for humility, the root of which – *humus* – means ground or earth.

Each woman's reconnection to earth and her own nature will take a unique course of reclaiming what has been denigrated or forgotten. It can help to see where this power is being lived unconsciously, so we know how near it is despite how far it seems.

When it comes to earth power, we can see its impact in the tremendous degree of materialism that has taken over our world, unconsciously shackling us to the earth through greed and desperation.

The world at large – and particularly western civilization – is gripped by matter, which pulls us to dominate the earth and consume its resources. But women live out a particular enslavement to materialism, a particularly way that our hopes and dreams tie us through an inescapable intimacy to matter. While the patriarchy dominates and degrades a separate earth, an earth that can be dismissed and denied its sacredness, women strangely imbue the material world with our love and our longing, with a sparkliness that we project into things and then reclaim through purchasing them. In other words, many men in this culture can push away and forget earth, while most women continually recreate ways of trying to remember.

It is an intimacy with materialism that mirrors our potential love affair with the earth itself. We fall in love with a pair of shoes and we so easily put our self-esteem into physical appearance. This particular type of projection into material goods is like a distorted magic that instead of freeing up earth energy in service of healing and growth ties us to it in continual patterns of deficit.

In these dynamics we can so easily see how the shadow side of longing – an emptiness that can feel like depression – cycles with the shadow side of our connection to the earth, compelling us to need more and more of the earth, as though ingesting and buying will help assuage our vulnerabilities and great need, while at the same time we strive to reduce the size and weight of our own personal bodies, heightening our hunger and emptiness.

The patriarchy, and the men and women who participate in it, encourages a domination of the earth that emphasizes its separateness and its objectifiable 'deadness.' But even through our shadow, women imbue the earth with spirit. All our psychic energies have a direct connection to the earth. Women have always been spell-casters. We work with the charms of the body and body of the earth in ways men generally find less natural. Even as we project into a pair of shoes or a new home our loves and our insecurities, we tend to bring earth closer and closer.

Our materialism has its own form of intimacy that we need to recognize in order to transform it into something more healthy. If we care for the earth, if we even consider healing or restoring the earth, this conscious understanding of how even our shadow relates to the energy of the earth is critical.

We will never lose this intimacy that compels our materialism, but we must rescue it from our neurosis and use it to enliven matter, not agitate it. This is where our connection to the earth desperately needs the empowerment that comes with a vision of life's sacredness. When we allow our longing and our need to work with an awareness that all life on earth is alive with light, women really can work our magic, bringing earth closer and closer through reverence, awe, true longing, and love.

This energizing of earth and our own earthiness will release us from another shadow dynamic – inertia – a sense of heaviness and sometimes confusion that keeps women sedentary and unmoving. Inertia is another form of powerlessness that reflects our closeness to earth. It is a mysterious and often debilitating combination of physical, emotional, and mental stagnation that gives a muffled expression to the grief and depression of being earthbound in a world pointed to the heavens.

Inertia can emphasize feelings of victimization. We might feel that we could do more or make changes, but we are lost as to how to move forward. Our own powerlessness feels oppressive, depressing, heavy, and we cannot take a step.

Inertia is an energetic stagnation particularly found in women, and especially women with lots of instinctual power. Women who are highly trained in academia or have a very well-developed intellect and/or sense of personal willpower are often not so susceptible to inertia, which is embedded in the parts of us that are close to earth and to matter, and less dominant when the intellect or spirit element is at the fore. In a world that is so focused on activity and achievement, inertia carries a sense of moral failing that encourages shame and guilt.

Materialism and inertia are two very different faces of the same great mother or *ouroboros* (imaged as a serpent eating its own tail), the primal level of life in which everything is undifferentiated and merged. In this dimension we see no growth or progress; rather, life cycles round and round, like a fertile womb that continues to create new life only to consume and absorb it, never giving birth to something new.

Many of us know this sense of trying to move forward into new territory but repeatedly finding ourselves back on the same old ground. It can be deeply disturbing and frightening, as any hope for progress or advancement dissolves into the realization that we are nowhere and have gained nothing.

A woman in England on the Sufi path remembers a dream about inertia she had when she first met her teacher.

> I dreamt that there was a beautiful golden Palomino horse that was just standing motionless in the corner of a field. There were many large black slugs stuck all over it. It was a shocking image.

Inertia is life energy at odds with life energy, like the *ouroboros* snake eating its tail, or the mother spider eating its mate and/or its young. The slugs of the dream are also part of life, part of the earth, but they keep the horse from running free. How do we remove the slugs from where they don't belong and release the power of the horse?

It can be important to remember that we do not necessarily have to do anything to break free of inertia. 'Doing' sounds easy, but this simplistic, generally masculine tendency often holds little power against the depths of earth energy that enslave us through inertia. It is a patriarchal prejudice that we need to break free of earthboundedness. Rather, the task so often centers around becoming more aware of this inner place that feels heavy and immovable and not in accord with outer standards of time or efficiency. And becoming curious about it, instead of fearful. Part of this waking up is seeing inertia as another way we are close to a deep, unmoving, largely unconscious dimension of life.

The dreamer above remembers her spiritual teacher not suggesting she use discipline or initiating new projects to move through her inertia. Instead she was asked to inquire where in herself she feels this immovability.

So often in a patriarchal culture women reach for traditionally masculine tools for transformation, and this is often the case with our inertia. We think we must 'push through' or force change. But discipline or willpower often has little effectiveness against inertia and even inhibits real transformation. Rather, we can ask: is there is a way to release energies from deep within, already present in this closeness with earth, that can be used from the inside out rather than brought from the outside in?

And what are the energies already present? They are many of the powers described in this book; one of the most relevant here is our longing. When we struggle with inertia, our longing to contribute to life, to live as ourselves, and to be empowered is a source of tremendous energy for change and realization. So is the longing to serve. If we honor our longing to serve life, then we are less likely to use the violence of discipline in order to bring about change. Instead, we work with energies that are with us, and we call energies to us, that can offer guidance.

These are small shifts of our attention with major reverbera-tions as we begin to move into a new worldview in which the earth itself holds tremendous energies for change, and women's closeness to the earth gives us unique access to these energies.

The Restoration of the Earth

Dr. Sun and the Grandmothers both emphasize that women are attuned with earth energies in a way that is unique to us. In a world that has been dominated by the universal yang, it is women as embodiments of yin that will bring life into balance. Part of this work includes the restoration of the earth, which will happen naturally as we live our power, as our power is uniquely connected to the power of the earth.

As we live our own spiritual nature, we come to know and honor the spiritual nature of the earth, and vice versa. The entry point is twofold, and the impacts go both ways. Just as women long to understand our own power, the earth seems to be calling for humanity to recognize its power.

Women's connection to earth gives us a greater responsibility in its spiritual renewal and restoration. As we consider this possibility, it's so important to remember that we might not need to 'do' much. The earth's power is in its life-force, its being. A flower does not try to grow. The power to generate life is not an effort. For women too, our power resides deeply hidden in who we are. Becoming more conscious and reverent towards who we are, how we feel, what moves us and what repels us on the deepest level is as important as anything we can do.

This quality and experience of living with and within earth are emerging more and more into our awareness. Women are hearing this call, which comes to us all in different ways. A woman from Germany had this dream:

> I saw a desert with the most beautiful soil. This is hard to put into words, since it was so drenched in feeling. But this soil was light brown, warm and receptive. I saw two female feet walking on it. The feet were gentle, young and beautiful, and around the left foot was a golden bracelet. There was warm sunlight everywhere and I saw that once a long time ago the light of God came all the way down, penetrated the earth and

then reflected the light back up, so people could remember God through their feet by walking the earth. And women were the ones who knew the secret of this remembrance. I knew that it was waiting to return but that it was not yet time. There was not yet a space in the world.

There is an initial work that needs to be done in individual women and in our general collective of preparing space for a return of divine consciousness – magic and mystery – related to the earth. This is not 'work' in a traditional sense, but a shift of consciousness that can allow space to be present. We will learn more about this in the upcoming chapter about the power of creative space, but it's relevant to know that this space is not in our heads; it is a space within our bodies and the body of life as well, and it will be created through our awareness of earth as a home for the divine, and our awareness of the sanctity of our own bodies.

Women's esoteric physiology gives us a unique responsibility on this planet – one that most of us have forgotten how to use. As we withdraw our energy out of our psychological shadow dynamics and take responsibility for how we have allowed the patriarchy to convince us of our own powerlessness, we can reclaim our most instinctual responsibilities, which have to do with sustaining the spiritual health of the earth. Women are so much part of the earth that we have always held responsibility for its health, and held the potential for its spiritual health as well.

The Naqshbandi Sufi Saint Radha Mohan Lal, known as Bhai Sahib (elder brother), once explained the power of this connection: 'If women became old, the whole creation would disintegrate.'[9]

We can see this disintegration all around us. Not because women have grown old, but because women have forgotten our closeness to the earth. We are not aware of how connected we are to the earth and to all life on this planet, and this unconsciousness denies the earth a main source of nourishment, energy, consciousness, love – all of which flow through a woman's energy system into creation directly. The great desecration of the planet might seem to be caused by our patriarchal systems' systematic raping of the earth and destruction of its resources, and of course this is true, but perhaps a greater force of destruction is women's forgetfulness of our own power and how it heals and sustains earth's living systems.

Today, in a time of such great imbalances, a critical work includes restoring the spiritual health of the earth, and receiving and grounding new spiritual energy as it is given. Why is this women's work? Of course it is the work of all humanity. But women's closeness to the earth gives us the chance and opportunity to respond now. We have the body and the psyche for this work. From Dr. Sun:

> How naturally and easily women connect to the land. And can recognize the spirit of the land and nourish and give it love. And women have a special connection to animals, which makes working with animal spirits much easier. The woman has the right body for this. She can channel the spirit – she can bring the spiritual in and give birth – in earth. Women can do that much better than men. For men, it does not come so naturally; it takes much more training and effort.
>
> If a woman does any spiritual or esoteric practice her body becomes more sensitive even, and her personal mind becomes more synchronized with the mind of the planet.
>
> Women can look around and sense what the land belongs to. Once you can identify – this land is an eagle land, for example – then you can use ritual to help bring that spirit back. You can make an eagle statue or buy one as an invitation and as a sign of respect. You can bring it to the land and invite the eagle spirit to touch it. As time goes by you can see the

spirit in the statue.

Sometimes the land is damaged and it needs an animal spirit to be with it for healing. But to start this healing you must ask: what is needed? What is needed for the eagle to be present? You might need to create a pond or plant a tree or change the land in some way. This all requires communication with the land and the eagle spirit. But women know how to do this. It is a natural sense – it is the simplest power of knowing. A powerful woman just knows. They trust their own bodies to feel what is needed and to know what to do.

It is important to not just keep this an inner acknowledgment only, but to bring spirit all the way down to earth through actions. It's like love – you can have love in your heart, but then in order to make the love become true you have to do something. Our action is like a bridge to make the love become true. This is the power of ritual.

More and more women are living this renewal in their own ways. It's up to us to find rituals or offerings and prayers that make sense and work for us. It can be anything that reminds us of how much we belong to and resonate with the earth.

For some, this kind of relationship to the earth is very natural. A mother from Seattle with a committed Buddhist practice describes how it is for her:

The natural world, fairies, devas, plant spirits – I've lived close to that world my whole life. Everything is animated for me and the spirit world communes with me on a regular basis. It's so basic to me, it's like brushing my teeth. I maintain this conscious relationship through gardening, honoring the spirits of the plants (I use flower remedies when I transplant anything or when there is other plant trauma. I talk to the plants – sing to them – and they offer songs and conversations back – although it's not at all required or even expected).

These days, the guidance is always about doing simple, gentle ceremonies to honor the earth and her waters, like blessing water with mantras from Tara [a female Buddhist deity] and offering to take it to the lake near where we live in Seattle. I call in the six directions daily, I pray for our good earth daily…

What is 'simple' for this woman might not seem so to others. We each find our own way. What's most important is that our attunement to earth not be entirely lost to our collective awareness. Many women live in this way that is natural to us and restorative and sustaining to the earth. We can follow suit and find our own simple gestures and prayers and offerings. As we take such steps, we begin communicating consciously with the heart of the earth – its 'seat of consciousness,' as Dr. Sun calls it. We begin to develop a very real relationship that can create what the German dreamer above says is currently missing – a container for the divine to come into the earth. All relationships are containers. Our commitments to another, our willingness to step beyond our own small needs to respond to someone or something else, a continual building of trust all create inner and outer threads that hold the lifeblood and energy within a relationship. We need to do this important work with the earth.

On the one hand, this is a big task: to reclaim energy lost in psychological shadow, to sense inside for our own genuine relationship to land and earth, to see through our own internalized fear or hatred of our own bodies, and to do all this with genuine longing to participate in the way spiritual life evolves for all of us on and with this planet.

On the other hand, it is so simple, requiring only that we shift our attention to the earth, to ask it what it needs, and to follow through as we would do with any friend in need. It is the asking, the shift of attention and attitude, that ignites the living relationship that already exists between us, waking us to our intimacy, empowering the flow of energy that has been dammed up and misdirected but not lost. We can, as the Grandmothers tell us, know that we are one with the earth and one with the power of the Mother that flows in our blood just as it fuels the earth's energy systems. As we begin to awaken to this oneness, we will find an ecstasy that is life celebrating itself.

A 64-year-old French woman living in northern California recently started a dialog in preparation for a woman's circle focusing on the earth. 'I wanted to learn more,' she explained. 'I wanted to discover the things that are hidden in being a woman. I want to be with what has been hidden.'

She sat down in silence and called out to the earth. She ended up in direct communication with Pachamama, the word used by the Andean people to describe 'Mother Earth,' or 'Mother World.'

The first thing that came to me was that my connection to earth as a woman is through my heartbeat – this great rhythm of ba-boom, ba-boom, ba-boom.

Then, I understood that when I take a breath and it's in my belly and I breathe out, I exchange this breath with everything around me. I connect to earth through my belly.

I became more aware that when I pray and send thoughts out around the world – this is earth wisdom. I am connecting to all life on earth. And there is a spinning to the earth that I can connect with as I dance and spin like Sufi whirlers…

Maybe more than anything, I felt so deeply that the earth is always sending joy and blessings and love – it is her nature – she is an outpouring of blessings all the time to all the universes!

As I move and breathe and live, there is a possibility for receiving all these blessings, to know the joy that is always there. And in her water, there is a cleansing. It is all movement and sound and cleansing and joy! Earth is happy by nature.

During this communication I felt transported. I felt right. I felt in awe. I felt tingling from joy like a child that found a treasure… and totally in sync with the earth's joy – I was saying YES to everything – Yes, Yes, Yes! And thank you, thank you, thank you!

Chapter 4

Purification

It is not menstrual blood per se which disturbs the imagination –
unstanchable as that red flood may be – but rather the albumen in
the blood, the uterine shreds, placental jellyfish of the female sea.
This is the chthonian matrix from which we rose. We have an evolu-
tionary revulsion from slime, our site of biologic origins. Every
month, it is woman's fate to face the abyss of time and being, the
abyss which is herself.
Camille Paglia[10]

Women's spiritual nature is pure and one of its main functions is
purification. This power has to do with how connected we are to
the earth, and how we are charged with the responsibility of
bearing children. In order to have children we must be the earth
itself, able to receive a soul into the world of matter. This requires
the capacity to clear a space so life can begin absolutely anew.

On the physical level we see how women's bodies purify on a
monthly basis, moving out the cells of the uterine walls and
preparing an inner environment for new life. This simple
function – attuned to the relationship between moon and earth –
is crucial for the entire process of human life, and it is a reflection
of a purification capacity that is essential to life's regeneration
even beyond procreation.

Women's power to purify functions with the power of creative
space, clearing out contaminants and creating space so that new
life can emerge. It is a deeply hidden power, since it precedes the
visible. It is the capacity to make sure life can continue anew.
This 'anew' aspect – the possibility of starting from a pure, clean,
or clear space – is central to the power of purification. Without it
life can't grow; it can't evolve. If we cannot start anew, we have

no hope of developing out of the old.

This capacity to create a clear and receptive space in which life can flourish is completely natural to women. The power to purify is linked to our esoteric makeup and the hidden spiritual purpose of our physical bodies, and it operates in ways that include and reach beyond our function as birth-givers. It is manifested both in our bodies – in our bodies' capacity to clear out the space of the uterus for procreation – and in our emotional makeup – in our capacity to take into ourselves negative or toxic energies around us with love and sacrifice to allow others, including humans, plants and animals, to thrive. It extends into all arenas of life.

Unfortunately, ideas about women's spiritual purity have long been used as a tool of oppressive patriarchal systems. The conflation of women's spiritual purity with patriarchal morality and ideas about sexuality remains one of the most destructive and oppressive forces against women and women's power around the world.

This patriarchal imposition has been predominant in most cultures throughout history. A focus on abstract or transcendent spiritual power often undermines the recognition and honoring of embodied spiritual power, and with the power of purity this is especially true. The patriarchy forces individual women to embody purity by disappearing into monotony – behind a veil or behind cookie-cutter images of attractiveness. And when women are truly embodying purity and the power to purify, as when we menstruate, for example, we are characterized as 'dirty' and 'unclean.' Women's purity and power to purify has perhaps more than any other power attracted the patriarchal shadow dynamic of an entire world – a sign of its immense, if largely unconscious, force.

To confuse women's natural purity and capacity to purify with patriarchal ideas about how pure a woman should be in order to serve men or God is a grave error with too many dangerous repercussions to count. But it is a widespread misunderstanding, carried by many women as well as men, and it prevents us from understanding the real nature and purpose of this power. There is a relationship between women and purity and the procreative powers within the body that needs to be uncovered if women are going to live their power more consciously and serve our planetary community.

Purification and the Menses

One of the most obvious aspects of women's power to purify, this capacity to prepare and maintain a clear and receptive space, is reflected on the physical plane in our menses. Hidden beyond cultural prejudices and personal confusion and shame, women's menses is a powerful force on many levels. The function of a woman's uterus on the most basic level is to support new life. But like so many physiological functions, it serves a more hidden function as well – a function that reveals a woman's hidden role in life around her. Dr. Sun describes a hidden purpose of the uterus:

> Like the ocean, the uterus has this amazing ability to bring energy in. That energy is more procreative, more creative, pure. Just like the ocean can absorb so much and break it down, so does the uterus. When a woman is on her period, an energy vacuum is created. It is actually like a vacuum cleaner. It is naturally open; it draws energy in. Energies are then cleaned out, along with the actual physical area.

This simple but profound understanding of menstruation as a physical and energetic purifier has largely been lost to our modern world. But it is still alive in some indigenous traditions. Larry Merculieff, Aleut elder, puts it this way:

> One of the primary purposes of menstruation is to eject bacteria put into women by men during intercourse. But as on

earth, so in heaven; the outer is always a reflection of the inner. In this case, the spiritual mirror to this process is the energetic purification of the individual, community, and environment. One of the sacred things women do over the month is absorb the negative energy of people around them. Menstruation purifies that. Most women are in pain during this time of the month, and this is because we've forgotten how to release the negative energy from the month.

There are tremendously important ramifications to this esoteric reality – for individual women as well as their families and environment. During her period a woman is processing energy and information from her environment through her individual purification system, usually entirely unconsciously and unacknowledged. Dr. Sun agrees that this unconscious taking in of energies is part of the cause of women's emotional disturbances and physical cramps during her period:

Sometimes a female practitioner will come to me and she will be having strong cramps and I will ask, 'Are you aware of being worried about something or someone?' And she will say, 'Yes, my sister is going through a hard time...' and it becomes more clear, more conscious. She will learn that the pain in her body is because her body is being used to help other people. It's a cleaning process. People don't know how much healing work is happening through this process. How many emotions are healed – one's own, or from another person or the family.

The menstrual distress that women so often experience as a problem, part of the 'curse' of our periods, Larry and Dr. Sun see as natural to us, a natural aspect of the capacity of the menses to purify and heal. This healing dimension is so little known that most women have not even imagined it. In some regards, purifications is at once the most obvious and the most hidden of our powers.

If we seriously consider the menses and the capacities it points to, we see it has ramifications for women most couldn't imagine. Understanding how this power works increases a woman's capacity to serve her family and community more consciously – and just as importantly helps her decide *not* to sacrifice herself if she feels inclined not to. Lived in full consciousness, this power to purify is amplified tremendously. Women can decide when and how to use it, and release ourselves both from the inner powerlessness and shame it often evokes in us, and from much of the physical and emotional anguish that comes from unconsciously taking in others' energies.

One way to become more conscious of this power is to watch and feel what is happening in your body and with your emotions during menstruation, and to sense where the cause is, just as Dr. Sun does with his female students. We can do this ourselves. Of course, this means allowing the deep truth that our bodies are spiritual vehicles with many hidden and mysterious processes. In order to consciously acknowledge the power of the menses, we need to acknowledge the spiritual power of the body.

In Taoism, Dr. Sun's spiritual orientation, the physical body and its organs are not just isolated physical parts of an isolated physical body, but are connected both to the physical earth and its seasons and to hidden spiritual aspects related to the earth. This attunement of organs to earth and to the earth's potentials also has consequences for the feelings and emotions a woman experiences during her period. As Dr. Sun describes it:

As the seasons change, the period also changes. In Taoism, every season has a dominant organ. For example, in fall, the lung and large intestine are dominant. If a woman is healing energy during winter, her lung and large intestine will be processing and purifying. And they are associated with grief and sadness. So a woman can feel grief during that time. But if it is summer, when the heart and small intestine are more activated, a woman might feel envious or jealous as she purifies energy through those organs.

We don't have to be Taoists to understand that women's bodies and their functions are part of a much vaster system of interrelationships that thread throughout the physical and spiritual dimensions. How could they not? In many ways, this is intuitive common sense that a veil of patriarchal oppression has distracted us from. As Dr. Sun suggests, we need only to ask ourselves why we feel how we feel, to look around at our environment and recognize how inner experiences are related to outer events. He continues:

> If you do energetic or esoteric practice you become more aware of what you are experiencing. You must ask – 'What is this cramp about, what is this PMS about?' You see it as communication, healing, sacrifice. It could mean lots of things. But once you understand what's going on, you manage the process better. You can bring love to it, or just release the toxins. Once you know this, you have lots of options.

Can we even begin to imagine the possibilities of putting this power to use? What if instead of working unconsciously, we attuned our menses with the power of awareness and of our longing to be of service? Could we consider the power of groups of women coming together with the intent to purify what needs healing on a planet suffering from so much illness and disregard? Dr. Sun confirms that we can apply the power of menstruation to greater healing:

> When you have the capacity you can take advantage and go where healing is needed and use your own body to clean your

environment through your system. If the woman is healthy and has the strength of course she can do that. It depends on where she is developmentally.

Women can be in pain during their period, taking in emotional energy or toxins from the environment and it can be unhelpful. It can make a woman sick or unbalanced. It is when she is conscious of what she is doing that she can really serve and live her power. Sacrifice is tricky. If you sacrifice yourself unconsciously then you are just a victim. But if you are conscious – if you are aware and choose to take in these negative energies in service – this is very, very powerful.

And again, a key component is to understand that the body has significant spiritual powers.

This is the significance of Chi Gong and Taoist practice compared to other religions that focus on the mind or say body is not important. For Taoists, the body is a vehicle. It purifies the spiritual, and it multiplies spiritual bodies. Just as we reproduce human beings, we can reproduce or multiply spiritual systems. This is part of Taoism's sacred internal alchemy. Through energy work, the reproductive organs serve the spiritual function of developing spiritual embryos and beings, increasing the capacity for energy exchange and giving energy back to life.

Women's individual development is not solely a personal issue, but has consequences affecting the entire web of life. The more women become aware of and attuned to our power, the more we can contribute. Our bodies' capacity to purify is one doorway into the multidimensional mystery of women's place in an unfolding world.

This is largely uncharted territory, requiring women to ask within about how we can serve and where we are needed. Once we turn inward with genuine need to understand, we will be shown. One woman from Langley, Washington had this dream after asking about the hidden purpose of her period:

> I enter a dark room or a cave and there are women in an informal circle. I feel like I am a guest here, entering some kind of sacred space, and I feel very alert and respectful. They seem to be like witches, dressed in dark or ceremonial clothes, their faces mostly hidden in this darkness. Most of the women are standing up, but there is a woman who is reclined and withdrawn on a ledge inside the cave area. It is as though she is not well. One of the standing women explains to me that this woman attracts negative energy and thoughts to her and then her body purifies them. I feel moved by this information, and want to say something. I feel like this is impressive and also somewhat dire, since this woman seems weakened or unwell. I say something awkward, like, 'This is so impressive,' and the standing woman looks at me a bit scornfully and says, 'No, it is just what happens naturally; she has no choice.' I stand a bit confused but then understand that this is a simple natural function. Then the woman says to me: 'And of course it is our job to purify her.'
>
> I glimpse how beautiful this system is, that one woman takes in this toxic energy, and then together the circle of women work to care for and purify her. It seems so beautiful, and I stand in awe.

Working with the Invisible

The power to purify is hidden, mostly invisible. To recognize and honor it means not using our normal means of perception, or our usual judgments. Just as menstruation cleans the uterus in a hidden space, purification can't be seen by ordinary eyes. But we can feel it, sense it, trust that it is happening and recognize its impacts when they reveal themselves. The dreamer, above, was shown something that takes place in her own body and perhaps in a shared body of a group of women. She now moves through life with a different awareness, which influences her relationship to everything and everyone around her, particularly during her period. We will all be given hints and signs if we ask for them, and then the task is to stay true to what is revealed.

A powerful story of purification and revelation comes from an organizer of international conferences and retreats focusing on healing conflicts between men and women and between masculine and feminine energies. He tells of a conference some years back in the Midwest that brought together men and women from several advocacy organizations. There were approximately sixteen individuals attending this five-day gathering. He recounts:

At the beginning of the conference we held an evening gathering to introduce everyone. These were professional people committed to deepening their capacity to work together in a particular field. We had been instructed beforehand to bring something meaningful or 'sacred' from our personal home environment for a collective altar. In the opening session as we introduced ourselves, we each showed what we had brought – a stone, picture, talisman, or whatever – and placed it on the altar. Then one woman present declared that she had brought her menstrual blood to the conference, explaining that she brought it because it was sacred.

Now, we were a group of professionals and this was not a new-age or traditional indigenous gathering. We were mostly educated middle-class American white folk. So I can say that this woman's words landed a bit out there for us and we were mostly just sitting in a somewhat stunned silence. She continued to say that her menstrual blood was stored in a special container in the freezer, which I think added to the slight discomfort.

She explained that she'd brought it because it had to do with the sacred mystery of the feminine, which seemed fitting to her since this was a healing conference around the topic of gender. Well, it ended there and other people moved on with their introductions and, honestly, I thought that was the last of it.

Later, during the course of the gathering we were in the midst of a sacred circle when one of the men came forth with a confession concerning his addiction to pornography. This was a very intense and deeply personal revelation, and he spoke about wanting to be free of his addiction. He brought out some magazines, which amplified an already very heavy atmosphere, as pornography can bring up a lot for men and women both. This was not particularly the focus of our workshops, and I did not feel entirely prepared for this. The feeling in the group was heavy and intense.

Then another man came out with his own involvement with pornography, and a few more pictures came forth. So, suddenly we were plunged into a very deep conversation about pornography and its impacts in people's lives. And of course pornography had, in one way or another, affected all of us.

Now, this topic of pornography was not totally welcomed. Not everyone wanted to deal with it, especially in mixed company. But what could we do? It had come out on the table and we really could not just move on. This was the challenge at least two of the men wanted to address. It was as if they had opened a giant invisible gate of some kind in the group and we all passed through.

During the next three days, this group moved into a deep level of processing around pornography and all that it entails. We were six or seven men, and ten or so women. In this process was a great deal of extreme discomfort and pain held by the women regarding being objectified through sexualized images of pornography, and the personal pain of feeling they had to compete with such images in their own lives with their partners. To really address the desecration, the sleaze, the eroticism in these magazines made us all uncomfortable. There were many tears.

The group went so deep. We worked with various forms of healing, including breath-work, and a great deal of grief and rage emerged. The two men were absolutely honest, raw, and vulnerable in their sharing. Just as the women felt tremendous sadness and anger, so did the men, as we were coming to terms with the ways that we ourselves had been conditioned around sexuality and masculinity in our western society. I can say that in the workshops I had experienced prior to this one, there had never been the depth and rawness and level of truth-telling that I was experiencing here.

Toward the end of the gathering we began crafting the concluding celebration, forming a way to recognize that we had all been through something profound and unique. In the course of planning the final day, two men made a declaration that they were through with pornography. They were swearing off it forever.

The idea emerged to use the magazines in the final ritual and to bury them in the earth. And someone made the suggestion to include the menstrual blood – which everyone had pretty much forgotten about but which was still sitting in the freezer. The ritual began to take shape – we would shred the magazines, 'anoint' each page with menstrual blood to somehow purify that image and its energy, and bury them in the earth as a primal offering.

So on the final evening we gathered in a circle and spoke an invocation, and then we brought out the magazines and the whole community ceremoniously tore out every page of the magazines. We did this in a powerful field of shared prayerful intention, men and women sitting together, and we sent healing thoughts and energies to each of the women (and men) in the pictures, and to all those who had been involved in creating these pictures, and to every person who had ever gazed upon these pictures for their own pleasure. Each of us had a small vial of the menstrual blood by our side, and with each page and each picture of naked women (and men) we dipped our finger into the jar and anointed the page with a drop of sacred blood. Then placed all the pages in a pile, and carried the pile outside where we buried it.

We didn't burn it. We had the feeling that burying it would be transformative, would return the detritus, the feces of a pathologized sexuality, back to the mother to be transmuted into a rebirth of a healthy sacred erotic communion between masculine and feminine.

The menstrual blood played this key role. It was the energy and life-force of the sacred feminine that would seed the healing. It would be in there with the rotted, erotic, and buried. We were planting the seed and then the porn would be the fertilizer. The blood would help grow the new healthy sacred erotic sexual union.

We ended that gathering with dancing around the fire. There was such a free sense of communion between men and women – an abandon of inhibition. Just connection. And deep reverence. Tears of radiant joy. It was as though the men and women were living archetypes or manifestations of male and female deities, representing a purified and powerful masculine and feminine. This freedom and celebration and deep healing were made possible by what had been shared. And the blood – what we had felt at first was bizarre and confusing – was understood absolutely as the way to close and consecrate the work of the five days.

None of us present could have imagined how this workshop was going to progress. It was totally beyond what we could have imagined. We were normal people, professional and hardworking westerners with not a lot of awareness of the forces of transformation and purification that had been evoked and released during those days. We were all changed by this remarkable experience.

One of the most important tasks for women at this point in time is to understand that our deeply personal bodily functions – many of which we feel ashamed of or confused by – have a role in outer-world healing and change. This is true with the power to purify, which is activated naturally through menstruation, and also through women's sexuality.

Pure... like the Earth

The spiritual understanding of women's power to purify and its origins is not limited to Taoism. In a lineage of Naqshbandi Sufism currently represented by Llewellyn Vaughan-Lee, we find a unique understanding of women's purity and its individual and collective potentials. The Naqshbandi Sufi Saint Bhai Sahib described women's purity to his disciple, Irina Tweedie, in India in the mid-1960s. Like Dr. Sun, he links woman's purifying power to the power of the earth:

> Woman is like Gold, she is like the Earth, she is never impure... Gold, even if it falls into the latrine and is taken out and is cleaned, it is the same, and its value is not less. The Earth purifies everything... the Earth is always pure and the woman after every menstruation is pure. So, they say, the Gold is pure, the Earth is pure, but the woman is impure... how ignorant they are...[11]

We need a reframing of the power to purify that points to a purity that is already present but not used. How do we use it? We consciously attune to its presence and allow it to be activated naturally. Just as when we menstruate we can become more conscious of how our bodies *naturally* take in and purify energy, and in doing so heighten and direct this power, so too can we become more conscious of how our pure connection to creation can naturally be activated through sexuality. Llewellyn Vaughan-Lee identifies an esoteric element:

> There is a substance within a woman's body and within her spiritual centers that is innate and belongs to her feminine nature. This has to do with her creative nature and is thus related to her sexuality. This is Virya Shakti, the Creative Energy of God.

Bhai Sahib explained to Tweedie:

> On the lowest plane of manifestation it [Virya Shakti] appears as seminal fluid in men; in women it is preserved in the Chakras.
>
> The more sex power the human being has, the easier he will reach God or Truth... Great sex power is a great help in spiritual life.[12]

We generally do not think that a woman's spiritual power is tied to her sexuality – quite the opposite in fact. In our patriarchal world, a spiritual woman is a chaste virgin. The more spiritual she becomes, the less sexual she becomes and vice versa. But there are other spiritual teachings that see sexual energy as creative, spiritual power. And for a woman, this energy is related to a pure and direct connection to creation. Llewellyn further describes these connections:

> A woman's sexuality and spirituality are both part of the sacred nature of creation. This pure substance within her is part of the purity of the earth. This substance is alive... It is a primal creative energy. When women are consciously aware of

this quality within themselves and how it is connected to the earth and creation, she infuses a sacred light into the earth – of course this used to be a central part of the spiritual work of many priestesses.

Through sacred sexuality, the pure substance in women can be given to men. There is a way that a woman can take a man into herself, not just physically but energetically, even spiritually. And in this sacred space that is created through this physical and spiritual intimacy she can share with him (if he is receptive) the sacred substance that belongs to sexuality. Mostly this is done instinctually – there is a deep and ancient knowing in woman about how this works. But certain women can make this conscious, can make a conscious offering of themselves. Of course in such a meeting the woman must want nothing for herself – which is why for temple prostitutes the partner was always a stranger.

From the very distant Aleut tradition of Larry Merculieff, we hear a similar description of women's sexual power and how it serves to transform and rebirth:

There's a sacred understanding that teaches that men can only be reborn by going back into the womb. The womb birthed us, but we need to complete the circle and be re-birthed through the womb.

Through enlightened sexuality, the man dissolves into women's energy field and is re-birthed physically and spiritually. This is the process of sex, death, and rebirth. If a man allows himself to dissolve into a woman he loves, in an act of total surrender and love, in that sacred field identical to the field at the center of the universe, he is transformed. This requires complete surrender of ego into the formless mystery we call love. Only then can the magic, the transformation, occur.

But a woman must be equally surrendered and open. What the man can bring through that union is a field of energy that helps the woman to open up. The opening up is not one-way, but it is essential for the woman to open up for spiritual transformation for both of them.

This discussion above about women and men is not meant to limit an understanding of sexuality. The Aleut tradition, Larry says, recognizes lesbian sexuality as well:

Gay women traditionally are called Twin Spirits or Two Spirited, containing both the masculine and feminine. In the spiritual sense, those born as Two Spirited have the ability to transform duality into oneness, where each aspect of duality works together to make the whole.

A woman's sacred energy field is always present, and while it can be activated during enlightened sexuality, Larry explains that, 'The main way of activation is through group ceremony.' We will learn more about women and ceremony in upcoming chapters, but it is important to understand here that we have forgotten how sexuality is a powerful vehicle of transmission between woman and man, and between spirit world and earth, and between woman and the whole of life.

Llewellyn explains that for a man, such lovemaking can be like finding 'a river in a parched land:'

I was once told by a wise woman, 'Man discovers himself through woman.' Making love to a woman can connect men more easily with their own real self, with life, with abundance, with joy, with wonder, with magic, with the mystery of creation.

The widespread, global pattern of persecuting women for our

sexuality, of shaming and degrading women and limiting our sexual expression, is a tool for spiritual oppression as much as a tool for physical and psychological oppression. It restricts women's spiritual growth and it denies men the opportunity for transformation through lovemaking. Sexuality is one of the most potent and direct ways we exchange energy – nourishment, love, consciousness – with the divine and with life. Cut off from our sexuality, women are cut off from this vehicle of exchange, as is life itself.

We tend to think of purification as work – like cleaning – not as a natural function. But women's spiritual nature is pure and has power to purify and renew. This takes place in the womb during menstruation and it takes place as part of 'enlightened sexuality' during which a man can actually dissolve into a woman's energy field and be spiritually reborn.

The sacred nature of sexuality has been forgotten by most women, and we have lost awareness of how our sexual power impacts life around us. The experience of sexuality as spiritual is not just an ideal but something that can be lived if we are connected to ourselves. A mother from California describes the experience of the divine while making love to her husband:

> Sometimes when I make love I know the divine is present. I do know that when the tenderness of a divine She is present, my husband's heart is touched. I just know that. She loves him very much and there is such tenderness in the heart. The man feels it back and responds with his heart. It really is beyond sex.
>
> My experience of sex is about being and sharing. I know traditionally or logically, the woman 'receives' and physically she does receive the sperm. Traditionally, the feminine longs and the masculine says, 'I love you.' But if you ask me, She loves him so much! And the man receives so much! They never know how much! Just that a woman allows a man to be

with her, wow, is he lucky to experience her – the earth. There's something real in her body that he doesn't have access to somehow in his own body by himself. It's there as it's always been there, but with time and history, it has been denigrated.

A woman who knows her value especially has something to give. In some ways this giving during lovemaking can happen because a woman is living who she is and what she longs to really do…

Understanding and valuing our sexuality for what it is, remembering its essential purity and power to purify and renew, empowers us and empowers life around us. Women have a direct link to creation, activated especially when our bodies are in sync with our consciousness and even more potently when they are in sync with our intentions to love, serve, receive, and nourish. To acknowledge and honor a closeness to life means to take responsibility for this closeness – attuning to what can be given and received through it.

Living our purity means valuing the depths of our being – of being-ness itself. This is the realm of women. It is the realm of the womb and of sexuality and of instinct and direct intuition. It is the knowing in our hearts and our gut that defies all reason. Llewellyn continues:

We are all part of the instinctual world, but generally only women can have conscious access to it. I think what is called 'feminine intuition' comes from this connection. Of course there used to be feminine initiations and trainings that enabled women to work consciously with the energy in this dimension, which is in some ways the energy of creation. This can be considered a natural magic, but one also thinks of the healing power of herbs, etc…, which a man would need a shamanic training to access, but a woman has more natural access to. Today most women are cut off from this energy and power, because our culture has focused on the light of consciousness rather than the darkness of the instinctual world, but some women retain a memory and understanding of this darkness, its power and wisdom.

Throughout this book the hints and the signposts are often so much the same – pointing both within to an energy flow of the body that is attuned to the rhythms of the earth, and pointing beyond any need for approval or success in a patriarchal system. The women who have reconnected with their instinctual power have gone beyond the limits of ordinary-world success, whether they have been taken there through loss and suffering into the depths of their being and reborn through touching into their creative power, or through physical illness and pain that draw their attention into the marrow of their life-body.

The journey of these women echoes the journey of those who travel to the underworld like Inanna and Persephone, who lose touch with the light of upper-world living to fulfill a deeper calling and to step into a vaster wholeness that always includes darkness – not just the darkness of human suffering but the darkness of the inner realms where no sunlight reaches.

The knowing here is the lamp of Hecate, the eyes of the owl, the glow of the moon, a luminous knowing that does not shine like a beam of light but emanates in waves of love and listening.

Body of Wisdom

The journey into the instinctual world is mythic in the sense that it is an archetypal imprint deep in every human being that has the possibility of being lived consciously in any point in time. This journey of consciousness, which is a descent into embodied humanity and an awakening into the mysteries of how the body and the spirit work together, is possible for all of us through many trials at the foundation of human life – like our struggles to conquer addictions or simply eat healthy food, to bear and nourish children, to keep our bodies safe from harm, and to acknowledge and respect our own beauty even if others do not see it. These are simple and ongoing struggles that we must attend to throughout our lives. For women, a key step is always to honor the body, attend to it, live within it, and know it as a miracle.

Today, when women are more cut off from their bodies than ever, we make this journey often through serious illnesses like cancer or auto-immune diseases, which leave us with one foot in the underworld, one eye at the keyhole of healing's mystery, one ear always listening for death's footsteps. The journey includes facing our own mortality and the ways we have not cared for our bodies or refused our bodies their sacredness. This process can happen often through facing – outwardly – a medical profession that itself takes the spirit out of healing and ignores the feeling essence of the physical.

A sculptor from San Francisco faced breast cancer and the many ways it challenged her to know and honor – and fight for – her body in a world that objectified it. From struggling with the grief of not being able to have children due to early menopause brought on by treatment, to the indignities of having tattoos on her breasts to mark treatment areas, she was called again and again to honor the emotional and spiritual aspects of her physical life in a world that seemed not to care. She explains what it was like to struggle through cancer in an uncaring environment:

The mechanics of breast cancer treatment just don't allow room for grief around what comes with treatment, including the loss of one's menstrual cycle, and the disturbing ways the body is treated.

When I went through radiation I was informed during my assimilation appointment that I was going to be tattooed so that the therapists could measure me most accurately each treatment. When I protested and asked to explore an alternative that would create a semi-permanent mark they wouldn't listen and tried to convince me to get tattooed. Not one of them could hear that I did not want to live with these marks as reminders of this experience. I already have two scars as mementos. I was shocked at how little attention is paid to the defilement of the body as one goes through this.

The outer world gives us opportunities to see and face our own inner barriers and prejudices. This woman's journey struggling against an objectifying culture allowed her to become more and more grounded in the wholeness of her being through honoring and protecting her body. In this instance, she was driven to innovate a more respectful alternative than the permanent markings that were being pushed upon her. She suggested technicians use henna as a way of marking the body so that it was not permanent. Her idea was implemented. 'Now they have an alternative,' she says, about all the women who will come after her through this difficult process.

This woman's attunement to her own body and willingness to honor it was a key ingredient in the purification of a toxic combination of unconscious thoughts and actions that perpetuated the objectification of what should be revered, and transformed the future experiences of other women.

The purification process includes the energetic clearing of toxic, old, or no longer useful material – physical and spiritual both – from the human being and the environment. This purification happens naturally and freely on the physical level but it also happens with greater ramifications when we are consciously involved, as when we struggle through life-threatening illness, and we allow ourselves to be taken through shame, disregard, and even violence into the areas that are hidden and unacknowledged. It is like cleaning out a closet where we have stored all our old junk. Today, the physical world and our own bodies have become this closet, the long-ignored repository of many of the fears that we don't want to face.

Today, our collective human community is being drawn into this purification process as we face the diseases we've brought to the earth, and as the earth energies shake off what is not needed. In many indigenous cultures, the earthquakes and other natural disasters we experience today with alarming frequency are seen as part of this larger purification process that brings our attention right back to our earthly life and our dependence upon earth's resources for the continuance of life. This larger purification process is not dissimilar to what happens in women's bodies monthly or what happens through healing of individual disease. It is a process of embodiment, coming into the earth, recognizing the spiritual nature of earthly life, its utter sacredness, and aligning with this sacredness against all that would degrade it.

This purification is paving the way for a new body of wisdom that is coming to consciousness, a body of wisdom that includes conscious acknowledgment of wholeness and the integration of spirit and matter. How we are part of this process is particular to each of us. But here women have a key role, as we are embodied in ways that include and depend upon purification. We are 'pure,' as Bhai Sahib said, closer to nature, to earth, to life-force as it moves within matter. This position means that our consciousness has a unique role in the purification process, a way of contributing that is direct and potent.

It is for each of us to honor this power to purify, to recognize its role in the changes taking place in our personal lives and in our collective planetary life. But we are becoming more aware of general ground rules. These include honoring embodiment, trusting our physical dimension as the seat of spiritual mystery, and allowing ourselves to follow our longing into this mystery and wholeness – which is the only place to discover the hidden realities of our human-ness and our place in the whole of life.

Chapter 5

Beauty

Homage to the Female Buddha beautiful with youth
Who sits on seats of white lotus and moon in nature
Spreading with stainless compassion and knowledge,
Who captures the radiance of snow mountains...

Homage to she whose face unites
The beauty of a million autumn moons,
Whose wide eyes gaze with compassion
Whose Joyous mouth smiles equally on all...

Homage to she of celestial raiment,
Whose shoulder-sash and skirt
Hug her body like rainbows
Hug the crystal mountains.
The first Dalai Lama (1391–1474)[13]

There is a beauty that makes the heart ache. A beauty that transforms and inspires, that brings us closer and closer... to what? To
a lover, to our selves, to nature, to the essence of life, to the
divine – it does not really matter. To some degree it is the
closeness that matters most and everything that is alive within
that closeness – the expansiveness, vulnerability, intimacy, and
tender belonging that are so often awakened by a genuine
encounter with beauty.

Like the power to purify, the power of beauty has to do with
women's closeness to creation. Through beauty, this pure
connection between earth and spirit is evident, for beauty shines
when spirit is clearly visible within form. It is a different aspect
of the same essential feminine power to unite the divine with the

material world.

A new mother in California illustrates this relationship between beauty and the union of spirit and form through her surprising first words to her newborn son, who was put into her arms after a lengthy birth: 'When I saw him for the first time, all I could do was laugh and cry and say: "Hello Beauty! Hello Beauty!" I just looked into his eyes – filled with light – and at his perfect little body and called him "beauty" over and over again.'

Like other powers in this book, beauty takes us right into this place where we know we are part of life and can consciously work with the eternal energies of existence, like love or peace. Beauty and love are almost inseparable. We love what is beautiful and with love we honor beauty. And peace is part of beauty because in beauty all things are in harmony with each other and the whole.

Of course great artists know the capacity to transform through the colors, shapes, and materials of this world, but so does a woman who holds her body with awareness of her own dignity or transforms the atmosphere of an entire room just by putting the right flower on the right table where the light hits it just so.

For so many modern women, beauty has become lost within an oppressive emphasis on attractiveness and the terrible pressure placed on us to fit in rather than express our uniqueness, where our beauty resides. While women have gained so much power and opportunity in the outer world, we have also let patriarchal ideals undermine our own ability to see, feel, and embody the real power of beauty, which is a deeply intimate intermingling of the inner and the outer, a way to live what is formless in harmony with the world of forms.

In the West, real beauty that is honored through love and craftsmanship has been traded in for efficiency and profits in everything from new buildings to clothing to everyday products. Bringing forth beauty takes time and attention, and a willingness to feel, and we are a world with a depleting attention, often turning us away from deep intimacy.

But beauty is an essential aspect of life – many traditions call it a divine quality. As we have lost touch with beauty, we have lost touch with our own selves at this deep and sacred level. This is a tragic aspect of our patriarchal culture – it has contributed to our forgetting the living beauty of existence.

A culture that has forgotten beauty has forgotten that human consciousness has a role to play in sustaining the sacred, in honoring that which is real through our bodies and our senses. A culture that has forgotten beauty has forgotten how to work with love.

Before this forgetting is complete, beauty calls on us to know and embody it. This is life itself calling to be seen and experienced in the most intimate ways, and to be protected for its true nature. As we honor beauty, we are brought into right relationship with life – one that includes a consciousness of harmony, humility and belonging.

The Dance of Beauty

Beauty's power draws us into a dance between the deep and formless inner all the way to the outer tips of form. Unlike other powers within life, it takes us in where harmony or love flows unrestricted through our heart and all the way out to the very most specific details of our world.

We smell the perfume of a flower, taste the perfect plum, or feel cool rain on our face, and we are transported into a place beyond words and time where our being is soothed on the waves of an inner pulsing ocean. But just as we are taken inward by the beauty of life, we also offer inner beauty outward for others to know and feel. Beauty is a channel that takes us to the inner real and insists we not hide there, but calls us back out again.

Beauty gives us endless opportunities to know life as it is. All things beautiful speak to our heart and wipe away the dust that covers our perceptions, allowing us to see and know what is real.

At the same time, as the eye of the heart opens it sees more and more of the beautiful. The power of beauty fuels and supports this back-and-forth of our unique, individual heart longing to know the world as it is, and the heart of the world offering so many ways to be known.

This dance of beauty moves to the song of peace, love, and unity. There is no beauty without unity. As Aristotle said, beauty is the harmony of the individual parts within and with the whole. In this harmony we also find peace, for all things come to rest in their proper place. This beauty is the beauty beyond attractiveness, where even darkness and everything we want to turn away from – ugliness, violence, failure, flaws, pain – has its place in the whole of life. Japanese art forms like *wabi-sabi*, which emphasize imperfection, reveal the beauty of a wholeness that includes that which we might want to ignore or deny.

The deep power of beauty is that it shines through the whole of life, including the bugs and the mud as much as the sky and the birds. It is oneness reflected everywhere it can possibly reach.

Beauty is a living invitation into the one heart that beats in time with all life. This invitation is ongoing. We will always be building buildings, dressing and caring for our bodies, watching the body of the earth become clean white in the winter and emerald green in the spring, having the moon shine on us at night like the open eye of eternity.

Because of its essential wholeness, beauty has the power to befuddle, to still the mind and free us from conditional habits. It is really too free and too inclusive to be constrained by thought or concept. What happens to us when we are in a beautiful building, designed by someone who understands the impacts of light, earth materials, symmetry, and scale? Or when we stand before a painting by a master? Or when we meet a person whose inner beauty shines outward? Or when we are alone in nature with no one watching or judging us?

Because so many of us are not practiced at working with

powers free from power dynamics, we tend to let the power of beauty work through our unconscious. Then its power manifests through shadow dynamics that try to own and control, and if not, then destroy, what is beautiful. When a woman is beautiful, other women often respond with jealousy or rage. Men want to possess her, and if they cannot, they want to destroy her – or themselves – so to not live without her. Remember Helen of Troy and the destruction caused in the struggle over who would possess her? The power of beauty – so potentially *complete* – often evokes our greatest insecurities, or our fear that we are not enough.

Beauty's shadow is so omnipresent in our culture that we no longer identify it as such. We think we can buy beauty or strive for beauty. We participate in a tremendous amount of violence against the real beauty of our bodies and the body of the earth and accept it unconsciously as status quo, ignoring how so many cultural norms – from how we keep our lawns to how much make-up we wear to how we destroy our health for attractiveness – continue to distance us from real beauty even as we are desperate to get closer to it. Beauty's harmony brings us *into* life. And we are a culture that cannot stand the vulnerability or need of this intimacy so we resort to the safer realm of control, ownership, and a sense of separateness.

But if we are with beauty and serve beauty, its power nourishes and empowers us. This potential was described by Rachel Carson, early founder of our environmental conservation movement: 'Those who contemplate the beauty of the earth find reserves of strength that will endure as long as life lasts.'[14]

The connection between love, beauty, and nourishment is also described by the 13th-century Sicilian poet, Jacopo Da Lentini:

Love is a yearning that comes from the heart
From a flowing over of great beauty;
And the eyes are the first to give it birth,

And the heart gives itself for bread.[15]

When the power of beauty bypasses the ego's shadow, it inspires us to act in ways that protect and support life. A photographer's assistant from San Francisco described a recent encounter with beauty and its very practical effects:

> I was working on a photo shoot with a model, and this woman was so beautiful. Something about her was just so beautiful I can't even explain it. And I had such a strong response from my whole being to protect her somehow – to make sure she was all right, that she was not cold, that she had what she needed. I was so surprised – it was like they were deeply connected – her beauty and my response of care and protection. I've never really had that experience before.

Mothers will understand this response to the beauty of a child. Conservationists know this need to protect the beauty of the natural world. And of course, many men will understand this response to a beautiful woman. In the Middle Ages, the ideals of chivalry and the practice of courtly love gave rise to a code of conduct for knights in service to a beautiful lady. This code of behavior is illustrated in Troubadour poetry from that period. Such poetry also shows the divine aspect of beauty, how it links to the power of longing, for the love of the troubadours was always accompanied by the knowledge that the beloved would never be fully possessed, the desire never satisfied. From the 12th-century poet Peire Vidal:

> As we gaze in awe at some great window,
> Shining in beauty against the splendour,
> Seeing her, my heart so sweet is rendered
> I forget myself in her beauty's glow.
> With the stick I cut, Love brings me pain,

For, one day, in his royal domain,
I stole a kiss for the heart to remember:
Oh, for the man who can't see his lover![16]

In this love, a troubadour 'forgets himself in her beauty's glow'
and this is perhaps a key to beauty's power. For a moment – or
longer – we are not isolated and separate and alone. Rather our
small sense of self is forgotten in something bigger and more
encompassing. This is a transpersonal power, taking us beyond
ourselves into another realm. The Troubadour is taken into a
'royal domain,' which is the domain of the heart and soul. Here
we discover all sorts of powers – love, longing, service, recognition of the sacred. In the domain of the soul, things of the
world mean little and service to love is all.

But in the practice of Chivalry, this dimension is lived fully in
life through actions and behaviors. It is not a state of being held
back from life as though only God deserves our devotion, but it
is a model that brings our devotion into society.

And from another 12th-century poet, Arnaut Daniel de
Riberac, we hear how this devotion nourishes and purifies:

Each day I grow better, purer,
For I serve and adore the noblest woman
In all the world – so I claim, and more.
I'm hers from my feet to my hair,
And even if the cold winds blow
Love reigns in my heart, and it acquires
Heat that the deepest winters hide.[17]

As we stay true to beauty we are sustained by love and heat
hidden in the deepest winter, a mysterious warmth that
nourishes and gives us ground for our lives. Beauty gives us a
way to honor and serve, to thread our deepest intimacies and
needs outward through daily life.

The deep connection between beauty and a capacity to love is articulated in a conversation that started in 1981 between a small group of children and an apparition of the Virgin Mary at a village in Bosnia-Herzogovina. Marija, one of the young visionaries, writes about one particular visitation with the Virgin:

> One day we asked Her, 'How come you are so beautiful? Because we have no words to explain to these crowds Your beauty.' Our Lady smiled and said, 'I am beautiful because I love.'[18]

Beauty and the Feminine

As Our Lady told the children, beauty is alive in love. If beauty does not evoke our shadow it transports us into the arena of the true heart, and into the heart of the world. The beauty of nature, for example, is not part of our heart alone, but part of the *anima mundi*, the heart or soul of creation. A walk in a meadow – light on the tips of grass, birds calling, enveloping summer warmth or vivid winter sharpness – can bring us directly into this dimension where life's divinity speaks to our own soul and calls us back into itself.

This divine aspect of beauty is represented in many different ways across the cultures of the world, personified in goddesses of beauty, or evoked through spiritual practices – like *ikebana*, Buddhist flower arranging, or visualization and mantra practices – that emphasize beauty and harmony as expressions of the absolute as well as a vehicle delivering us to the absolute.

This aspect of the absolute has generally been understood as feminine. Beauty is expressed through the great Goddesses like Aphrodite and Venus whose power is intertwined with their sexuality, or Kuan Yin, whose beauty is an aspect of her spiritual freedom and compassion, or even the fierce and wild beauty of the Tibetan Dakinis, consciously awake within the primordial wisdom.

In Sufism, beauty is known as the immanent, feminine dimension of God. Sufi teacher Llewellyn Vaughan-Lee explains:

> For the mystic this world is a place of divine revelation: a place where we can come to experience and know the beauty and wonder of the Divine. In the many faces of creation we can see the single face of our Creator. This is the drama of revelation, how the hidden face of God becomes visible, tangible, in the multitude of this world of forms, the many forms of creation that embody the feminine mystery of the Divine made manifest—what the Sufis call the mystery of the word 'Kun!' (Be!)
>
> A central quality of this revelation of the Divine is the beauty of creation. Within the wonder of creation the beauty of the Divine is most visible, from the fragility of a butterfly's wings to the grandeur of a snow-capped mountain range. Beauty also belongs to our human creativity, how music touches the soul, a painting stirs the heart. Being part of the mystery of creation, beauty is a quality of the divine feminine. It is said that even in the angelic world there are angels of power and angels of beauty: the angels of beauty are an expression of the divine feminine.

Beauty is a feminine aspect of God, and like all things feminine has a special connection to women. This connection is not just cultural or conditioned, but is an aspect of women's being. The connection between women and this divine quality is well articulated in Sufism. Llewellyn continues:

> When the soul is touched by beauty it turns towards God; it remembers the unrivalled beauty of its Creator in Her feminine aspect. And in the myriad expressions of divine beauty it is said that the form of woman holds the highest essence because she is the most beautiful creation of the Great

Artist. According to the great Sufi Ibn Arabi, 'Woman is the highest form of earthly beauty, but earthly beauty is nothing unless it is a manifestation and reflection of the Divine Qualities.'[19]

In Sufi poetry there is a rich symbolism of how each of a woman's features has symbolic significance representing qualities of the Divine. For example the eye symbolizes the quality of the mystery of God's vision; the mole or beauty spot signifies the Divine Essence itself; the twist or curve of her curl is a metaphor for Divine mysteries:

By the fragrant breeze from your tresses' ringlet
I am forever drunk;
While the devastating guile of your bewitching eyes
devastates me at every breath.[20]

Through the beauty of creation we can come to know the beauty of the Creator. For the Sufi the Divine Being is in Itself unknowable; 'no one knows God but God.' But through the Creation we can come to know the Divine, and a woman is the highest, most perfect manifestation of this Divine Beauty.

And in Rumi's words:

a woman is God shining
through subtle veils[21]

This connection between women, the divine, and beauty is part of every cell of a woman's being. It is an aspect of a woman's own divine potential and her divine gifts and responsibilities in life. It is tied to women's purity and sexuality, what Llewellyn articulated in the previous chapter having to do with the substance in women's chakras and 'the potential to give birth, to bring the light of a soul into the physical world.'

The Sufi Muslim Shaykh Muhammad Hisham Kabbani
further illuminates the relationship between women and beauty
in his description of the Prophet Muhammad's ascent through
the heavenly realms, guided by the Angel Gabriel. In the 'Night
Journey' Muhammad is led through the seven heavenly realms,
the fifth of which is described as the 'Garden of Beauty and
Felicity':

> The Prophet asked: 'Gabriel, what is the secret of this
> Paradise?' Gabriel said: 'God created this Paradise to reflect
> the beauty and perfection of women. The light of this Paradise
> is the source of the angelic lights of all women on earth.
> Women have been created to carry the secret of creation in
> themselves. God has honored them greatly by making their
> wombs the repository of His word, which represents the
> Spirit. He looks at the most sacred place and there descends
> His mercy and blessings. He perfected that place and covered
> it with three protective layers to shelter it from any damage.
> The first is a layer of light, the second a layer of love, and the
> third a layer of beauty.
>
> Women are not created weaker but more generous than
> men. They are created more beautiful, and less fierce, as
> beauty hates to hurt and harm others. That is why they seem
> weak to people but in reality they are not. Angels are the
> strongest of created beings, and women are closer to the
> angelic nature than men, and they are readier than men to
> carry angelic light.[22]

In this story of the Night Journey, Shaykh Kabbani links women
to a number of the powers described in this book:

> God gave women five angelic qualities which men rarely
> have. They are the source of peace, as God said that He
> created them 'so that ye might find rest in them' (30:21). This

is the attribute of the first Paradise, which is named 'the Abode of Peace.' They are oases of constancy in the midst of chaos and change. That is why they give birth as the mother nurtures and shelters the baby more reliably than the father. This is the attribute of the Second Paradise, which is named 'the Abode of Constancy.' They perpetuate generations. Through their offspring God creates angelic prophets and saints who establish His perpetual remembrance on earth as the angels establish it in Heaven. This is the attribute of the Third Paradise, which is named 'the Abode of Eternity.' They are generous and bountiful. They are described as 'a fertile land' in all Scriptures because they give without counting, including life. They sacrifice themselves for the sake of another creation, and this is the attribute of the Fourth Paradise, which is named 'the Sheltering Garden.' Finally, they are the source of Beauty. Through their softness and subtlety, God has crowned the earth with the diadem of angelic grace. This is the attribute of the Fifth Paradise, which is named 'the Garden of Beauty.'[23]

This passage is deeply mysterious and is easily misunderstood as it can be seen to paint women into very traditional boxes. But there is a need for women to look into these 'angelic' attributes in themselves and rescue them from cultural distortions. We can learn to value a natural, inner ease with life as an expression of divine peace rather than psychological complacency. To reclaim a connection between motherhood, so often discounted in our culture, and our divine equanimity during chaos and change. To acknowledge that a willingness to sacrifice ourselves for love might not always be co-dependence or self-destruction, but a divine quality having to do with a capacity to create and shelter life. And it is the same with our 'softness' and 'subtlety' – to bring those qualities out of a cultural garbage bin of 'lesser' and 'weaker' and reclaim their divine potential.

In beauty, women understand and live the power of softness and openness, because beauty cannot flow through closed doors or through psychological hardness. It needs an open channel from inner to outer, and it thrives in our attunement to subtle changes and shifts in energy flow that we *feel* in our body and through all our senses.

The Inner Truth of Outer Beauty

A key part of honoring beauty includes recognizing the reality of our true nature and remaining open and vulnerable to deep inner reality. Pamela Wilson, teacher in the non-dual tradition of Advaita Vedanta, explains the relationship between beauty and the essential non-being that is our true nature.

> Beauty is the radiance of formlessness sparkling with potentiality. Beauty is the formless in full devotion to itself. It is the formless saying, 'Look how much I love form! I make everything beautiful!'
>
> It is the exhale and the inhale both. The exhale is radiance and celebration; the inhale is the coming to rest, the satiety, the contentment.
>
> In the word 'Beautiful' is 'full.' Here's something that's already full. It is full with potential! There's an absolute humility in seeing this. It does not need mind to add anything to it. It doesn't add anything to itself. It is already complete.

Women, according to Pamela, are naturally attuned through humility and openness to this formlessness that manifests through the beautiful. She continues:

> Women have this natural humility. We have a formless, open 'yes' that allows everything. Innocence is our true nature – the openness that drinks everything in. But if we don't know our true nature, then everything is on automatic. We don't notice

this beautiful innocence, which is related to our emptiness, our inner no-self, our 'I am-ness' that is just barely manifest, that is just radiating from non-being.

This divine innocence just coming into manifestation is easily projected onto by the mind as having no-value because it really has no qualities; it is so close to formless. It is seen as deficient and then the editing and the enhancement begins.

We tend not to look closely or deeply through that deficiency into that formlessness. Instead, we think it's a personal deficiency. I have met with some of the great artists of our modern time, and they have this amazing gift, but underneath is the same 'How am I doing?', that same insecurity. Or mothers who have such a natural serenity and calm and giving, and underneath is the same questioning and doubt.

But I always invite friends to notice that this innocence has ultimate value. It's so precious.

To live beauty means to allow our hearts to be open, to allow ongoing vulnerability and care, even as we get hooked into believing that our sorrows and openness are problems, says Pamela:

Women are the heart of hearts. We are wearing really sensitive instruments. We feel so deeply and care so deeply. And then, since we carry everything the way the heart of heart carries everything, families, humanity, animals, eco-system, with a deep true unshakable love – that's why we get overwhelmed. Then, thought can use that being naturally overwhelmed by the infinite to make a story of 'You're not Awake!' That's when we get hooked. We allow ourselves to doubt this compassionate sadness, this naivete that opens to everything, and return to a solid story about ourselves being deficient, so that in our deficiency it really feels like we are someone.

At our women's gatherings women see this tendency to make solid what is really empty very quickly. A woman sees the openness and shows her body and mind the value of this naturalness.

Women have a different sense of this no-thing than men, who deal with it differently – through gazing and pushing. But with women it's just effortless. Through honoring the veils – they all just fall away.

Much meditation training is to withdraw from nourishing of thought. Innocence has been feeding thought through listening to it. Meditation weans you off thought. If you want to fixate on something, try fixating on the space. Then, after a while, once the naturalness sees itself, it sees everything is arising as a spontaneous act of intelligence.

While women can see and know this natural formlessness within, the challenge according to Pamela is to live from this place, to know its strength and its power.

Women know themselves as love. But they don't know love's strength. There is big strength in this love. But women are afraid of relaxing into it.

We get in trouble when we try to contain that full heart in order to protect ourselves. Generally, love has been projected on by thought. And thought looks down on love and sees its formlessness. The next assumption is that because it's formless, it's frail, and it needs to be defended. We create containment around the heart, which from the point of view of mind and body and innocence is good, because it keeps the deep, true openness from being hurt, but then the love doesn't spread its wings through the beauty of life.

Why do we contain the heart? Not because we are afraid of being hurt, but because we are protecting ourselves from hurting others. The panic arises in this relaxation, as the big strength starts to root itself. The panic is saying 'We're not going to hurt anyone, are we?' Once it has our confirmation that we're not going to hurt anyone, the beautiful rootedness reveals itself. Then a woman can relax and reveal love's strength. This lets the embodiment be unshakable.

Then there's a way to live in the formless. There's so much strength in formlessness. It holds up all the planets!

A woman knowing she is the big strength of uncontained love, deeply rooted – WOW! That's what we are all longing for! With unshakable strength and clear seeing!

The mind is just a vast spacious no thing. The heart is pure love. Then the gut is pure strength – mountain strength. The head rests in heart, the heart rests in the big strength. And now you have a woman who is divine, moving through her own creation with strength, grace, and clarity. Beauteous! This is how we get our majesty and dignity back. Her longing – she wants to know herself as divine. She wants to live what she knows is true down to her toes. She is beauty itself.

If you don't understand beauty, you can ask! I like asking – asking inside – anything I'm curious about. 'Let me feel your divinity.' The door is the asking. It's important to not try to trudge through life all by yourself. It's an act of great humility to say, 'I'm tired. Please reveal.'

The divine bows and says, 'All is yours. Let me show you.'

A Time for Beauty

Beauty is like other natural powers within women in that it connects the formless inner dimensions with the outer world and invites us into an experience of wholeness, and in that it honors the created world as sacred. But beauty is unique, as it really cannot stay hidden away. We see, feel, hear, touch, and sing beauty. It is interdependent with the senses. We can try, but it is not easy to hide beauty in the same way we can hide our longing, our recognition of life's sacredness, or our ability to work with creative space. We can honor the earth and reclaim our under-standing of earth's spirits in private, but when we walk with beauty through life, we are exposed. This exposure can feel uncomfortable, even dangerous, and we'll often go to great lengths to avoid it.

Pamela tells an allegory of hidden beauty:

I was in a little shop and was drawn to this strange ring and picked it up. It had a weird gnarly metal covering – chunky and thick. It wasn't particularly attractive, but I was drawn to it. The clerk said that I was the only woman she'd seen pick up the ring. She said it was a 'traveler's ring.' She showed me – she pushed aside this thick metal covering and below there was a pearl and an emerald. It was so beautiful!

People used to wear jewelry like this while traveling, to make sure nobody stole it. The metal covering hides the beauty and deflects the gaze.

So you see – the gaze – women deflect the gaze. It has been dangerous to live our beauty. We still think we have to dim the shine, veil it, to deflect the gaze.

To some degree, women are still like travelers in this world, trying to hide what is real for fear that it will be hurt or stolen from us. But it can't be stolen; our beauty and our power are so deep that they cannot be taken from us. And the more we cover it, the greater the chances that we, ourselves, will forget.

It is time for women to reclaim this capacity to uncover our inner beauty and to serve what we know is beautiful. To step into the strength of our being. The beautiful earth has suffered from our willingness to forget this gift and responsibility and to participate in the trading of real beauty for economy or attrac-tiveness or other things that can be bought and sold. We have let life suffer because we haven't stood up for the truths that we see and know.

Living and protecting beauty will bring consequences. A woman who honors the power of beauty is likely to feel ongoing sorrow at the desecration of our material world – the McMansions and the strip malls, the common-denominator element of all that our society builds and sells and that we buy. She will likely not be able to bear the destruction of the natural world and she will likely feel the need to protect it.

But there are even graver consequences to not honoring beauty, including a deeper and vaster covering of the dust already dulling the treasures of our earth and our hearts. The breath of beauty clears away this dust, allowing the ecstatic intimacy of divine presence. More and more of us are hearing beauty call to us, asking us to listen, reaching to us through our dreams and through our longing and our loves, as though it needs us as much as we need it. A German woman who has practiced in both the Buddhist and Sufi traditions tells a dream of beauty's return to a land that waits for it:

A man, full of dignity and strength, is steering two horses with a wagon attached. He looks tired because he has been looking for something that is the most important thing for him. He has been to many countries and places and almost had given up hope that he would ever find it. But now he has found Her. And he enters the New land, which also was the Old land.

He is riding the horses and then he looks back to the end of the wagon with so much love. I follow his look and I come to see the most beautiful woman I have ever seen in my life.

She is sitting gently, full of light at the end of the wagon. She is dressed in a simple white garment. Her hair is long and black as the color of a raven. Her skin is fair and soft. Her eyes are big and the color olive green. Her gaze looks into a distant reality. She is completely surrendered and belongs to God only. Her hands are gently folded in her lap and she wears a simple ring with an olive-colored stone. In front of her face she wears a translucent veil and around her is a light, warm wind. The man is looking for a safe place in this world for her to live but there is no place where he can take her. In this recognition they both disappear and I am left alone.

For this dreamer, and for so many of us, there is yet no safe place for real beauty, the kind of beauty described here that is part of the divine and lived through our own soul and reflected through our being, that is beloved and protected. But how can the dreamer honor the need for beauty, knowing it is not safe yet for beauty's return?

Many of us feel this tension – the deep need for a personal as well as collective recognition of how we have erred, how we have destroyed, how we have denied the beauty within life, along with the deep need to return to beauty and live in harmony with beauty. This tension can give rise to frustration and helplessness, but it can also empower our longing and confirm our instinctual knowing that a world in which beauty is truly honored is possible.

In the dream, the land is a new land and an old land. The dreamer describes it as a land that is 'waiting for life to return, waiting for life to flourish.' But *we are this land*. The land is our own body. The land is a longing waking up through our individual and shared body, reminding us that we need something more, something else, something that is coming. And like a farmer preparing the land, we prepare our bodies as though waiting for a lover. Nourishing the soil, planting the seed.

We attune our conscious remembrance to the forgotten earth, bringing together something of what has been nearly abandoned with what is promised for the future. The dreamer writes about her dream:

The remembrance of this quality of the Soul and the Divine can bring with it an unbearable pain and grief as one looks into this world of human creation in which everything has been desecrated. But of course on an everyday basis one can maybe live this quality a little bit.

I can live it in my home and in my garden. First one has to clear out the garden, clear out the space. Then one needs to create a protected space from the animal world, a fence or shrubs that keep the unwanted friends out. Then one digs the earth, opens Her up. And then there are the seeds, which carry the secret. One never knows how they will reveal their potential – some might sprout, some might stay dormant for a long time and come up for an unknown reason one year later. One can create all the right conditions but one cannot control the outcome. Nature has its own way, and I think we can never understand Nature; one can only feel it from the heart and pay attention. Attention, humility and space are what allow beauty and harmony to come into this world. Of course to know that beauty exists, to be conscious of it without wanting it, allows it to reveal its magic, and a space, a container, is necessary.

Women can build this container, each of us working in our own lives as well as working together for the sake of the whole. We understand about creating space and working to protect space so something new can be born – we live this reality as mothers who birth children. We take care, protect our body – which we know is also our child's body – stay healthy, rest when needed, listen within, feel inner movement, wait for the right time, and allow the miracle of birth to take us over.

Creating a space for beauty depends on clearing away our dependence on false beauty, the substitutes we accept because they are either easier or safer or because real beauty seems so hidden right now. Honoring real beauty means not allowing the substitutes to take our time or resources, or to distract us. And it means developing our sense of knowing. Real beauty is here, but we have to look and *see*. We need to look past the places we are conditioned to look and turn to where our heart senses it resides. Our heart sees beauty all the time, but do we listen to our heart and look where it is pointing?

A woman on Whidbey Island, Washington remembers an encounter with two belly dancers, which left her aware of the clear difference between real beauty and it's imposter:

I was at a dinner celebrating Moroccan culture, and after the delicious meal a belly dancer came out to dance for us. The music was wonderful, and the dancer was very well trained. She was American, and there was some aspect of her dancing that felt over-trained or forced. She was very fit. She wore the beautiful flowing clothes well and her brown hair was flying. She clearly knew all the steps. She had a big smile but her face wasn't relaxed.

Then, in the background, near the kitchen area, the cook's wife, from Morocco, started dancing too. She was quite overweight and her stomach was showing through her traditional clothing. Her hair wasn't done particularly well and she didn't have the same beautiful costume as the paid dancer. In fact I think her clothes were dirty from cooking!

But when she started moving I couldn't keep my eyes off her. She was just so beautiful. So natural. Every movement came from the same inner place of confidence and love, though those words might not be right. It was like the movements of a snake – its body moving in all different directions but it is going one place and it is in total harmony... It was like that. She was connected to something and was moving with it. Actually, she looked like she was in love or being seduced but it was so beautiful and tender. Meanwhile, the American dancer kept at it in the center of the room. But it was the dancer by the kitchen that I could have watched for hours and hours.

This woman was seducing and being seduced. But by whom? By what?

Every woman knows that we look, act, and even think differently when we feel beautiful and want to be seen as beautiful. We tap into that innate connection to beauty and offer it to our beloved. And this deep power of beauty is activated more fully as we acknowledge that all life is divine and sees us at all times. When we are in a love affair with all life, we allow the power of beauty to work with other innate powers like the power of community and of recognizing life's sacredness. When we show ourselves to a lover, we reflect our inner beauty outward. But all life is our lover when it is sacred, when the divine wakefulness is watching and being with us.

The unveiling of our beauty is not something we need to do just for ourselves. We do it for the world we live in, for the entire community of life, which includes earth and spirit.

The Navajo people honored the living potential of beauty and understood that ceremony was needed to honor and renew the power of beauty in personal and community healing. The Navajo 'Night Chang,' one of the most sacred of all Navajo ceremonies, includes ongoing reference to beauty. Our dominant culture has lost this understanding of beauty and ceremony both, but this restoration can find many forms. We can start by acknowledging the need to return to beauty and our power of prayer.

In beauty may I walk.
All day long may I walk.
Through the returning seasons may I walk.
On the trail marked with pollen may I walk.
With grasshoppers about my feet may I walk.
With dew about my feet may I walk.

With beauty may I walk.
With beauty before me, may I walk.
With beauty behind me, may I walk.
With beauty above me, may I walk.
With beauty below me, may I walk.
With beauty all around me, may I walk.
In old age wandering on a trail of beauty,
Lively, may I walk.
In old age wandering on a trail of beauty,
Living again, may I walk.
It is finished in beauty.
It is finished in beauty.[24]

Chapter 6

Community

Do we know the people around us?
Mother Teresa[25]

Community is a matter of consciousness. We are aware of our connections to others and to life or we're not. And of course the level and degree of awareness changes, increasing and decreasing depending upon many factors. One minute you are not aware that there is a person on the street below your apartment, and the next you hear someone call out and you know someone needs help. Awareness is the foundation of relationship. Without it, you do not know or see and cannot give or receive.

The power of community is highly tied to shifting awareness. Mother Teresa pointed out this connection as she advocated for caring for others by first asking, 'Do we know the people around us?' Without awareness of others, we cannot care about others or even develop an understanding of our responsibilities to them.

When it comes to the power of community, we can step back from a literal way of thinking about 'community' as a fixed group of people, like your family or your neighborhood, and appreciate that our sense of 'community' is highly flexible, changing as our awareness of others changes.

As our sense of community expands or shrinks, so do many of the resources that flow through community. For example, if you need to borrow a rare book and you only have a small group of friends to borrow from, it is likely you will not find a copy of the book you want. But if there is a local library near by connected to a wider library network, your chances improve. The bigger your community, the more resources become available to each member.

In recent years, global communication and the Internet have significantly broadened much of the world's sense of community. The now everyday expansion of awareness directs our attention and resources beyond our local sphere. Once that door is opened, we have a powerful channel of attention that is the basis for actions, experiences, and empowerment.

Key to working with the power of community is recognizing that our sense of community shifts with awareness, and as it shifts our communal resources also expand or contract. Power is tied to this shifting resource bank. We are empowered when we receive what we need just as we are empowered when we can give what is needed. Perhaps we can even go so far as to say that the more we give and the more we receive, the more powerful we are.

It is also important as we learn to work with the power of community to realize that we are not just speaking of physical resources. Yes – money and other resources like clothing, food, or medicine all are important resources, and are key to the health of a community. But inner resources are just as important.

There are many inner resources that exist in community and need to flow through community. They include love, belonging, trust, the power to contribute and the power to receive. These inner resources and capacities add a critical dimension to the physical world, influencing the physical flow of resources. For example, when we give another person a birthday present, we might also give love. The gift is given and received, and so is the added resource of love. The outer world is naturally a vehicle for the transmission of this hidden inner dimension of energies and experiences. Imagine being given a gift without love. How much does the gift lose or gain value when you feel – or don't feel – the energy and intention behind it?

As we consider the power of community, we need an open mind that can hold these different dimensions at the same time.

We need to value not just the outer resources but also the inner resources that flow through the community. And we need to sense how our conscious awareness influences both kinds of resource exchange. This is not an easy task. But women instinctually have the wisdom to work with the power of community in this multidimensional way.

Women's relationality is already multidimensional. We know the power of community deep in our bones and blood, which are not separate from our hearts or our minds. We know how to create – and destroy – community through energies like love or envy. We know how to nourish others through immediate, physical connection as well as from afar through intuition and through the powers of the heart. We know how love is brought down all the way through the body to a child, and we know how to live that love despite seeming physical separation as that same child grows older.

All these aspects of community can be revived and honored by women, not just so we can live what is natural to us and to life, but so we can offer our natural wisdom to empower the whole.

Individualism and the Patriarchy

The power of community is natural to women. It is part of our emotional makeup, an aspect of our natural relatedness. We are consciously and unconsciously involved – through feeling and through our bodies – with life around us. We build relationships and then we pass energy and resources through those relationships. We care for others; we suffer for others. Our bodies become the container for new life and then sustenance for our children.

Women's instinct toward community has an important role to play in our collective evolution, which is taking us all into a new world that increasingly values and understands the interdependence of life. As the world comes to honor relationship, women will find more space to live our instinctual ways of connecting. But in order to ground ourselves more consciously in the opportunities of the present it's important to see how this shift has been developing throughout the last centuries and sped up through the last decades.

When Carol Gilligan wrote about women's psychological tendency toward relatedness in *In a Different Voice*, she called into question the patriarchal worldview dominating the field of psychology at the time, which emphasized individuality, autonomy, and separateness as pinnacles of human development. Her radical suggestion that men and woman develop along different psychological lines revolutionized how we collectively understand men and women and their relationships to life. Her work galvanized the questioning of a value system that prioritized individualism over community. This questioning continues. Today, neuro-scientific research into the male and female brain supports the view that women's brains and hormonal systems create a ground for experiences of relatedness in ways that men's don't. And evolutionary scientists suggest we are moving along an evolutionary trajectory that is increasingly valuing many of women's natural capacities for relating, including empathy and emotional attunement.

These scientific inquiries and the changing attitudes they support are part of a slow dying away of patriarchal values that have largely devalued many aspects of women's experience. It's important to consciously acknowledge that many of our collective assumptions about human maturity, morality and spheres of responsibility are born from a patriarchal worldview that is not compatible with women's natural wisdom.

Exalted ideas about autonomy have strong religious, economic and political functions in the global patriarchy, and were highly intertwined with the decline of the power of the Catholic Church in Europe in the Middle Ages and with the Renaissance, Reformation, and rise of capitalism. The decline of

Church absolutism, the Protestant Reformation's emphasis on individual choice and scriptural interpretation, the increasing interest in humanism with its recognition of the power of individual will, and the rise of capitalism and accompanying promises of upward mobility all supported values of individualism that pinnacled in modern times and our ideas about 'self-development' and the 'self-made man.'

But this was largely a European phenomenon, while many other parts of the world remained more oriented toward a sense of community intertwined with spiritual views that emphasized divine power over personal power and divine power as fully present throughout the created world as well as beyond. The culture clash of individualism and community was lived out violently through colonialism when European settlers brought their ideals to foreign lands.

When settlers came to the Americas, many were initially impressed by Native Americans' sense of community. In one journal from the early 18th century, that of German settler Friedrich von Reck from Georgia, we hear admiration for this sense of community:

Their table is open to everyone, and one can sit at it uninvited. When an Indian wants to assure someone of his friendship, he strikes himself with his right hand on his left breast and says, my breast is like your breast, my and your breast is one breast – equivalent of my and your heart is one heart, my heart is closely bound with your heart...[26]

But by the mid-to-late 1800s, the community aspect of Native life was largely seen by settlers as backwards and less civilized than the individualism of the Europeans, which was deeply tied to political and economic ideas about private property and competition for resources. The conflict between individualism and community is well articulated by Joseph R. Brown, a Sioux agent and US government official participating in the national agenda to destroy Native culture in the United States in 1858: 'Give a man a separate tract to cultivate and he does not hesitate to labor in the common field… The common field is the seat of barbarism; the separate farm the door to civilization.'[27]

Today, few would equate community or the 'common field' with barbarism as we are coming to realize not just how shared our global resources are but also the damage that can come from seeing natural resources as separable. Nonetheless, our culture is steeped in assumptions about what is more civilized or of higher value, and a sense of individualism and self-determinism tops the list, while a genuine need for community is often misinterpreted as co-dependence, inability to stand on one's own, or lack of personal willpower.

To say that this dominant cultural ideal of individualism has held women back and also held back our global (and particularly western) society from developing its sense of collective responsibility is an understatement. But that ideal and its foundational place in our global community has slowly been crumbling, and a door has opened to a greater valuing of women's innate qualities that have been misunderstood or ignored for so long. Simply by honoring what we know and how we naturally live, women will support the global changes already taking place, changes that are propelling the planet along a specific evolutionary trajectory that is in part increasing our awareness and respect for traditionally feminine wisdom, like the awareness of relationship and connectedness and the feelings – like care and compassion – that arise with this awareness.

The growing scientific support of the intuitive sense that women are naturally relational is not separate from other emerging feminine perspectives and experiences gaining ground in our collective consciousness. Among these are an increased sense of the sacredness of the earth and all life forms, not just human; the need to treat the earth as a living home, not an object;

and the newfound appreciation of non-rational modes of intelligence like intuition and emotional intelligence that bypass Newtonian science and Enlightenment-era prejudices that favor reason.

More than ever, women need to recognize that our instincts and our unique ways of experiencing the world – including our experience of life in community – are aligned with a future that needs our help to manifest. Recognizing, honoring, and learning to live in community is in many regards the task of the next century, as we understand more and more that we will be thriving or suffering *together*.

In order to activate and work with the power of community, we need to understand how the inner and outer dimensions work together. For this, it is helpful to look to traditions with a strong shamanic element, which value both worlds and their interdependence.

Inner and Outer Resources

A key element in the power of community is to understand that the bigger one's community, the more resources are available to us. Sobonfu Somé, elder from the Dagara tribe in West Africa, whose work of bringing African Wisdom to the West includes an emphasis on the importance of community and the emerging feminine consciousness, puts it this way: 'Two eyes see fine. Four eyes see more. Think what 1,000 eyes can see!'

But the availability of resources is not just about objects but includes energies and experience. In a culture that focuses so much on outer resources, these inner resources are often missing in our understanding of what can be exchanged in community. But they are really the basis of our humanity. The experience of feeling that one belongs within a caring world is exponentially powerful. A woman from Connecticut remembers how being helped as a young girl left a deep and lasting impression:

I was a teenager arriving in New York City for the first time to visit my mother who had just moved there. I flew into New York with only 20 dollars for a taxi, and I was conned by someone pretending to be a taxi driver who took the money. I was standing on the corner with no money and no way to get where I was going (and this was way before cell phones)! This was a horrifying feeling. But after a few minutes, a taxi driver got out of his car and asked me if I needed help. I told him what had happened. He told me to get in and he drove me home for free. I'll never forget how it felt to be so scared and alone and confused and just have someone do the simplest thing like help. It changed everything in my psyche. It made me aware of how much power we have to influence each other, to connect, to determine circumstances in both good and bad ways.

The inner resources that become available when we are attuned to community grow when we share them and increase the flow of outer goods. As love grows, it creates more ways for us to give and receive, and our giving and receiving supports love's expansion. The more generous we are, the more likely we are to feel we have something to share. In this way, generosity creates a sense of abundance and undermines the power of scarcity. Gratitude, with its beautiful understanding of how vulnerable we are to life, grows as we open ourselves to receiving, and does not exist if we isolate ourselves. This also applies to the realm of imagination. As we collaborate with others, instead of just working alone, our capacity to imagine and innovate often expands. 'Two heads are better than one,' after all.

These invisible inner resources have big impacts on our lives. You don't see generosity, but you certainly recognize its effects. It is the same with the vulnerability and humility of gratitude.

Through honoring and living these inner energies, we are transported into the realm of the soul – the deep inner, the center of beauty, love, and power where we know and live what is real.

The inner experience of community and its impacts on our daily life free us from many of the delusions society has convinced us of, like the idea of scarcity, the need to compete, and the need to hoard resources. Through living the power of community, we taste the reality of the deep inner soul, which is free, whole, and full. Through honoring the dimension of soul we have the opportunity to harmonize the inner and outer worlds – bring together what is real with the practicalities of life. It is this harmony that undermines the imbalances of living in a society that continually tells us we do not have enough, or that we need more and more in order to live a life of value.

This is not a grand plan or giant project, but depends only on simple willingness to be honest about what really matters to us, and continue to attune our consciousness to the hidden reality of what is available and possible in a shared world. Can we admit that genuine belonging is a deeper need than a new car? Can we honor how much we need to feel connected and how isolation harms us and others? Can we admit how much we want to love someone? Can we live according to these deep needs and change our daily lives to honor them? This is how we develop the capacity to remain attuned to the soul and the soul of others despite the distracting and often damaging messages of the modern world.

As we value and live these inner needs and experiences through outer connections, the power of community grows and grows. It rarely diminishes or contracts. How big can this power get? How skilled can we become at working with this power? When we do not limit 'community' to a small, defined outer group, and allow our awareness of connection to grow, we naturally awaken to a greater and greater sense of belonging, an expanding understanding of responsibility to others, and a finer and finer-tuned capacity to both give into community and receive from community what is needed. As we develop this power we become more synchronized with the whole of life. We see the parts integrated into a whole; we can give to one in a way that nourishes all and receive in ways that do not 'take' from the whole but actually strengthen it.

Through the power of community, we find our place in the whole and discover our own ways to give.

Individuality and Community

Honoring the power of community does not mean we diminish our sense of individuality, though many of us fear this is true. But it's just the opposite. The power of community awakens and empowers us *individually*. We don't find our individual strengths and purpose isolated from the world we live in. We find them when we recognize and honor the needs of the time and place of which we are a part.

We are not born into the world randomly or accidently. Rather we come with things to learn and to give that are realized through acknowledging and working with circumstances of the moment, our own needs, and the needs of those around us. The great innovations of all time are responses to the needs of the community and the challenge of contributing. One's individual destiny is forged through living in relationship to the hardships of this world, and through the challenge of aligning what is inwardly sustaining in relation to outer circumstances. This realization of destiny, discovering and living our individual soul-purpose, is interdependent with the time and place of our lives.

The individual and communal aspects of destiny are described by Rainer Maria Rilke: 'Destiny itself is like a wonderful wide tapestry in which each thread is guided by an infinitely delicate hand, placed beside the next and held and supported by a hundred others.'[28]

The relationship of individuality and community is not easy to understand or honor in a world that tends to downplay community as well as to deny the inner truth of the soul, from where our destiny is birthed. To fully live as ourselves, we need to remember the spiritual dimension and value the ways our spirit or soul depends on and interacts with the outer world.

Sobonfu Somé explains the Dagara understanding of individuality, community, and spirit in a way not unlike Rilke's:

> Every person comes to the world from a circle of spirit from before we were born, which fully supports that person and his or her purpose. We come with gifts, and these gifts are for the world. This means we have the right and the capacity to provide a space to everyone in order for their gifts to bloom. Community is what enables us to be human, and to be accepted as ourselves. Without community, the individual becomes extinct. Without individuals, there is no community.

According to Sobonfu, when there's an imbalance that undervalues community, isolation, pain, strife, and illness follow:

> There is something in the mystery of the Self that binds us to each other; we need each other. If that glue fails, we all feel it. And the energy of disconnection will create pain. If it's not addressed, the pain becomes a weapon we use against each other. When the glue that binds us together isn't functioning, it sends everyone busy licking his or her own private wounds and we are blind to everyone else's pain. This blindness grows.
>
> When someone's gifts are locked up or muffled they have the capacity to work against you. The energy of the gift can become dammed up, and toxic. Then, it might become an illness that devours your life.

Sobonfu explains this 'glue' that binds us all together exists not just here in the world of shared outer resources, but also has a spiritual dimension. Today, our modern world is suffering both in the outer and the inner because we do not bring the spiritual dimension into our outer community:

> All relationships and every community exist because spirit is at the foundation. Spirit is radiating light at the soul of community. Without spirit nothing can exist.
>
> But there is a hole in the soul of the world. In part, this is because we don't see the spirit world. There is no energy being put to feeding the soul of humanity, so we have homelessness and hunger. We go shopping. We might try to tap into the soul of community but all we come out with is muck.
>
> The 'Occupy' movement seems to be about money but it's not. It's really people asking – Who is going to see me? Who is going to talk to me in ways that spirit is accepted? Who will meet me where I need to be met? These are personal questions and questions about community and about spirit.

To repair the hole in the soul of the world requires honoring both the inner spiritual realms and the outer worldly community of life. As we attune to the spiritual through our own heart, instinct, bodies, and perceptions and live the spiritual outward in community, we fulfill a key role of human consciousness – to weave the inner and outer worlds together to create and sustain a harmonious and multidimensional web of life.

Dangers for Women

A danger for women as we seek to repair the illnesses of modern community is that we honor community in a habitual or conditioned way and lose track of spirit, which we can only access through our deeply individual instincts, senses, and intelligence. We must not forget to carry this inner dimension into outer life.

In the West, we have a strange situation in which a false community overlays the real thing. The false community depends on women sacrificing their own knowing to fit in. This is the community of patriarchy that is perpetuated in part by women unable or afraid to honor their own knowing. As Sobonfu says, 'In the West, women do hear spirit, but they are willing to deny spirit to fit into the status quo. They want to conform to a man's world.'

What gets in the way of women honoring spirit? Pamela Wilson, who leads gatherings and retreats in the Advaita Vedanta tradition, describes a dynamic that keeps women from attending to our inner wisdom:

We are trained as women to be community oriented. And it's our joy to be of service. But this means that so often awareness is focusing on the needs of others, and not listening to what's true inside. But if we don't know our true nature, then everything is on automatic.

So, it's funny, there is a habitual service and focus on family or community or job. But the greatest gift that women can give humanity, community, and families is to relax back into their naturalness. That only takes a few moments. Just looking a little deeper than normal. Looking within the movements, and into the space that allows all the movements.

For Pamela, honoring spirit is a matter of looking inward, past the habitual into what is genuine and natural. Sandra Ingerman, American teacher and writer on shamanism, describes the need for women to move past cultural habits and align with the inner, from a shamanic point of view:

For women really the number one myth that you are supposed to take on somebody else's pain and sacrifice on their behalf needs to be broken.

I am an empath – and most women I know are empaths, which means we feel for others. This makes it so easy to take on the emotional pain if we are around someone who is depressed, or even some of the physical symptoms of someone who is sick. Many women don't know how to create boundaries between what is my pain, what is my feeling, and what is being felt by loved ones, friends, clients.

We look at pictures of Mary and other goddesses and see that they are crying on behalf of the pain and suffering of the world. But we really have to understand that they were able to hold the pain and suffering of the world without sacrificing themselves in the process.

Being empathic is a wonderful trait as long as you are not burdened by others' emotions. It doesn't help anybody to sacrifice yourself in the process of helping another.

In our family system there's an unspoken teaching that as a woman you should give away a piece of your soul to your children, to your husband or partner because that's just the sacrifice women make. That's how you protect your children and that's how you protect your loved ones.

From a shamanic point of view this is an extremely unhealthy stance to take because what happens when you give a piece of your soul to somebody else is that you end up burdening them with unusable energy. You can't use another person's soul for your own energy. So if you give a piece of your soul to a child or a loved one, you end up pulling back on that person's creativity because they are being burdened by this unusable energy.

And I'm very challenged when I work with mothers because mothers often say to me 'I don't understand the big deal about giving a piece of my soul to my child – I want to protect them, I want to hold them, I want to support them.' And it's very challenging to be able to teach them that when you give up a piece of your soul to someone you really love, you actually end up pulling them back and restricting them instead of being able to protect them.

To be able to support and love without actually giving a

piece of yourself away is something that many women don't really know how to do in this culture. And it's a work in progress and it has to do with learning boundaries between yourself and somebody else, learning how to be supportive while somebody's in pain without taking on their pain or sacrificing a piece of yourself thinking that by doing that you're actually going to help them with their pain, which you're not.

The highest evolution of my work has to do with teaching people in times of crisis to see a person in need in his or her divine light. We all have a central essence that's perfect within each and every one of us, and as we can acknowledge the divine light and divine perfection in another person – what we do is we stimulate that other person's radiance to really come through. And we end up helping to energetically and spiritually lift them out of the hole, where giving a piece of our soul away or acting with pity we end up pushing people further down. It is time for us to bring through the power of universal and unconditional love.

During a time on the planet when so many of us feel disempowered, it is crucial for us to understand that we have power right now to create positive change by incorporating spiritual practices into our lives. And we magnify the results when we focus our work together as a global community.

For Sandra, the key to living one's power in community is living with awareness of divine essence in yourself and others, and relating from and to this essence, which is highly individual. This is how we avoid giving parts of ourselves away in false community. Pamela Wilson describes the same task in different language, as looking within to feel a natural movement of energy and the space around the movement.

It is through this inner connection to divine essence, inner movement, or the world of spirit as Sobonfu calls it, that the power and energy of our individual self or soul enhance and enliven the spirit of community. In turn, our power is amplified when we find a way to contribute from our essential and natural selves.

Women's Healing Gifts

Women's tasks include disengaging from false community determined by our patriarchal world and connecting to the sustaining energies that can help us restore and live within genuine community. According to Sobonfu, this is our responsibility and we have gifts to help us fulfill it.

Women are the backbone of community. This is throughout all cultures, not just Africa. The people who send updates or family cards are women. The neighbors who reach out to other neighbors will be women. Our power to sustain community is connected to our capacity to give birth. We connect spirit into the earth. Women are able to weave community, to create networks that are life-sustaining.

A woman's body, consciousness, heart, and everything in between is made differently than a man's. Women are wired differently; our energy flows differently; we think and feel differently. We even breathe differently. Women tap into a different way of existing, into a different world. Women's gifts are used in order to see what energies the community needs for its own growth and for its survival. That's why women are prone to survival – that capacity to root into the earth and hold the natural goodness from the earth, to survive atrocities and various harmful energies.

In Dagara tradition one of the main roles of women in community is ensuring the survival of the human species, to protect life, to create a web or links between our world and other worlds less known to everyone. Women can bring the energy of survival into the center of community so the community can make use of it. Why can't men do this so easily? Because women have an open channel through our emotions – we can use our emotional channel. Our intuition and our senses enable us to tune into something that is not known or seen yet. Women see what's coming.

In my tribe, for instance, when a stranger comes to the community the women sit quietly and watch, not to just look but to see in how you walk and how you hold yourself what it is that you are bringing that is not apparent. So they can prepare how to receive you and so on. Lots of time when you go to a woman diviner she will ask you to walk – how are you carrying your gift? Your pain? How is all of that potential going to impact the community? This is something that is not evident to normal eyes, but women tap into that.

A key task for the survival of the global community, which includes all living beings as well as spirit beyond time, is for women to reclaim their awareness of this intuition and emotional knowing so we can access a sacred, hidden dimension. Sobonfu speaks of specific ways women can reclaim their gifts and begin the work of restoring community.

The hole in the soul of the world is a collective issue, and it needs a community response, which is to bring the sacred feminine energy and the energy of the earth back into the community. But the West is an individual culture and individual work is needed to recognize and participate in community and give community what it needs. Women must contribute.

Sobonfu's wisdom, which traces back centuries, fully lived and honored in Dagara tribal society, emphasizes some of women's powers identified in this book, described by other teachers and healers – like Dr. Sun, or Llewellyn Vaughan-Lee – from spiritual lineages seemingly distant and distinct. These teachers concur with Sobonfu, that women's powers have a key role in maintaining and restoring the community of life. These powers are not isolated in the lives of individuals, but when honored and lived play a key role in the whole of life.

From a tradition that has never ceased understanding and valuing women's spiritual responsibilities and gifts, we hear the need for women to be who we are in order to serve the present and the future:

Are there collective gifts of women? Yes – the gift of motherhood, the gift of sisterhood, and the gift of community. How do we live these gifts? If mothers could regain the sacredness of giving birth it would create healing and it would create a different way women see and value themselves and help humanity see and value itself.

We need to treat motherhood as a sacred act. Not put it in the world of the mundane. The way we birth needs to be reorganized; something needs to change in the way birthing happens. Now, our methods make women disconnect from this very important being that they are bringing into the world. The hospitals, the lack of breastfeeding, these create wounds. That's the beginning of the loss of humanity. This is the huge gap in the soul of the world, which is the damage done to us all from conception to children. If you are able to damage a woman, more likely the wound will be passed on to the child. That's a hole right there. It needs a lot of addressing. All the psychological help or medical help cannot make up for that loss.

Women need to understand the simple fact that the womb is not just a place for babies. It is a very charged magnetic center for a lot of energy that comes from many different dimensions, so that we need to take better care of it, and value it as a very delicate and powerful tool that we have been given. The womb is a gift that has been bestowed on us, and we are the caretakers of it. The womb is one of the entry points of spirit for women. So when we are fed bad energies we feel it in the womb.

Most women in the West don't know that there is an automatic mechanism in the womb that releases the toxicity of what we have taken into our systems – this happens during menstrual time. When we have PMS we are releasing energies we should never have taken in.

Western women don't understand the power of the breast, but we receive and emit energy from the breast as well. The breast is sacred – it is a sacred source of energy, enabling life to continue. The West's fascination with breasts is because people aren't breastfed, but in our tradition the breast is used to restore balance.

So there is a need to restore the sacredness of motherhood. And also to restore the sacredness of sisterhood. In my tribe we honor the gift of sisterhood. Women have their own quarters to help strengthen the identity of women as a whole. So we can create health and deal with the things that are not working – as women.

There are ways that women talk that don't need words. It's innate to us and it's why it's a challenge that when we are with men the vibration – the electrical connection – is not working because we do not talk to men the way we would talk to a sister.

Between sisters there is an understanding in the way we carry ourselves, in the way we carry our energy. Between sisters there's a lot of communication that happens through our body, through our eye contacts or spiritual contacts, which enables us to converse without words.

Creating Healing Energies

Part of women's work is to work together, *as women*, Sobonfu says. Through trusting other women and honoring sisterhood we amplify feminine energies and introduce them back into community. But we need to stop competing with each other:

> Women can recognize we are not on survival mode; we do not have to struggle for resources and compete with each other. What happens when we are put on survival mode? We fight to survive! And then we live in a world based on scarcity and competition.

In order to move into a future that empowers genuine community, a way of living together that supports the truth of abundance, we do not just withdraw from false community, but we have to become *creative*. Sobonfu explains this next step:

> What we take in from the scarcity-world creates frantic community. So we have to create energies that enable us to recognize there's enough for all of us. It's time to begin healing all this wounding that we do to each other.

Sobonfu's suggestion that we create energies that undermine and bypass fears of scarcity and remind us we have enough – is so important. We don't always understand that we can create energies that can benefit us all. Buddhists understand the potential of generating compassion for the sake of ending suffering in the world. But in the western spiritual mindset, so often we are not truly committed to serving the world; we tend to want to generate compassion to help us feel better.

Love, compassion, peace, generosity, awareness of life's abundance are all healing energies that come from and strengthen the community of life. And while formal spiritual practices like prayer or meditation help develop these energies, so do all the powers described in this book. Women have forgotten how creative we are. How what is natural within us is always working to bring forth and nourish life.

We have forgotten how truly alive life is and, as with anything alive, how it needs us to work with it, care for it, join with and give to it. This is the deep meaning of the now popular term 'co-creation.' As human beings we have the power to work with life-force and the energies within life. Our hearts are the gateway and the generator. But for women especially, our creativity generates energies that heal life all the way down to the ground, as our bodies are connected to the earth in a unique way as bearers of children.

As mothers, we can remember how creation happens, and how it involves the power of our longing and our love, and our bodies and our hearts both. The energies released through the birth of a child – the immense love, the nourishment, the care, the conscious awareness of life's utter holiness – all are available to us at other times too.

Just as Dr. Sun describes how women can use prayer and spiritual practice to activate the chakra in their breasts after breastfeeding, women can, through conscious intention, learn to use the natural wisdom and power of our being to support the larger community.

The powers in this book, like the recognition of life's sacredness, our capacity to nourish, our longing, our instinctual connection to earth, are the living truths of our lives. They are natural to us, and through coming to recognize and honor them, we access, activate, and empower these forces of life.

For many women, it can feel that if something takes work it is not 'natural.' But that is because we limit our understanding of 'work' to effort and willpower, and forget that we can work with the energies of life through love and through care, through longing, through openness and receptivity. 'Work' includes allowing ourselves to need what we need, and honoring our needs as they shape our inner and outer lives both. This honoring is an act of consciousness, a shift of attention, a willingness to know ourselves.

Helpful in this process of changing our ideas and our practices around creative 'work' is to revive the power of sisterhood, as Sobonfu describes it. Through being with other women, we can confirm and reflect what is natural to us. Women's power is so deep and so fully embodied that it can be transmitted without words and without willpower. It is as though we can remind each other of what's real and alive inside us just by being together. Sobonfu explains:

> Part of this means remembering the gift of sisterhood. The best support for another woman is another woman. But the enemy of a woman is another woman when she doesn't know the value of sisterhood.

Women contain so much of the wisdom that is needed to create the future. But we must work together and not against each other, reminding each other of what is important and supporting each other as we move with what is natural further and further afield.

Women have always understood a deeply simple and powerful aspect of community, the reality that needing each other is sacred. We have lived that awareness in our most private relationships as mothers and children, and as wives historically dependent upon husbands' strength. And somewhere we know it with our sisters, as Sobonfu says. This too we need to reclaim – to rejuvenate and restore our identity as women, which has been nearly lost in the homogeneity demanded by a dominant patriarchal value system.

Sobonfu says, 'The wound is where the healing is,' and this is so true today in our communities that have nearly disintegrated in the corrosion of extreme individualism and self-interest. But women know another community – a more genuine community. If we are willing to restore this inner knowing, and align with it as it does its own creative work with our attention and our commitment... who knows what can be born?

Chapter 7

Longing

As the sun from its highest zenith,
Sinks down into the night,
Thus also do we sink,
Soul and body.
Mechtilde of Magdeburg[29]

A woman's heart rarely breaks out into the universe – into the realm of ideals or heavenly abstraction. It breaks into life and bleeds into the earth, into the many details – faces, hands, grasses, and rivers – of life. This outpouring nourishes the entire web of existence. To live with a willingness for this heartbreak, and even a need for it, is to live our longing, which is one of the greatest powers in all creation and one of women's most important spiritual gifts. It gives a way for the soul to be part of life in greater and greater measure, and gives way for life to enter us more and more deeply.

Longing is a state of vulnerability and deep need. It can be like a cry in the heart – or a whisper. It can feel like a tender sorrow you want to watch over and protect – like when a lover is away and you await his or her return. It can feel like a haunting homesickness for a faraway place. It can be an anguish that tears you apart – as with the death of someone dear to you – and it can be a terrible sense that something is not right in the world, no matter what you do.

You can hear the longing painfully sung in the old slave song:

Sometimes I feel like a motherless child,
Sometimes I feel like a motherless child,
Sometimes I feel like a motherless child,

A long way from home...

And you can hear it as regret in a contemporary Emmylou Harris song:

There's a valley of sorrow in my soul
Where every night I hear the thunder roll
Like the sound of a distant drum
Over all the damage I have done...[30]

We mostly hear about 'longing' in a spiritual context, such as in the longing of a heart for God, as described in Psalms 42:1: 'As a deer thirsts for water, so thirsts my soul for you, O God.'

At the same time, longing is not just our own need; it is also a need of the divine. This is the mystery of the Islamic *hadith*: 'I was a hidden treasure and I longed to be known, so I created the world.'

Longing is deep within us and it needs to be recognized and honored. As we look into the core of our many sadnesses and see them for what they are – our deep need for something real or enduring – we allow them to grow and lead us through life, shredding away what does not matter and aligning us, like a compass, to our true north. Women's longing is key to this moment in time. It is critical in recreating communities, restoring the sacredness of the earth, and purifying life so something new can be born. If we honor this hidden power, we release and generate tremendous energy for change.

The Power of Longing

What is the ultimate point of longing? It brings us closer and closer to what's real and brings what's real closer and closer to us. When we long for love we search for it. When we long for meaning we engage with life to find meaning. When we grow tired of games and superficialities, we look and pray and work towards what is more enduring.

All of these things we do for our own sake as we move from the surface to the depths. At the same time our searching and our commitments serve life. As we relate to life through our genuine need, our attention, our care, our consciousness all engage with life. Longing is about connection. We long to bring things to and into us and as we follow our longing we create deeper and deeper connections.

As we move through the amusement park of our world to find meaning, meaning itself *is found*. As we work for peace, peace becomes more and more active. As we open ourselves to love, love has more places to thrive.

But this power must be recognized and lived in order for it to be activated. 'Ask and ye shall receive,' says the Bible in Matthew, and this asking is the voice of longing. Without it, we do not receive – nothing comes together; nothing is revealed.

This deeply spiritual truth of 'asking' is an obvious everyday reality. When we talk with our friends or partners about our most genuine innermost needs, often this is what compels a heartfelt response. When we look on the face of a suffering human being or animal, compassion is called forth often effortlessly. Very little takes place from within a closed heart. Rather it's our openness, our vulnerability, and real need that transform a moment.

To live our longing means to honor the suffering in our lives and at the same time give ourselves to what is needed in the moment. We can follow longing until it reveals that what we thought we needed was a covering over of something more important and then have the courage to let go of that veil. This is a process of letting go – but letting go into something deep and real.

This process is at work in so many areas of our lives. We allow our longing for justice or peace to fuel our work – against all odds – for social change. We long to be healthy, to feel a vital life-essence in our bodies, so we let go of our addictions to unhealthy food. We would not make that passage through absence or withdrawal if we did not have access to life-force itself, which is so intertwined with our longing.

We are drawn into a love affair only to find in it destructive elements. We allow our longing for something better, deeper, and more enduring to ferry us through the loneliness of breaking up.

We can even leave behind a spiritual teacher when his path or light becomes an impediment to knowing what is uniquely ours. We allow a longing for truth to lead us into the unknown with no guide.

In all these cases, longing drives us deeper in and further on, all the while supporting us as we allow the old to pass away. This support is possible because longing is an essential life-force. It is not an abstract 'idea' or a 'concept' that sustains us for a bit but loses energy or appeal when a new idea comes on the scene. It is not like an object of desire that ends up being of no real use. Longing is one of the greatest powers in the universe, always at work through us, with us, for its own ultimate purpose. It is given to help us come home.

As we live the power of longing, we are at the same time building our strength and endurance, and honing our power to discriminate. Longing is this same need that draws to us the most basic nourishment of life. But we can ask – What do we really hunger after? What do we really want? What do we really need? And why? With these questions, we begin to sort out the substitutes from the real thing, and give longing's power a central role. We understand that eating a big meal might help in the moment, but within our relationship to food lies a deeper hunger to feel whole in our own bodies and to connect to the earth around us through its nourishment. There are many things in our world like a 'big meal' and we need to recognize and move past them.

This discrimination is a key step in a woman's development toward wholeness, and it is fueled by longing. In the myth of

Psyche and Eros – which is often interpreted in our modern day as an archetypal description of the development of women's consciousness – discrimination is the first task Psyche faces as, pregnant and longing for her beloved Eros, she works through a series of seemingly impossible tasks set for her by Eros's jealous mother, Aphrodite. In this first task she must sort into separate piles a huge heap of different kinds of seeds all mixed in together. It is her longing for Eros that drives this task of painstaking discrimination, and it is her longing that attracts what she needs in order to complete it.

Longing pushes us to use our discrimination. It compels a search and a sorting. As we let it drive us, it provides the clarity we need to sort out the false from the true, the necessary from the wasteful, and carry us deeper into the essential center. By using discrimination with our longing, we can start to see all the ways we compromise what is most important for an instant fix of safety or satisfaction. Once our consciousness is attuned to these subtle compromises, we become less able to indulge them.

Longing is eternal. Its objects are often of momentary interest. We forget the bad habits once they're gone. We forget the bad boyfriends. We put the useless to the side and move through and move on. But the longing with its promises and its heartache both becomes a most trusted friend.

Longing in Women

The journey that longing takes us on is process-oriented, not object-oriented. Our yearning carries us through life, ripening our experience, developing all the while a strength, endurance, and devotion that grows and grows as we give ourselves and endure our losses. What are we devoted to? We can call it 'Truth' or 'Love' or 'God.' But for women, these labels are often too abstract. Instead, we call it 'my children,' 'the garden,' 'our family,' 'my art.'

This is one of women's spiritual gifts – we have so many

names for the Sacred.

In many of our patriarchal religions, we find a strong distinction between relative and Absolute, with the sense that Absolute is not part of the relative world. The Absolute is a transcendent, distant force absent from life. It leaves a taste of divinity in our hearts, and we look only to heaven or 'liberation' for the promise of more.

But while the divine Creator exists – and our hearts long for Him – there is also the Divine within creation, and our hearts also long for Her. This is generally women's natural orientation. It is not less or more real than men's. But in some ways, in this world, today, it might be more relevant.

This does not mean that women don't have a yearning for a transcendent Absolute. Of course we do. But it is also the case that we long for intimacy with the immanent. And since the divine immanent has not been equally valued in our dominant religious systems, that longing is also not honored.

The stripping away of ordinary life as we step toward the transcendent Creator is a male model, which often does not work for women. But it also does not work for *life itself*, which has been left in the dust of the race for transcendence.

In a traditional male search, perhaps decades of practice and often austerities can bring union with God, which then leads us back to earth and to the divinity that is present here. This is the state of 'oneness' described in spiritual literature – realized during a long journey.

But this journey takes place in time, and in all the years that a man – or a male society – is focused on the transcendent, the immanent is ignored. And if not everybody makes the journey to the divine oneness that is ultimately revealed, then still the immanent remains unacknowledged.

This is very real danger in a patriarchal model. We hear this perspective in the title of a popular Buddhist book by ex-monk Jack Kornfield: *After the Ecstasy, the Laundry*, which chronicles the traditional male journey of a monastic approach including years in retreat and subsequent return to the world with new awareness.

But who has been doing the laundry during all those years?

Most women do not have the luxury of leaving the laundry behind in a search for ecstatic union. Women are the homemakers and the caretakers of children. We live with tons of laundry! If ecstasy is to be found, it will be found before, after, and during the laundry. In the little objects found in pockets, in the unfolding of socks, in the untangling of a sleeve, in the repair of an elastic tie loosened during the spin cycle. This is in part because these tasks are natural vehicles for our love or care, natural reflections of the immanent dimension of the divine, but also because if women did not know how to bring love and care to these tasks, we would go crazy. And many have. But those who survived with all that laundry, all those denied opportunities for outer expansion, all those restricted choices, all those *earthly* chores, know a secret we all need to hear – the secret of how the ecstasy is always with us, and how there is no before or after when it comes to divine presence.

This is not a gender-specific secret; it is a secret of life and of the divine. But women's historically restricted outer landscape and our natural and embodied wholeness work together to offer a continual – if not terrifying – invitation into this secret.

Today, the dominant paradigm of the spiritual search is losing ground as women's natural instinct toward recognizing the immanent nature of the divine has come to the fore through more and more women's involvement in spiritual life, and as all of us recognize where this paradigm has left the planet – in a shadowy degradation.

The era of honoring divine immanence is upon all of us, men and women both. The world as a whole needs the renewal that comes from having its divine nature acknowledged. And women need the opportunity to live our longing in ways that are natural to us. This symmetry is no happenstance. But men still resist women stepping into their power and women still hesitate to claim what is ours. Our hesitation comes from both an internalized historical blindness to our uniqueness and a fear of what it will mean in our lives. For as we live our longing, what is not real – what is not truly alive and resonant – will have to go.

We must be bold and honor messages of longing without the need for affirmation from the outer world or even other seekers or teachers. Our dreams and our hearts will guide us, and other women can affirm our instincts. Longing will come in so many ways. It will come in dreams and through regrets; it can come in a sudden need to engage with life in a new way, or an exhaustion with an old way.

In a dream from a woman in British Columbia, the dreamer is approached by an ancient archetypal energy:

I am standing on the back deck of my house looking out at the ocean. I notice a pod of pure black orcas swimming into the Bay. I feel the excitement of seeing them. There are three or four of them and I can see their beautiful dorsal fins and sense their majestic presence. Standing beside me is a woman I recently worked on a project with; she is actually an Orca researcher and much more knowledgeable about these creatures than I.

Suddenly the orcas transform into large, somewhat intimidating pure black dragons that emerge from the water. Instead of going to her – the expert – surprisingly, they approach me. As I stand there in awe and some concern, one of them says: 'We need your help.' I back away, explaining that I'm pretty sure I don't know how to help dragons.

This dreamer associates the orcas and then the dragons with feminine energy, 'what is in the darkness, unspoken, yet alive, somewhere seen in the unseen,' she explains. This 'unseen' realm is confusing and even frightening, and the dreamer backs away from this invitation to help. Her psychological dynamics are at the fore of her experience, revealing to her psyche that she is not yet prepared to relate to this depth. But after contemplating the dream and feeling into it, she evoked a greater willingness not to doubt this part of herself that is alive but unknowable. 'I went from feeling almost guilty and uncertain and doubtful (weak) about things I knew, or sensed, to accepting them as part of my life and just another aspect of who I am.'

Women's instinctual nature is connected to the archetypal energies symbolized by the dragon, which in the past had to be slaughtered on the male heroic quest. By connecting to it, this dreamer finds a new way to be with this deep energy. A way that is more confident, more centered in herself. And she discovers this place by feeling, and acknowledging, the need of the dragons for her help. It is a need here, a longing, a desperate call that connects her to herself.

Longing comes from the depths of our being. It is not the need for the insights of the 'expert' knowledgeable friend, but a cry for help from the darkness of the ocean, the inner hidden terrain of feeling and instinct. For this dreamer, what is important is that she feels, knows, is moved by these cries, that she recognizes and responds to the dragons. It is for her to come closer and closer to this dragon energy, this primal earth and spirit energy that has been lost to consciousness, killed by the princes and heroes of the past as they have lived out their own quests within her individual psyche and throughout our collective psyche. It is for her to become intimate with the dragon; but the first step in this intimacy and this honoring is the longing to which she responds.

For a writer from Seattle, longing came through a very different dream image:

I enter a coffee shop. I notice that President Obama is in this shop too. He is waiting his turn to order, and I hang back respectfully giving him space. He sees me and sits next to me on a bench. He greets me – speaking my name, which I am very touched by. His face is so close to mine, and he says, 'Can you do more? You can do more! You can do more!' At the same time, I say to him: 'You can do more! Please do more. Be bold! Things can change!' I see in the lines of his dark face that tears are starting to flow. I feel on my own face this flow of tears. We sit, crying, in this intimate, tender, and heavy sadness.

For this dreamer, it is the need to contribute in the world, imaged by the President, that calls to her. She is reminded that she can do more to help people, the country, the world – not in an abstract or 'spiritual' way, but in a worldly and political way. For her, the time had come to go outward and contribute.

For a 70-year-old woman from Washington, longing takes on a new form after years of living a certain way:

You know, I have always been such a thinker. I've been a scientist. I've lived in my head. I've done spiritual practices that seem to be about my mind. It's only now that I understand that all this has been missing something. I look at my life now, and what I really long for – what I really want – is to connect with the earth, to the land, and my body. To know and feel more of that. I spend more time in my garden. I am trying to listen to what my body needs so I can feel healthier. I just want this connection to the earth. Sometimes, when I realize what I've missed all those years, how I've stayed in some abstract space all the while this other beautiful thing was happening, I just feel so much regret. But as soon as I really turn to the earth and say – I want this, I want to know you – it is like She embraces me completely and all that time away didn't matter at all. I can't put in words how this feels – how it wipes away all the sense of loss that could otherwise be so painful...

This woman is being called into deep relationship with the earth, after a lifetime of ignoring it. As she honors her longing, she is taken into a place of wholeness where the disconnect of the mind and all that comes with it – fear, regret, separation – is somehow dissolved in intimacy.

It is so important for women to allow ourselves to long for what we long for and not to deny our longing or try to fit it into a small box created by past ideas or other people's models.

In our modern world, so many of us are feeling such unease about life and civilization. We feel the pain of struggling to find a place in a patriarchal world, and the pain of a soul trying to go home. For many women, there is no distinction between these two – between the spiritual and the world. It is so important for women to let their longing live regardless of any kind of 'spiritual' or 'worldly' duality. Otherwise, we keep our power locked in a closet where it cannot serve.

Longing and Attachment

Culture at large has little place for women's longing. But perhaps more undermining is the lack of awareness of longing's power in spiritual communities. For too long, women have been denigrated for their multitude of 'attachments.' But what might seem like attachments from a male perspective are often simply ways that women live their longing – in life. Emotional attachments to other people, to objects, to experiences, to animals and plants, to our children can be vehicles for service, not impediments to spiritual achievements.

We read and are told that attachments are indicative of a life controlled by our desires and excessive needs. Emotional ups and downs and sexual desire reflect strong attachments. The need to be with other people – even to be loved – and our need to help others in order to feel OK are also attachments.

In contrast, detachment indicates a state in which we are free from all these ties that bind. This freedom has long been associated with a life of renunciation, a sense of cool reserve achieved through leaving behind family and society and ordinary concerns. Jesus left his family, the Buddha left his wife and children, and following in these footsteps yogis, monks and nuns have long associated detachment and spiritual freedom with isolation or turning from worldly life.

But 'detachment' seems quite a lot like the 'autonomy' and 'separation' that have been heralded as critical aspects of human psychological maturity, and which Carol Gilligan so astutely pointed out as male values in a patriarchal field. Women and girls develop differently, she argued. More recent research in brain chemistry and evolutionary psychology confirms this. Of course this is relevant spiritually as well.

What happens through attachment? Two beings share energy and experience. A woman attached to her dog shares herself with her dog, and experiences her dog as part of her world. A woman attached to her job gives herself with a commitment not present if she is not attached. A woman attached to a man opens herself and lives *with*, allowing nurturing and love to pour through the container of union.

Attachment with our children is a necessary element in their development, and it is no surprise that attachment disorders plague many young people today in a western culture that has denied the power of attachment and emphasized individualism even in babies and young children. We still do not understand that an emphasis on detachment and individualism is a cultural construct, not active in other cultures. It's time to look at attachment anew, and see it as a necessary vehicle for energy exchange and for the forces that can only come to life through connection, community and need.

Through too much emphasis on detachment, we can easily activate subtle energies and attitudes that might look like spiritual discipline, but are actually harmful, not just to our spiritual awakening, but to life around us, which depends on our connection and yes, even attachment to it. Instead of freeing ourselves from our limited point of view or desires, we solidify our psychological or spiritual prejudice against being fully involved in life. We turn from the vulnerabilities and responsibilities that come along with that involvement, we leave ourselves cut off from life's nourishment, and we leave life cut off from powerful gifts inherent in human consciousness.

Women, particularly, who struggle to find their place in our worldly as well as spiritual systems often don't realize that they are often struggling against our own nature – which is to value attachment, connection, and the primal instinct to hold others and life itself close.

Women are not just attached to caring – life is attached to women's care.

Longing's Shadow

Like all powers, longing has a shadow side. When we don't live our deepest attachment to love, life, nourishment, we become attached to imposters and quick fixes. If we don't acknowledge our genuine needs, we become psychologically desperate and compromising. If we don't honor the inner weakness and vulnerability of our souls, we become weak and powerless. The longing of the soul when it is not acknowledged fuels many psychological habits and addictions that keep us powerless and afraid, and at the same time distracted from the power within us.

With longing, the shadow side has a great deal to do with needs that are never met or resolved. Longing is the need of the soul for what is real and truly transformative or nourishing. But if longing is not recognized and lived, its energies emerge through life-destroying forms of attachments like addictions, which is perhaps the most dramatic example of psychological, physical and behavioral patterning that just goes round and round, undermining the possibility for growth and development.

The life-serving attachments of longing – the ways we are drawn deeper into connections and relationships through genuine need – are negatively mirrored by addictions' life-destroying attachments to substances or experiences that trap us. But the deep life-force is the same, and the trick is to become conscious about the true nature of our needs and develop the courage to stay true to them.

One man on the Sufi path had a heroin addiction. But his Sufi teacher told him that it could be resolved since the need for heroin was essentially the need for love. In a loving relationship with his wife and through his commitment to his spiritual path, which works with love, his longing could be released and channeled in life-supporting rather than life-denying channels. A Buddhist woman suffered from eating disorders much of her life, but when she discovered the love that was present on the level of the soul she could finally stay true to her need for that love and let go of self-destructive habits.

There are many ways we live a confused and twisted longing unconsciously. Many of the afflictions that plague modern women, like depression, substance abuse, eating disorders, abusive relationships, and self-destructiveness, can be expres-sions of a confusion about longing and how to live it. This confusion is amplified in modern society that has little reflection of the power of our genuine longing, and continually feeds us alternatives that distract us.

Our hunger for real nourishment in a world that does not fully support breastfeeding, sells us Twinkies, Coke, and foods filled with toxins, and makes organic food unaffordable turns up in eating disorders and endless dieting. Our longing to be loved is hidden under our compulsion for romantic relationships or sexual situations that offer fleeting fulfillment but nothing that lasts. Our yearning to connect drives us into any form of partnership we can find just to relieve an aching loneliness. Our longing to experience our real power keeps us demanding material security to stave off the fear of powerlessness.

Often relationships or situations in which we feel like a victim are twisted ways of living our longing. We stay in situations that evoke in us that sense of being tortured or martyred because there is a pleasure to it. Unfortunately, this is not longing's real sweetness, but a distorted version that distracts us from the real thing.

There are many ways we try to put an end to the great need that often seems to roar within us like a terrible hunger. But they don't work, because these are not what we really long for. As Carl Jung said, 'Neurosis is always a substitute for legitimate suffering.' He understood that there is a legitimate suffering, pushing us toward awakening and transformation that is easily thwarted by substitutes.

There are so many ways that our longing can get tied into psychological patterns of impotence and self-destruction. And this is why discrimination is so important. We need honesty and clarity to see the threads of our longing and untangle them from our psychological patterns. Longing is from the soul, carries a different note and feel than our psychological needs. To be willing to let go of the psychological needs and feel into the often more frightening needs of the soul can be painful and even horri-fying as this domain is vast and deep, so much bigger than anything we have known.

But the alternative of not valuing our longing, not following where it leads, exacts a price we should not be willing to pay. The self-immolation of women in Arab countries as a last resource in a life that has no place for them is perhaps the most horrifying example of what happens when the burning of our souls to be ourselves has no outlet and we turn this burning against ourselves. This horrifying self-destruction is taking place not just in Arab countries but in other forms across the world even in countries where women have rights and opportunities. Still we self-destruct; still we do not honor the power within us; still we give in to the forgetting that swallows us up and spits out a silly substitute.

Women will burn one way or another. We can be aflame with love and devotion for what is real, or we will burn out or accept the slow self-immolation of a meaningless life of materialistic distractions or romantic delusions. It is up to us which kind of burning we will allow.

Women and Pain

One of the main reasons we ignore our longing is because its pain is deep and unending. Lesser pain, pain that we create and control, is much more palatable.

To live our longing means to understand something about women's pain. Pain is part of all of our lives, but for women this is especially true. Pain is intertwined with our longing and how we live our longing in life. Our bodies are often in pain monthly during menstruation, a physical reflection of emptying, purification, waiting – and longing for new life and love. We are in pain on and off throughout nine months of carrying a child, and then when our fertility comes to an end we can suffer the pain of years of menopause. Our hearts carry the sorrows of our family and the sorrows of life around us. We are touched, moved, and saddened in so many ways that many men have difficulty understanding. Our sorrow and our despair are expressions of our longing and also our instinct toward community – reflecting how our feelings reach down into our bodies, and how they stretch out into the community of life.

Women have filled mental hospitals for centuries because a patriarchal world cannot see the wisdom or meaning in our heartache. But our pain – so much a part of longing – is a key to the healing of all of us. It needs to be rescued from our cultural waste-bin that holds so much of women's experience, taken out and looked at anew.

Like so many feminine mysteries, longing is a mystery of

wholeness. It appears as a lack, as a need, but in truth it is a living sign of unification and nearness. When a woman follows longing to its source, she experiences her need as not solely her own, but a need that belongs to life itself, just as longing for partnership and children is an expression of life itself needing to continue. Longing reveals how we are connected to and vehicles for the whole of life, how our deepest needs are actually individual expressions of forces much bigger than ourselves.

Similarly, the pains we feel are tied consciously and unconsciously to the pains of life and the pains of a collective civilization. A woman can dream the dreams of her children and her family; she can know the currents of potential that need to be lived by her children and partner. She can also hold the dreams of the earth and the dreams of life around her. Her longing is the longing of a civilization and of a God trying to find expression through its creation. Our longing and our pain are part of the pain of an entire world. And they are the birth pains of a civilization struggling to awaken.

When women stop individualizing and internalizing our longing and the pain of longing, when we see them as expressions of something much bigger, we take a step into longing's power, which is connected to the power of community, a power activated only when we see ourselves as part of a bigger picture. Our pain is a realistic response to living in a world that has lost touch with what is real to us. It is the pain of wanting and needing something different and not knowing how to manifest it. It is also a historical pain, passed through the actual blood of mothers to daughters, from which sons are spared. It is a pain that, once acknowledged, becomes fuel for change, just as our own individual pain often wakes us up to the need for a different way of living.

Women's pain has a key role to play during this moment of history. It has been denied for a very long time. But our pain does not only belong to us – it really isn't ours to deny, on either a personal or collective level. It belongs to the whole. It has a place in the whole. It has energy and wisdom for the entire community of life. The power of longing and the power of community cannot work together until we see our heartache in a new light, recognize its wisdom, and understand it is life working through us and not our own personal problems.

Women's history of oppression and abuse, our broken hearts and our broken bodies, our missed opportunities and our struggles for dignity, our dying children and our dying earth have left us with a unique suffering and a unique longing, with a key role in the evolution of the whole. Our attachments have created threads of attention and consciousness that can give and receive nourishment and healing – if recognized and used.

There is an important need for women to bring our deepest longing into alignment with our natural connectedness and see how they can work together. This includes and depends upon a willingness to bear the pain of how we have ignored our connectedness and broken our attachments to life in an effort to survive or succeed in a world that does not honor them. It depends upon a willingness to bear the pain of how we ourselves have compromised what is most natural and real. Does this mean more pain, more suffering? Not exactly – it means letting go of the neurosis and swimming in the ocean of longing that is our nature, which is the nature of life and the divine.

In a mysterious recognition of the role of woundedness and longing in the unfolding of the divine throughout life, the great Sufi, Attar, speaking in the voice of another great Sufi mystic, Bayazid Bistami, wrote:

They called to me in my innermost interior: 'Oh Bayazid. Our treasure chambers are filled with approved deeds of obedience and pleasing acts of worship. If you want Us, offer up something which We don't have!' I said: 'What is it that

You don't have?' The voice said: 'Helplessness and impotence, need and humility and a broken spirit.'31

Women's brokenness is not the same brokenness as the patriarchal collective's. Just as subcultures that have been oppressed – Native American cultures, African American cultures and others – have their own unique constellation of pain, so does the collective of women. It is a unique brokenness with unique consequences for life around us. As Sobonfu Somé said, 'The wound is where the gift is,' and this is relevant to women. Our wounds are part of the whole and need conscious acknowledgment by the whole. Just as we as a collective will benefit from deeper acknowledgment of the holocaust of indigenous peoples and the recognition of continued suffering of those peoples and the ancestors of slaves, so will we all benefit from becoming more aware of women's suffering and its hidden meanings.

The power of our pain cannot serve its purpose if it is unlived, dishonored, forgotten, or unclaimed. This is an imperative for women – to see the hidden nature of our wounds, to acknowledge them, to see them for what they are – a passageway of power that has not yet consciously been released into life.

Years ago, a Buddhist woman from Boston had a vision of a constellation of lights:

In my mind's eye I saw a vast constellation of lights, hanging and blinking in the night sky above the earth. They were like stars, but they were not stars. Somehow I knew that this constellation was the longing of individual women – interconnected, creating a whole web or container or vehicle. But there was a clear sense that it needed to be on earth, in our bodies. It was as though the stars were our hearts projected outward and upward, disembodied and somehow useless up there.

I was left with the sadness of this situation, and the dire need for women to honor the ways our longing works with and serves life on earth.

Chapter 8

Receiving

I felt my lungs inflate with the onrush of scenery: air, mountains, trees, people.
I thought, 'This is what it is to be happy.'
Sylvia Plath[32]

Receiving does not seem like a power, but it is. It is to giving as longing is to love. It is the building of momentum before manifestation, the hidden aspect of everything in life. It is the bringing in that allows the giving, the wave curling back to its ocean before sprawling out to the shore, the inhale of the spiraling breath of creation.

Receiving works with every other power in this book. We cannot be nourished if we cannot receive, and we can't nourish others if we have nothing to give. We cannot know the power of beauty if our eyes, ears, or hearts are closed. We cannot know love if our longing has not carved a space for us to receive it. We cannot work with the energies of the earth if we do not allow those energies into and through our being. And receptivity is a critical aspect of community, as when we receive we participate in the resource exchange that creates and sustains all aspects of community.

Sobonfu Somé explains the importance of receiving in real community:

Part of the work of community is to make sure we know receiving is an aspect of community. We don't know the difference between taking and receiving. 'Taking' leaves a hole. Receiving reassures you of abundance. Receiving doesn't mean you are taking away from someone; there are no scarce resources. In community, there is enough for everybody.

There is little reflection of the power of receiving in the outer workings of our world – so few areas where it's truly understood or valued. Listening is one of those areas, though most don't do it very well. And when we want to get pregnant, our physical receptivity to a man becomes critical. But generally we focus so much on expressions of power that we have hardly any sense of what precedes, creates, or drives those expressions – we have no eyes to see what comes before, what allows and holds. Morally, we value 'giving' more than 'receiving' and we do so in a way that often diminishes receiving as part of a psychological inadequacy or neediness, when in fact it is a spiritual power that makes every gift possible.

If receiving is so widespread, so much a part of life itself, why is it a 'woman's' power? All of us can acknowledge the power of receptivity. Receiving is a feminine counterbalance in the great play of opposites with masculine expressiveness. It is the receiving valley in the *Tao Te Ching*, to which we are advised to always return, steering clear of too much time with the rising mountains.

We can all value receptivity and bring balance back into a world that has been guided by patriarchal principles. We can learn the tools of listening, intuition, attentiveness without action, and deepen our capacity to take in nourishment on all levels – to allow ourselves to feel and be loved. We can learn to bring energy into our bodies so that we feel stronger and more alive, and into our awareness so that it can expand our consciousness and make us 'bigger' people. Without receiving spiritual guidance through the messages of our life, we stay stuck in repetitive habits and old ways of thinking. If we cannot take in spiritual energy, we do not evolve.

But there is a significant difference in how women and men

live the power of receptivity, which like other powers is grounded in and interdependent with our bodies and our role in procreation and also in our spiritual responsibilities in the process of creation and divine revelation.

Women and Receptivity

How does a modern woman, often still struggling to live in physical security free from violation, welcome life energy inside her? How does a woman so overfilled with conditioned thoughts and values sense an inner space of natural openness? How can a woman whose voice has rarely been heard practice listening? How can she give herself to the feminine power of receiving without losing ground or losing herself?

The short answer is practice. Because as soon as we consciously practice receiving, we feel and know how powerful it is. We experience receiving not as a place of instability or weakness, but as a foundation of great strength.

Elizabeth Frediani, who has worked with subtle energy for healing and spiritual practice for over thirty years, explains the importance of receiving:

> Receptivity incorporates many layers of experience. It is how you connect with your body in a way that is present and awake to sensory feeling. It is about your willingness to connect with another person and feel what moves between you and her or him.
>
> Receiving also applies to your connection with the earth, nature, and transpersonal and elemental forces. Receptivity to self, to others, to the environment, and to spiritual energies literally nourishes your energy system. Receiving is an integrated experience of connection, presence, and taking in.
>
> Every time you feel exhausted, afraid, creatively stagnant or spiritually uninspired, you are suffering from a lack of receptivity! Your energy system, body, and heart are not in a

receiving state. You are not connected, present, or taking in. When you receive, you are full.

Helping individuals learn to receive energy is a central theme of the subtle energy work I offer. Women most often understand the importance of receiving and appreciate it from the start. The first step of developing receptivity has to do with the heart chakra and allowing the love that we would willingly outpour to others back into self. When women allow the flow of energy and love into themselves their response is immediate – they feel elation and bliss.

Women recognize and celebrate the feeling of energy coming in. They are so highly attuned to this. Women recognize it as replenishing, awakening, and grounding. The recognition is instantaneous.

This often immediate response means that right away women understand and relate to the power of receiving, and quickly attune to it. So from one point of view, it just takes a bit of practice. This practice is part of Elizabeth's work, and helps women begin to open to an inner life, which is closed off if we cannot receive. This inner awareness, and the process of bringing energy in, is critical to health, happiness, and spiritual growth.

A longer answer has to do with levels. It can be helpful to understand the issue of levels when we look at women's power to receive. We are always engaged on various levels of existence, each with their own rules and patterns, its own ways of working, its own energy flow. For example, our physical bodies must take in food to survive. For psychological health we need to be able to take in love as well as criticism. For spiritual growth we need spiritual energy and we need to be able to listen for guidance from the soul.

At times, all these levels come together in an integrated moment. But often, they work independently, still with the possibility of being in harmony. For example, a nun living in a convent is not going to receive a man through intercourse, but she can receive divine nourishment through her heart. A businesswoman in a boardroom needs to listen to other people's ideas and thoughts, but she will lose herself if she is not trained to listen inwardly, to her gut intuition. A woman on a fast will not be taking in food, but that does not mean she is not receiving love from another person. From these examples one can see that there are times to create boundaries in one area of life in order to open channels in another.

At other times, barriers on one level can get in the way of receiving on another. A woman whose capacity to listen to other people is compromised likely will not be able to develop her capacity to listen spiritually. Sometimes a woman needs to receive spiritual sustenance through her intimate sexual relationships and through the food she eats. It takes listening and attunement to sense when and how we need to be receptive.

Why is it important to understand there are many levels and ways of receiving? Because as we practice working with this power it's important to know that receiving does not necessarily leave us vulnerable to violence either physical or emotional, or the violence of ideas. Women can – and must – build boundaries where boundaries are needed in order to protect the place where we will be open to receive.

Building boundaries where they are needed also allows us to hold what we receive so it can become an effective creative force. It is of little use to be receptive if we cannot hold and use what is given. We don't ever give birth if we cannot hold first sperm and then the growing fetus. A vessel with holes in it cannot hold water. In a similar way, our entire being can only hold so much when we are unstable.

Attuning to our receptivity – knowing when and how to be open and take in – is not an easy task. It includes and depends upon an increased willingness to be responsible caretakers of our entire being – to watch over our bodies and our souls with discrimination, care, and lots of common sense.

It can help this process to understand more about how receiving works in women, how it is multilayered, how it functions in different aspects of life, and how it is different from men's experience.

Esoteric Underpinnings – Energy Fields and Fluctuations

Women's receiving role in procreation reflects our fundamental place in the process of life's continuing and sustaining itself. This role is multilayered and multileveled.

It's not easy to recognize the many ways women are receiving and bringing energy and information inward. One commonly referenced way is 'women's intuition,' the often uncanny way that women receive ideas/hints/messages from life. Our intuition can come in the form of a feeling in the gut, or an image in the mind, or just a 'knowing.' Women are intuitive in part because our esoteric makeup – the way we receive energy, the way energy circulates through our energy field – is generally non-linear and very open.

Dr. Guan-Cheng Sun, Chi Gong practitioner, teacher and researcher, explains how women's receptivity is part of her energetic makeup:

> First, women and men are different. A woman's energetic system is more open. It's more open to new energy. When I teach a Chi Gong class, and we do a practice, women almost always are first to feel energy. Women are two to five times more sensitive; it is much easier to bring energy in. They have a stronger capacity to receive. And greater body awareness.
>
> Men's energy fields are focused around the head, and especially at the front of the head. This is connected to how the brain works – a man is focused on a task and the energy field relates to that focusing capability.

For a woman, her energy field is not usually as focused. It radiates out in many directions, especially from the chest and the back of the head. This means she is more receptive, as her field is more open, less restricted.

Women know! They just know! A powerful woman is one who takes in this wisdom from the earth and all around. She just knows.

Elizabeth Frediani concurs. She works with men and women both, and has noticed some differences around receptivity.

Subtle energy practices require willingness to go inward. In working with both men and women, I find that men often do not register the feeling of energy coming in and/or they equate receiving with being 'out of control.' Consequently, men generally do not feel the pleasure and excitement from the energy practices that women do.

Generally women are thrilled with the experience of energy coming in. Women not only respond quickly and positively to receiving energy, but they understand how receiving energy can serve them. They feel the energy – and through feeling, they know.

Women's openness might be related to a unique field, as Dr. Sun suggests. But Elizabeth links women's flow of attention inward with both our connectivity and the flux that is always taking place in our being. She explains:

Connection is key to receptivity. You cannot receive if you cannot connect. Overall women are adept at connecting – as a feminine culture we cultivate this ability. We recognize our connection to the earth. We connect to our children through our bodies, nurturing, and long-term guardianship. We foster connections with our partners, friends, and family.

Connecting fulfills our basic physical expression of how to be on the planet.

Men have grown more isolated in many ways. The modern, male culture draws men away from home through work/career, which can be quite demanding, competitive, and separating. Generally 'making money' does not fulfill the physical expression of living on earth. Often men are challenged to stay connected to home, partner, children in a strong, attentive way. Urban life contributes to this sense of separation, making it hard for anyone to feel connected to the natural world and basic life drives.

Women's biology gives us a wonderful advantage for developing inward focus and our ability to connect. Our bodies are fluctuating, stimulating us in ways that men do not experience. From puberty to the cessation of menstruation, we are in a rhythmical state of flux – a 28-day hormonal cycle. And then, as we continue to change, we come into another phase of experience at menopause. These rich and amazing physical cycles draw us to know ourselves on many levels. Through our bodies and our cycles, we discover ways of emerging and giving birth to ourselves, to our children, and to our connection to life. Our female body tells us – 'You are on a journey.' And fortunately, for us, a substantial part of our feminine culture encourages us to fully engage in our journey.

Our bodies, our energy systems, our brains and hormones all uniquely contribute to a life of flux. Women's physical cycle moves in sync with energetic and emotional cycles of fullness and depletion, love and longing, leaving us one day desperate to be filled and the next overfilled and overwhelmed by all that is in and with us. We only need to develop a willingness to accompany the journey already taking place in our being.

Nurturing and Receiving

Women's affinity for receptivity and our ongoing invitation to listen inwardly does not mean we're good at it. One participant at a woman's circle near Seattle recently shared a vision she'd had in meditation:

> I saw a beautiful, big, empty clay vessel, and water was being poured into it. I understood it to be about how as women we receive – we are vessels. We take so much in.

At this point, she seemed to grow uncomfortable and she added, as if uncertain: 'And of course we give so much!'

After she spoke, she was asked by another woman why she had added this final part about women giving so much, since it didn't seem to have to do with the vision. The first woman laughed and admitted that it made her uncomfortable to just talk about receiving, as though receiving was only OK if we gave away everything we were given.

As human beings alive at this time in history, we are largely uncomfortable with receiving, and instead are conditioned to express and give. But this conditioning denies us what is natural. Elizabeth continues:

> Taking in is so deeply basic and so much part of being a physical being. Most physical things on the planet – trees, cats, whales – they are in the act of taking in all the time – food, oxygen, life. And we humans for some reason are the opposite. We produce, exhale, do, do, do. And we don't take in anything. We are just falling apart.
>
> And even though I feel that women or certain men will say they're receptive, I get that they are not. They intellectualize the idea of receptivity and think of it as a form of being cooperative or a form of being nonassertive, but they don't understand that it is an act of taking in.

Our society does not value receiving, and one way women avoid it is through an ongoing, habitual involvement in nourishing others. For many women, this over-reliance on nourishing comes from an inner territory already set up to support an outpouring of energy. Elizabeth works with chakras, which are energy centers positioned along a central vertical channel of the body that reaches above the head. The first (lowest) chakra relates to our physical being and our connection with the earth. Our second chakra, located in the area of the belly, governs our ability to connect through relationship – to partners, children, and ourselves. She explains the connection between the second chakra and women's receptivity:

> The second chakra is where the baby is held in the womb; it is the energy center through which we express nurturing and open ourselves to merging. These two aspects are critical in terms of understanding why women are more receptive. The nurturing drive is more alive in a female body. And while it might seem that receiving and nurturing are opposites, they are, in fact, interrelated. We nurture because we take in information about the needs of another person. This receptivity to others is tied to our capacity to give what is needed.
>
> When a woman carries a fetus in her uterus, mother and baby are merged in energetic and physical ways. This bond is deep and spiritually intricate. And, it has the power to override a woman's concern for herself.
>
> When you are so attuned to another being, it is easy to forget that you have a self – a self that needs to be maintained – contained. This forgetting can perpetuate a continuing and/or habitual outpouring of nurturing. Depletion of physical, emotional, and creative energy can result.
>
> The second chakra also governs self-containment and the recognition that 'I have a self.' When a woman is over-involved with caretaking, she no longer recognizes or contains

self.

Elizabeth's perceptions echo both Pamela Wilson and Sandra Ingerman's comments about women and community and the way that mothers can easily sacrifice parts of themselves for the sake of others. But as these teachers emphasized, this tendency serves nobody. Each person must have her own sense of self; only with a strong self can she give and receive deeply.

Women's natural and instinctual responsiveness to a child contributes to unconscious patterns of giving and receiving that easily become unbalanced. And when this intense openness to another – and to another's energy and needs – is combined with wounding related to one's sense of individual self, the combination is dangerous. Elizabeth continues:

> Think of yourself as an energetic container, holding your inherent life-force. Now, imagine that when you were young, you decided it was safer to please others – Dad, Mom, etc. The choice to please others quite literally sends energy out of your body and energy system – and you begin to externalize your focus. You give up an inward connection to maintain outer ones. This can cause chronic energy drains, compromise chakra function, and create loss of self. Instead of knowing what you are passionate about or what makes you happy, you are more aware of what makes others happy.
>
> You can see that this kind of wound can easily develop into an ongoing drive to over-nurture others and merge at the expense of connection to self.

Of course it is a vicious cycle, not being supported as a girl and losing oneself further through motherhood, and reinforcing an incapacity to return to Self.

Women's woundedness comes in many forms, from extreme closing down due to terrible violations to the simple habitual nourishing of others. But the signs are easy to read, and most of us don't recognize them as issues around receiving. Elizabeth explains:

Fatigue, depression, lack of creativity, and a lack of direction are all signs that a woman is in a state of deficiency. From an energetic point of view, it is important to recognize this, so you can begin to inhale and take in energy. It is very simple: when you are taking in/receiving, you will be nourished. And when you are in constant outflow, you will become depleted.

Any person who has been hurt on a deep level, through physical, emotional, or sexual abuse, through abandonment, through a controlling relationship, is often unwilling to be receptive, because receptivity does not feel safe. These individuals often survive by being defensive, vigilant about self-protection, and/or being numb, disconnected.

Deep wounding can also result in a habitual self-negation, self-criticism, and/or putting everyone else before self. Through self-denial a person keeps disconnected internally.

Receiving awakens a person. When you are receptive you actually feel! A constant outflow of energy contributes to numbing. When a woman begins to be receptive and feel again, life begins to change – it will demand change. She begins to discern what feels good and what does not – who and what supports her and who and what does not. When a woman starts receiving, she opens to a whole new paradigm. This is the paradigm that women – everyone – need to step into. And receiving is the key.

Healing Wounds

The physical reality of penetration as integral to procreation leaves women tremendously vulnerable in ways that most men could not imagine. Women's bodies have received men's violence, penetrated when we have not willed it, violated and harmed and betrayed. Violence against women has created a block to women understanding and living the real power of receptivity. As Elizabeth says:

> In terms of sexuality, the true power comes from receptivity. Sexual energy flows through the same energy system as spiritual energy and consciousness. When both men and women are receptive – to each other, to earth energies, to their own hearts and spiritual energies – sexual energy flows in a full, balanced way through their bodies. If either person lacks in receptivity, true, complete sexual energy is diminished and so is the sexual act itself.

Healing our wounds so that we can empower ourselves, each other, and life is a task for women across the world. Nobody is going to do it for us. But critical to this healing is the capacity to receive, to take in information and life-energy on every level and through all our energy centers. We need to take in life-force through eating good food, and take in spiritual energy through eating healthy food with gratitude. We need to make love with people we trust and who truly see us, so we take in on the physical level as well as psychological and spiritual energy. We need to take the time to bring the energy of the earth through our bodies and to listen to what is needed from our environment – how else can we care for it?

Elizabeth encourages women to put attention into various energy centers in the body – various chakras – and take energy in through those centers. The next step is learning to hold energy in the system, which takes place as the energy centers become stronger. Rather than any great effort, this requires a shift of attention inward.

> While healing begins with receiving, women must also learn to contain or hold their energy so that it will sustain them. When women come to see me, it's clear that many do not

know how to check in with themselves or how to hold energy. Containment is also part of the second chakra function. Holding and conserving your energy is a form of nurturing self. It does no good to receive energy, if you are going to outflow it all.

As you learn to hold energy, you will recognize how directly it influences you on a consciousness level. Your sense of self, power, will, and spiritual connectedness will grow in strength and clarity. Energy, after all, is consciousness.

As one receives energy and contains it, one grows fuller and one's consciousness expands. Energy will replenish all aspects of who you are, healing depletions, catalyzing the release of blockages, waking shut-down aspects of self, activating creativity, and opening spiritual connectedness.

Receptivity and the Heart

Issues around merging and loss of boundaries from cultural conditioning, wounding, or the natural challenges of motherhood, are only some aspects of the ability and inability to receive. Another level of receiving must also be understood and activated – receiving in the heart. Without the capacity to receive and hold energy in the heart, through the heart center, we are unable to find meaning in our lives, to make sense of our lives, or to develop spiritually.

Elizabeth describes the purpose of the energetic heart center:

The heart chakra is the meeting place of self and soul. It is the energy center that most expresses the balance between our engagement in life through love of self and others and our connection to the infinite nature of our being.

The heart serves as the seat of our spiritual consciousness. Through the heart, we integrate the personal and transcendent aspects of our consciousness. And when we are able to hold both of these, we are home, spiritually grounded – and capable of powerful receptivity to self, to life, to others, to knowing, to soul.

Through this depth of receptivity, we become able to digest our life experiences, extracting their essential meaning and wisdom. This aspect of the heart chakra consciousness is powerful and fulfills the soul's inherent drive toward evolution. The heart chakra is our greatest spiritual ally and resource. Through the healed, receptive heart we establish stability within our energy system, our consciousness, and our life path.

Our western culture is ignorant about the heart as a center of consciousness. We do not understand that the heart is more than a Hallmark-card ideal of romantic attraction or a new-age image of world peace achievable through superficial affirmations. The heart is the doorway to the infinite, to the endlessness of love's power, which does not serve romantic pairing as much as it provides access to the essential fuel of life itself and the forces behind the conscious evolution of our planet.

But to be receptive to the heart, we need to practice self-love.

To strengthen our connection to the heart chakra, women – everyone – must also heal their hearts. A healed heart chakra is a natural outcome of self-love, self-recognition, and self-honoring.

Some people believe that self-love is a cliché or even selfish. It is neither. Attendance to self is the primary way that one establishes receptivity. If a woman rejects or denies herself, the core flow of energy into the heart chakra is compromised, making true, deep receptivity impossible.

The heart center is a powerful container – vessel – for guiding all levels of our being in this life. We often forget, however, the tender nature of our hearts, of our beings. Treat yourself as you would treat others you love. Respect yourself as you respect others.

Care for self in the manner you would care for those closest to you. This is how to care for your heart. If you dishonor yourself through poor self-care or self-denial, your heart will not remain open. And heart chakra consciousness will not deepen.

Women can wake up to our needs for all these things – our need to be seen as we are, to be known and honored for who we are and what we offer, to be able to contribute our greatest gifts. But often we need to see ourselves before another can see us! We are the ones to recognize and honor who we are inside, just as we ask that others do. If we do not take the time to listen to our own needs and to give to ourselves, then we are truly limiting our capacity to help create a world that will listen to us. These are basic responsibilities of self-care directly linked to serving life itself. And without satisfying these various levels of responsibility, we will never enter the heart, where we truly long to go.

And again, according to Elizabeth, women are blessed with a natural capacity to enter the heart, and to do what is needed to get there:

The need to own the heart and the need to be receptive are awakened drives in women. As women, we are fortunate to be bonded together – to have established a feminine culture that promotes self-awareness. This circles back to our bodies and their invitation to know ourselves through the flux of our own cycles and through the mystery of birth, whether physically actualized or not.

There is an ongoing potential for women to draw inward and be receptive to self. If we listen to our bodies, this will translate into listening to our emotions, our truth, creativity, will, and knowing. This listening happens throughout the entire energy system from the root chakra to the crown – but the heart is the primary center.

Listening to self is a radical practice. Given all the things that draw us outside ourselves, listening is radical. Listening takes courage, commitment, and time. Listening to self is being willing to discover – to be self-referencing, self-validating. Women thrive through listening inwardly. It enlivens us – and we align to our own delicious wisdom through listening!

Neutrality and Sacredness through the Heart

Elizabeth reminds us that the heart is how we hold and digest life experiences. And when we deepen this receiving process, we connect to life's essence, finding equanimity and the wonders of being open to everything that life brings us. Elizabeth discusses this neutrality that is part of the heart's consciousness:

Heart chakra consciousness is layered and includes love of self and others, acceptance of self and others, digesting life experience, and weaving together the partnership of self and soul. One aspect of heart consciousness that most of us recognize as essential is unconditional love. To love unconditionally you have to transcend the superficial and the façade identities of self and/or the others. You then are able to connect on a soul level with self and with others. In unconditional love, there is no fixation on things being a certain way, no control dynamics.

Once you see beyond the superficial and ephemeral aspects of self and others, you reach a deeper level of inner stability and spiritual grounding. You now can experience life without judgment. You are open to seeing what is and being with what is. Inwardly you have developed a place of neutrality – and also deepened your receptivity.

This frees you to accept life in a new way, allowing your

heart consciousness – not your karma, not your wounds, not your projections – to meet your experience and bring you into right relationship with it. Through this depth of heart chakra consciousness you intrinsically know and honor the sacredness of all life. That's the neutrality. There is no favoring... Instead, you are looking at life through the eyes of your heart.

This neutrality of the heart is key to many powers in this book. Sobonfu Somé stated about community:

> In order to work as a community, we have to let go of judgment. Lots of times we use the word 'tolerate' or 'tolerance.' But this word has an energy that says 'I'm keeping you out of my life and I don't know what else to do...' It really suggests they need to change in order for you to let them in. Instead, we need acceptance to another person in whatever way they come. You create a place in your heart where they know they can rest. They know they do not need to change for you.

This true acceptance of another person is a form of receptivity. It is taking in another human being as he or she is. We know what it feels like when we are accepted; we know how acceptance reflects back our own wholeness, the sense that we are fine the way we are. Being received for who we are is a true gift.

And there is a way our neutrality and openness can work to receive all life. It is as though when our hearts are truly open, life's essential wholeness is received. This creates a spark of sacredness between the depths of the heart and the depths of life – a way for the spiritual essence of life to come all the way into a human being and be seen and known for what it is.

This essential role of humanity in the revelation of the sacred through life has been hidden to most of us. It depends on receiving into the heart. Through receiving, much can be given into life. Light, spiritual energy, and love come through the inner planes into the outer world through the heart. But if they are not received, they cannot be known for what they are, nor can they be transmitted into the world.

In this process of receiving divine energies into life, women hold a unique knowing. We do this through the miracle of birth, though often we are not sure what we are 'doing' since it is so natural. But the process of receiving a soul into the material world is not just limited to childbearing – just as we've come to see how physical aspects of child-rearing have mysterious implications in other arenas, like purification or nourishment.

Receptivity and the Meat of the White Buffalo

A Sufi woman living near Seattle described a vision from meditation that included traditional Native American imagery:

In this vision, I saw a huge buffalo with long, white hair standing in a vast open landscape. The buffalo was majestic and its long hair was tangled with age. It was so massive and still that it looked like a snow-covered mountain.

Then, the scene changed, and a few women stood together with their mouths full of something white. At first it seemed they were eating white rags or paper towel, but then it was clear they were chewing the meat of the white buffalo. Then, suddenly I noticed a group of men were present, and they approached the women. The women leaned in as though to kiss the men, but instead they were passing the white substance to them.

This vision is mysterious and in many ways beyond understanding. The woman herself was struck by its distinct Native American reference – a spiritual system she was not overly familiar with. But a review of writings about the white buffalo,

which is a traditional image in the spirituality of many Plains
Indian tribes, reveals a Native American prophecy that has
relevance to today.

The white buffalo is a symbol of spiritual wisdom and energy,
initially introduced to the Lakota people through the appearance
of a spirit woman called White Buffalo Calf Woman. She came to
the Lakota people with ceremony and ritual, the purpose of
which was to maintain spiritual balance. She also brought with
her a prophecy for the future of the world, which foretold a time
of spiritual harmony and unity, an era that would be signaled by
the return to earth of a white buffalo.

In the woman's vision, the white buffalo, looking so much like
an ancient snowy mountain, suggests a spiritual energy that is
also an earth energy – white and pure, but totally manifested
through the physical realm.

Larry Merculieff, Aleut elder, is a member of a group of
indigenous leaders called the White Buffalo Messengers who
have been called to write and teach about the meaning of the
return of the White Buffalo. He comments on this vision:

The White Buffalo is the symbol – in energetic form – of the
sacred Divine Feminine. White Buffalo Calf Woman is coming
back as the White Buffalo. This means that the Divine
Feminine knowing, which comes through women, can come
to men. In my tradition, women initiate the shamans. Some
things come through women. Then there is the process of men
harmonizing the sacred feminine in themselves.

You have to become the sacred feminine. Once a woman
becomes that, the men are going to heal through her energy
field. The sacred feminine has to come through women. When
I was born, it came from my mother. My mother was a very
highly evolved spiritual being. She accepted me no matter
what. She always loved me unconditionally. She just held the
space of love for me. The process of that was a profound

teaching. She downloaded her energetic space to me while I was in the womb.

Where we are headed is anybody's guess. But it is about transformation ultimately into light. Any physical object can be measured in quantum physics in levels of light. We are moving into a formless state of consciousness. And the knowing and the depths of the vibrational field of formlessness are feminine. That's where we're moving.

It was clear to the woman who had the vision that it is *women* who can receive the energy associated with the White Buffalo, and are responsible for transmitting this energy to men. Larry concurs. What is most important then is that women understand and use their receptivity in a spiritual context in order to serve their own transformation and the transformation of men and even of the planet. The White Buffalo story is a story of global change, the return of the sacred feminine into the world.

Llewellyn Vaughan-Lee, Sufi teacher, also sees women's capacity to receive and transmit spiritual energy as beneficial to the transformation of the planet. He refers to a process of 'spiritual photosynthesis,' through which light is received and used to transform life. He has spoken about the 'spiritual substance' in women's bodies before; he speaks of it here in the context of this process of spiritual photosynthesis:

Women have a particular spiritual substance in them that men don't have. This substance is pure. This has to do with the fact that through the birth process, women are able to be a place where the light of a soul takes on human form while remaining true to its own essential nature. Most women don't understand that this substance, which plays a part in the birth process, can be given back to the earth so to help light enter and revitalize the earth. The earth has been horribly damaged and has lost its ability to transmute spiritual light. By offering this pure substance within them to the earth, women can help revitalize the earth.

Just as there's a physical photosynthesis, there's a spiritual photosynthesis... The earth can and must absorb spiritual light and transmute it, so it can grow as a spiritual being. Because we've treated it so badly, we've actually damaged the light cells of the world.

But just as a soul can come through a woman into manifestation, a higher energy can come down through a woman's spiritual vehicles through her body into the physical body of the world, bringing with it this sacred substance that a woman has which is always completely pure.

Llewellyn explains that women's bodies, which have the capacity to receive a soul and birth it into the world, can take on the work of bringing light into life in order to revitalize and heal the earth. This is a work that men cannot do. 'Men don't know how to heal the world in this way,' he says.

Women and men both can acknowledge that women's capacity to receive a soul into the body has a spiritual purpose beyond the very personal and familial realm of childbirth. This power can be activated in service to the healing of the earth, which we can consider to be connected to the return of the White Buffalo and a time of spiritual revitalization that includes humanity and nature both.

Women can take responsibility for what we already know, that the miracle of birth is a spiritual experience, and as such ties us to the spiritual life of the entire planet. The next step is to trust that this miracle can be offered back to life – not only through the particular form of giving birth to children, but also through our attitudes around being of service to life birthing itself. We can awaken to this power within us and become curious about and committed to it.

Llewellyn predicts that to do this work, women will meet in

groups across the globe. Larry Merculieff also suggests that women's ceremony plays a key role in a process of birthing something new into life. These general suggestions are part of a wisdom that is emerging at this time, a wisdom that recognizes an important spiritual work that only women can do. There likely will be few directions to this work; rather we will have to figure it out by following our longing and trusting what we know.

Women's circles are growing in popularity around the world perhaps as part of this movement. One yoga teacher from San Francisco started a women's circle not with a clear sense of why but because it felt right. She was not certain of how it would turn out or who would come, but at the first meeting she had the following experience during the first minutes of meditation: 'Soon after we closed our eyes, I felt like we were all holding hands underwater and swaying like kelp. It was a beautiful feeling, which felt nourishing and I felt blessed…'

This image – so strange and mysterious – of connected women, swaying like kelp, deep on the ocean floor – suggests a connection between women and plant life. Was this a glimpse into the 'spiritual photosynthesis' that Llewellyn describes? If such a photosynthesis can take place it would likely, paradoxically, happen down in the dark, hidden from the upper realms of our man-made world, in the ocean floor where the light is the light in darkness, under cover and hidden in matter, the way the womb is hidden from the outside world and yet receives the most holy light into it.

We can remember that while men and women alike need to be able to receive, women have a unique power to receive spiritual light into their bodies and offer that light – that soul – into the created world. Isn't it time to honor this power, to ask what role it has in healing the world around us? Isn't it time for women to explore this power and how it can serve?

Receiving is a natural power with great ramifications for life.

And to explore and use this power we need only recall what is natural to us. This is the first step to the more esoteric work described by Llewellyn and Larry both.

As Elizabeth reminds us, receptivity is right here with us:

Being receptive is as natural to us as our in-breath. When we love or find pleasure – when we feel grateful or inspired – when we linger at sunset watching the last bit of light transform into darkness – or when we cannot turn our eyes from someone who is most dear to us – we are receiving. Receiving awakens our hearts, ensures our physical and spiritual wholeness, and transmits a message of feminine wisdom to the world.

Chapter 9

Creative Space

There is a sacred vibrational field inside of women that is the place of all things born. What women have done before time began is to take that sacred vibrational field and move it outside into ceremonial space to create the womb on the outside, so something new can be birthed into this world.

If women don't do this, human beings as a species are done for.

Larry (Ilarion) Merculieff

There is a creative power running through the core of life like a river of mystery. This power has a feminine quality, as it lives in an inner formless space and can only be approached through a consciousness that is not fractured by rationality. To consciously be with this power means surrendering into not-knowing and embodying love.

All of us can approach this space if we allow our minds to take a back seat to our feeling intelligence, but women have natural access to it and affinity with it, as it is part of our own nature, and of the feminine nature of life.

Women even contain this life-giving space in our own energy systems, though we've largely lost awareness of it. Larry (Ilarion) Merculieff, Aleut elder, calls this aspect of the sacred feminine 'the womb at the center of the universe,' which he says also exists in women's own individual energy fields. Our patriarchal culture fears and denies the creative power of the universe, just as it has suppressed women's creative power through so many socio-political, spiritual, and psychological forms of oppression. This has left our culture imbalanced, and it has left women consciously disconnected from and fearful of our own power. If women don't overcome this fear and learn to work with this energy source *that is part of our very nature,* 'nothing new can be born into the world,' says Larry. And if we look around at the many challenges of modern life, we truly must acknowledge that something new is needed.

It's not easy to talk about the power of creative space, since it is formless. It is not something to name or know with the mind; it is a living mystery that we can sense into and allow our human consciousness to be with. It is hidden from us yet it is the source of all life. It is not the nothingness before life exists, but life before it moves through the prism that shows off form.

To work with the power of creative space is itself an energetic experience of being with the forces of creation – the eternal life-forces beyond and within everything we can see and know. This experience is possible to varying depths and degrees, depending upon how capable we are of knowing power beyond our will, putting our psychological needs aside to attune to the sacred, and surrendering to life beyond our control.

And while the power of creative space is a power available to all humanity, just as the 'womb at the center of the universe' is the sacred feminine principle accessible to all, women are especially near to it, as it is alive – like a 'hologram' of this universal feminine power, says Larry – in our energy systems. It is activated naturally when we become pregnant. Women have unique access to this womb that is both universal and present with us, an ongoing invitation into the vessel that is life's heart.

The experience of pregnancy illustrates women's embodiment of this power, and what it demands from us. Men's contribution to the creation of a new human life is directive, linear, and essentially competitive (only the strongest sperm survives) and is over quickly, limited to the planting of a seed. A woman's part, on the other hand, is to receive, protect, and hold what is given, a process that takes time and on a psycho-spiritual level great patience and perseverance and an intuitive capacity to be completely involved and yet not interfere.

Pregnancy is an experience of being part of something much bigger than yourself and of becoming aware of how powerfully body and spirit interact. It is a miracle that a child grows inside a mother dependent on the mother's energy system all the while forming into a being absolutely unique and distinct from the mother. When the child is born, a new constellation of creative power takes place as we watch, protect, nourish, and give space for a child to grow outside of us.

Women's power to receive, contain, and birth new life in the physical world is a mirror of a spiritual power, which has been imaged throughout history. In many forms of art, Mary Magdalene, 'the woman with the alabaster jar,' is depicted with a vessel of healing herbs, pointing to an instinctual knowledge of how life regenerates and renews itself within a feminine container.

In ancient Greece, the initiate who worshipped the Goddess Cybele, a form of the Great Mother, declared:

I have eaten from the timbrel,
I have drunk from the cymbal,
I have borne the sacred vessel,
I have entered into the bridal chamber.[33]

In this beautiful description of ingestion, receptivity, and partnership with an invisible bridegroom, we feel a feminine capacity to be a vessel, surrender to love, and create life imbued with the sacred.

These images abound in all cultures across the world and across time, signifying a feminine power to transform and regen-erate through receiving, holding, and birthing. Today, the great Kogi civilization of the Sierra Nevada in northern Columbia still honors a collective recognition of the power of the feminine vessel through the ritual lime gourd, carried by all men as a reminder of the Great Mother and her power. Myths describe the first lime gourd being given by Aluna, the Mother, to her son as symbolic of a wife. The gourd holds the energizing coca; it is given along with a stick to collect the cocoa from the gourd for ingestion, the length of the stick indicating the man's standing in society. This ever-present reminder connects individual men to the reality of the sacred feminine, so he remains balanced and connected to Her power – the fertile container of new life.

This power of creative space exists in so many dimensions of life, and is accessible to those who can stretch consciousness beyond the mind's chatter and our immediate psychological or physical needs into the hidden worlds where regeneration takes place. Perhaps the most powerful work with creative space is conscious participation in revelation – the birth of spiritual power into physical form in full consciousness. This process and practice relates directly to the power of recognizing life's sacredness.

We can give birth sometimes with no love for a child and sometimes with such a great love that we unconditionally want what is best for it. Both reflect the power of creative space, but the latter includes the conscious sanctification of life, a process of knowing, honoring, and regenerating the sacred in physical form. In this latter example, a woman is *with* love and all the wisdom it contains – wisdom pertaining to the spiritual sustenance of the child. Symbolic of this deep level of revelation, we find the image of the Virgin Mary, whose total surrender to God's will was a condition of birthing God's son into the world.

During the great second turning of the wheel of Dharma, a period during which Buddhism re-invented and reformed itself in accord with new teachings on the nature of reality, Mahayana Buddhism introduced the female bodhisattva, Prajnaparamita, whose name means 'the perfection of wisdom.' Described in the Heart Sutra as the experience of 'emptiness as form' and 'form as no different than emptiness,' Prajnaparamita is a great mystery of emptiness and creative potential. As Mary is known as the

Mother of God, Prajnaparamita is known as 'the mother of all Buddhas,' birthing pure compassionate action from her womb of living, intelligent emptiness.

Not many can be consciously awake to this level of creative space, for it requires a surrender of the unreal into the real, a capacity to put the ego aside entirely and be with the great spiritual process of revelation and rebirth through which the sacred pours into and infuses the created. The Virgin Mary and Prajnaparamita are similar to what Larry Merculieff describes as the 'womb at the center of the universe,' which one experiences only through complete surrender and dissolution of ego consciousness.

While this might sound intimidating or unreachable, it is at the same time so accessible and especially accessible to women, who carry this womb with us like a portal to the infinite. We can become familiar with this power, learn to work with it, learn to give ourselves to it. Women need to sense its presence in our day-to-day lives and honor it so it can grow through our consciousness and our embodied experience. This power is active when we listen and take energy in or hold an idea or need before acting out or expressing it. It is active in how a mother watches over a child, allowing the child to learn seemingly on its own, while her love and attention are present and protective like a container. It is active in how an artist works, how he or she receives inspiration and walks the very fine line of openness to further inspiration and the use of personal will to act on what is given. It is always active when we love free of conditions, for in love we are conscious and awake while also pouring energy outward as it is needed, like a stream naturally quenching the thirsty without any personal preference or direction.

In these activities we are putting our controlling selves aside to recognize, honor, and work with something much bigger and vaster. What is this bigger and vaster energy? What can be born through the womb of the universe?

Pouring through Space

On all levels, creative space is an in-road to and out-road from the sacred. Space is sacred because it is empty of our own personality and needs, and alive with the ineffable, unceasing, eternal energies of life. But creative space is not just absence; it is a cauldron of life-forces beyond our own personal will or intention, like unconditional love, peace, and other divine energies. These forces are accessed and expressed by our own individual sacred attributes and experiences, like compassion, gratitude, humility, reverence, and awe.

Far from being a remote spiritual ideal, creative space is accessible in every moment that we put our personality or control dynamics aside to experience the transpersonal dimension, which is always present. Sometimes this takes discipline, as when we 'hold our tongue' in an argument so to not violate a deeper communion. Often there is a strange tension when this power is at work as we step aside to allow energy to rush through us, like when we are in the throes of a creative process, and inspiration and the energy to create almost take over. It can take discipline and intense attention to stay with these processes, because we have to be fully present with forces beyond our control.

Spiritual transformation seems to always depend on creative space, on knowing when and how to watch and protect space for transpersonal and divine energies to emerge. In individual practice, meditation and prayer are containers for just this kind of process. Both require a time and space to turn inward, away from outer distractions of the day and inner distractions of mental chatter. They open our being to what flows from the inner worlds. Churches, monasteries, and nunneries are themselves protective containers for spiritual energies, as are all sacred places on the earth where human consciousness protects and honors the potentials of grace and revelation.

In ordinary, daily life we honor the divine energies of life through commitments and vows, including marriage vows, which serve as a transformative container, like the retort of medieval alchemists. Vows to another person serve as a transformative protector of a creative process in which base energies and needs can be transmuted into psychic and spiritual gold and contribute to new life, not drain it. In the container of marriage or deep friendship, we put aside some of our personal demands and give space for transpersonal forces of unconditional love or deep respect to flourish, and the symbol of this new life is the child – the child of the future.

The nurturing and protection of transpersonal life-energies are a potential and responsibility that human beings struggle to recognize, and so often ignore, even as we so clearly see what gets in the way of this responsibility. We know that reactivity, control and power dynamics, and personal agendas all violate the sacred that can bloom through space. We can deny love its place with an angry word; we can push aside peace with our personal demands. Respect, honoring, and non-reactivity, on the other hand, all give a way for unknowing, presence, and humility to play a part in any relationship. Through honoring space, we allow miracles to happen. Grace can be given and received, love can grow, and life-force can build in creative momentum. These forces are beyond what we can create on our own. They require a devotion to the unknown, an attunement to magic, a love for possibility, a commitment to give despite not knowing what will ever be given in return.

Because the living template of pregnancy and birth is present in every woman, our instincts are attuned to working with the power of creative space. This power is highly connected to women's power to purify and to restore harmony, as we do this in our bodies every month. Traditionally women use the power of creative space and the power to purify in order to create a home that protects and nurtures family. The old saying, 'Behind every great man is a great woman' no doubt reflects this capacity to hold space and nurture mysteriously from behind the scenes.

This power is also highly linked to woman's recognition of life's sacredness. We recognize life's sacredness because we are part of it during the miracle of birth, and we honor and live that miracle through unconditional love.

In the modern world, the last thing women should do is take a back seat to men and to the patriarchal destructiveness taking place all around us. But we do need to remember our power and live it in any and all circumstances, and the power of creative space, which is as invisible as the power in the womb, demands that we develop deep trust in inner, hidden processes that might or might not ever be acknowledged by the outer world we live in.

For many women, the imperative to work with creative space will feel natural. We already long for what takes place in this space, just as we long for love, just as we long to be ourselves. The power of what exists in space, what grows in space, is so alive that our bodies ache for it. We long to give ourselves to creation, transformation, and healing, to all the hidden creative forces of life. We long to know the fruits of sacrifice and the joy alive in the marrow of creation.

We can be more conscious of our own longing to work with space, to give ourselves to creation as it creates with us. We can practice seeing past our immediate desires into the infinity of the future, which calls to us. We can practice discriminating between when to receive and hold and when to guard and protect and when to participate in bearing forth.

We can practice in all areas of our lives – during physical pregnancy and birth, during collaborative or artistic endeavors when we know something is trying to come into manifestation, in relationships that we hope will evolve and grow, and in the most seemingly mundane parts of the day when we simply want life to feel fresh and new. Birth is part of every moment. Life is always renewing itself. Reminding ourselves of this helps us orient toward this inner space where we are in reverence and awe of the miracle of life, and where these deep aspects of our consciousness

– gratitude, love, or willingness to serve something bigger than ourselves – can be activated.

Space in Receiving, Transforming, and Giving

Working with the power of creative space requires an understanding of when and how to receive, when and how to hold, and when and how to give forth. All these activities require awareness and respect for space – for a creative process beyond our individual needs, beyond even our understanding. The more awake and aware we are with space, the more we participate in transforming what is taking place in that space. This has nothing to do with control or domination; it is a genuine participation based on listening, watching, being with, and giving.

Receiving and creative space are deeply linked. Listening is perhaps the most simple and profound example of how these powers work together in the most seemingly ordinary situations. Listening is a creative act. We don't just allow information or energy to come in; we allow it to come into us and transform. Transform what? We don't always know. This transformation happens in the deep inner space that is open and clear of personal agendas and contributes to deepening relationships, the emergence of wisdom, and the honoring of life.

Deep listening creates opportunities and understanding, and supports energies like compassion and empathy, which arise naturally and are infused into what we say or what we offer outwardly, transforming others and the potential of the moment. Listening allows us to start anew, from outside the prescribed and often predictable box of reactive defensiveness or personal agendas.

Larry Merculieff describes how space allows for learning. Larry was raised in a traditional manner on the twelve-by-five mile St. Paul Island, one of the five islands that make up the Pribilof Islands north of the Aleutian Islands off the coast of Alaska. The Pribilofs were occupied in the 1700s by Russia and later in the mid-1800s by the United States. After experiencing what Larry describes as a holocaust at the hands of the Russian fur traders, the surviving Aleut people were taken as slaves to the Pribilof Islands to kill fur seals. St. Paul Island was the center of first the Russian and then the US fur seal industry before seal slaughter was ended by Congress in 1983. Before occupation by the Russians and Americans, the Aleut people lived in a spiritually advanced and sustainable relationship to the earth and sea. And after occupation, pockets of traditional indigenous culture remained. Larry was part of the last generation to be raised in a traditional manner. He was identified at age four as the one Kuuyux of his generation, whose duties include holding ancient indigenous wisdom and extending it like an arm or a bridge (the meaning of the word 'Kuuyux'). Traditional culture on the Pribilofs included deep respect for and knowledge of how to work with the sacred feminine and its expression through the power of creative space. He describes being taught these values as a young boy on St. Paul Island through his relationship with his mentor:

The traditional mentor relationship is based on inner knowing, inner feeling. That knowing is essential for mentoring to happen. From age five to thirteen, my mentor taught me what I needed to know about being a man, what it means to be in relationship, Aleut ethics and values, hunting, fishing, reverence for life. But in that entire time, he said no more than two hundred words to me. Something else is happening in the mentor relationship, including communication on a different level, which is essential to understanding communication with creation, with the sacred.

He gave me my first rifle and shotgun at age seven. He was responsible for creating space for me to learn, and he never instructed. I would just sit, watch, listen, learn. We'd get out before sunrise, stay out till four or so in the afternoon. I'd get up at three a.m. to get out, and I would be up for over twelve hours – sitting and watching the hunters. Listening and learning. I'd sit quietly for six, seven, or eight hours at a time. Today kids can't sit for five minutes.

Learning – bringing in information and transforming and grounding it through direct experience – flourishes when we are not distracted by imposed ideas. Larry describes his mentor 'creating space' and not using words or instructions to help him learn. The listening was taking place throughout the whole human being – not just the mind, but also the body and the heart.

We don't listen just to words; we can listen to life and we can listen to our intuition or our heart. Listening activates the creative processes within space, as we take in, receive, and allow – all activities that do not fill or clutter space but honor it.

Sandra Ingerman, author and teacher of shamanism, describes this capacity to work with space during the creative process of writing:

I constantly hear people talk about writer's block. What I realize now after about eight books is that when you think you have writer's block, it's often the most important part. A silent germination is going on in the inner garden. If you try to rush the birth you will be dissatisfied. I've learned as a writer that if it seems that nothing is happening (for five years I had three pages in one book!) it is often a good thing. After those five years, I finished the book in two weeks. There is such a potent process when you think nothing is happening – everything is happening. When students say they're in a fallow period, I say it's a fertile time and something is growing inside you.

We want things instantly now, but birth – doesn't happen that way.

Working with space creatively can require great patience and awakeness. We don't just create space; we also need to consciously acknowledge and honor that space, often for hours or days or even years before something happens, respecting that more is going on than meets the eye. We don't fill the space with compromises just because it seems as though nothing is happening. Sandra's reference to birth is a potent example of how women are involved and attuned to all these stages – receiving, holding, and giving.

Each stage requires different energies and attitudes. To be given the seed for new life, we need the power of deep, inner longing, manifesting in its most physical reality through sexual desire or through the psychological or spiritual longing for connection and belonging, to live our human destiny through relationships of giving and receiving.

Holding and protecting the fetus requires that we use the powers of attention and self-nourishment, as well as the power to sacrifice ourselves in love to another. How many women give up coffee, drinking, or other bad habits only when new life needs it?

Finally the push of birth can include incredible physical suffering, but also the natural attunement to impersonal forces of the universe that are participating in the birth. We need to know when to push and when to hold back. This heightened attention and the feeling of connection to something bigger than ourselves can be so appealing that many women can become addicted to the birth process.

All these stages and powers are at work at all times, not just during birth. We allow our longing to carve a space in our hearts and our lives for something new. As stated in an earlier chapter, longing works best when we are conscious and respectful of what we really want and need. Longing is generally useless if we cannot bear the empty space of our need, and unless we can notice when we are being given what we need, and receive and respond.

The woman whose dream about crying with Barack Obama in a café about needing to do more to help the world, which was included in the chapter on longing, had spent months feeling unsettled about where she lived and wanting something new, when suddenly out of the blue she was offered a job in a town 2,000 miles away. Interestingly, she says she didn't realize that the job offer might have been connected to her longing to do more in the world. 'It took me by such surprise, and I had so much resistance to taking the job, selling my house, losing friends, moving my entire life somewhere else. But I only had a few days to make a decision, and I went for it. But now I see that all along my longing for something different was creating a space so something really new could be given. It's just I almost didn't recognize it!'

Often we are unconscious of how our longing creates space that draws new opportunities. Too often we reject what comes along since we aren't aware of what we really want or need or of how life responds to that deep need more often than to our superficial desires. It's up to us to become more conscious and respectful of what is taking place deep inside us and protect that process so we can respond with what's needed. This is how we can work with life as life works with us.

We need to honor the power of longing, which is deeply tied to life itself wanting to bring itself into existence, and spiritually speaking to the divine wanting to know itself. Creation is an expression of the divine manifesting through its world, and we play a part in this creative process by honoring divine needs and powers as they live through us. We work with longing, receptivity, nourishment, beauty, and the conscious recognition of life's sacredness in this process of birth. These inner divine qualities, which are also powers so naturally lived by women, have their own place in the bigger unfolding of the divine into life.

Filling the Space

A big deterrent to working with creative space is an inability to endure times when there are no solutions or no outer signs of what's happening, no indication of what to do or how to act. Imagine being the first woman ever to become pregnant. You would have no idea how long the pregnancy would last. You have a sense of something truly remarkable and strange taking over your own body, but little way of knowing exactly what is going on, or when the process will be finished, or what will come of it. You get bigger and bigger and more and more sore and increasingly uncomfortable, with nothing more than these strange signs of what is taking place. Until that moment of birth that reveals that something very specific was at work all along, you would be called upon to endure, watch, and trust. This kind of trust, attunement, courage, and willingness to be uncomfortable with little or no understanding and no end in sight is very often what's needed as we work with creative space.

Each of us can become pregnant even if we never carry a physical child. Pregnancy – the process of birthing new life – is always unique and without precedent, just as no two children are the same. But too often we just don't respect the process taking place in the inner recesses of our being, and we have lost the ways of sensing into that space.

Most of us in the modern world keep our conscious attention on immediate needs that can be satisfied with effort and usually very quickly, needs most often based on fears – fear of the unknown, fear of being out of control, fear of vulnerability, fear of not having enough, and fear of loneliness, etc... For women, especially, quick fixes take the form of emotional or psychological satisfaction. We do not want to acknowledge that some opportunities are diminished through emotional quick fixes. We want to make others and ourselves feel better, but often this impulse interferes with deeper processes that require unknowing and respect before any appropriate solutions present themselves.

Sandra Ingerman, who has spent years working with women in a healing practice, describes how women can interfere with the power of creative space:

This holding is the feminine part – where there is no response needed, nothing to do. We change the world by who we become, not what we do. The feminine is the allowing and the holding and acknowledgment of what's taking place. The dynamic or masculine part wants to analyze or show what we know. Or, we want to jump in to take care of someone else – the rescue response. Not everyone is comfortable not trying to make things better, but just being fair witness.

Even though it is 'feminine,' women have little practice with it. Women have a need to rescue and to make better. But we need to learn not to jump to that, but to be witnesses instead. To be present. This is one of the hardest concepts I've run into in training people. I can talk about the power of holding space and being an anchor, so something can happen naturally, and they either get it or they don't. I've been doing teacher trainings for more than ten years now and I still see that people either get it or they don't! Too often, women's need to rescue is making people sick. We aren't allowing ourselves to be nourished by deeper aspects of life.

I tell people it is a feeling in the body, where you just sit and you just hold the space, anchor the energies, and let them flow through without judgment. It helps to be able to quiet the mind and to experience something deeper than the mind and our emotional habits. But not everyone understands how to do this.

Sandra continues, describing a time in her own life when she understood that holding space was required:

Fifteen years ago I went through a real crisis. I felt dismembered completely. I went through such a loss, and I didn't think I was going to make it through. But a part of me knew it was a powerful initiation. The only people I told were people who I knew were just going to listen and not try to make it better. I needed people to just hold the space. I knew if I called on friends who loved me and were going to try to make it better for me – I knew it wasn't what I needed. So I asked others to be with me – women who could help hold the space. That was a very powerful teaching for me personally. How I felt held by these women and nobody tried to rescue me in any way. I asked people to do this for three months. It was so potent.

We need to remind ourselves so often that there is much more going on in life and in our own individual lives than we know through our habitual emotions or feelings. The soul works in very different rhythms to our emotional ups and downs, and when we work with creative space we are with the energy of our souls and the soul of life. Sandra continues:

Transformation and healing happen through presence. Your own radiance gets stimulated. There is no effort – no trying and no taking. This presence can transmute poison in water, pollution in air; it can change and transmute anything. I described this in the context of community and relationship – there is a way to be with something and someone that reflects and stimulates their divine essence. This is how healing and transformation happen. It is not us doing something, but what I call fair witnessing. A star in the night sky radiates light. It does not send it. By simply radiating light we become an energy of transformation.

To work with creative power means having a developed inner awareness. Sandra echoes Larry's earlier words, about listening to our feelings and our bodies to sense what is needed:

> It means having a very deep and rich inner world that is then reflected through our bodies. This cultivation of an inner garden creates the inner sacred space so we are not dependent on the outer world for peace or joy.
>
> The power of creative space is how we create sacred spaces and take care of our selves as sacred – as the temple of our spirit. Our house, garden, land – all are temples. We can acknowledge life as a temple consciously, and to do that promotes beauty to burst forth. But it takes time.

At its deepest, creative space is a sacred power and it brings out and empowers the sacred in us when we attend to it. No mother believes it is she alone at work in gestating her child. Yes, she is the pregnant one; at the same time, she is fully engaged in the sacred process of life happening. As we learn to value creative space, we learn to let go of our control dynamics and include – with our conscious attention and reverence – the living mystery of creation as it moves with and through us. This is a challenging way to live, but it can be how we live in so many ways. It is how we allow spirit to participate in our lives – we recognize the space for spirit and understand the intentions or energies that welcome spirit into that space, just as we participate in the creation of a child.

Sandra explains the way women have traditionally known how to keep space empty while at the same time allowing divine energies to enter and transform:

> Women put spirit into everything. I'm a spinner – I spin fiber into wool. I teach spinning workshops occasionally. What we try to teach is that spinning is a natural process; it's natural to do it with care and love. How do we bring back our knowledge of how to make material things with love and

spirit? Food cooked with love tastes different than mechanical and factory-made, where there is no love or attention. Caring for one plant – as you feed one plant with love, that space inside you wakes up to how to do that with everything. It's all in there! Open to space to allow it to happen. The deep mysteries have always been about how this power is in you already!

In traditional times before modern times – before technology – when women cooked or made clothes it was with love and attention. It mattered who they were making or cooking for. Women kept the house with an intention to make a loving space. In all these ways we worked with space and knew how to bring love into that space. So it was…

Entering the Womb

Nothing reflects the power of creative space as much as women's womb. But the womb is not just about creating new human life. It is about creating new life of many kinds.

According to Dr. Guan-Cheng Sun, Chi Gong practitioner and teacher, a woman's creative process in the womb is ongoing. When a woman is not creating a child, her uterus can become the container for various spiritual forces and formations.

The uterus is a powerful assembly of energies. The lights of the uterus are amazing. There are three dominant colors and energies – one is like dark blue or shiny black. Then in that there are lots of dots like white energies blended together. And also there are pink or fresh red energies. These are the dominant energies and they are very beautiful.

If one is pregnant, the energy is there. If not pregnant or if you don't do energetic practices, the energy is available but doing nothing. This energy is about creation and synthesis – synthesis and creation.

Larry Merculieff also describes the womb as a powerful assembly of energies. He calls the womb a 'hologram' and a 'matrix of energies' that are the exact energies at the center of the universe, or the 'womb of the universe.'

> What is the womb at the center of the universe? How is it reflected in the woman's body? It is not just reflected; it is identical. A woman's body contains the same field of energy that is found at the center of the universe. It's a field of infinite potential. It is the formless void.

From this universal womb genuine wisdom is born, according to Mahayana Buddhists who identify Prajnaparamita as the 'mother of all Buddhas.' This is also the teaching of the Aleut people, among whom Larry Merculeiff grew up. According to Larry, at the beginning of time, humanity was given 'original instructions' for how human beings should live on the planet. The instructions included wisdom about how this energy matrix functions in women and in human transformation. Traditionally, it was a woman's responsibility to work with this energy matrix in her own life and in ceremony with other women, during which 'the womb is brought out from the women into the ceremonial space to birth something new,' says Larry.

As Larry explained in the Purification chapter, women can activate this energy matrix through their sexuality as well. Another way is through the development of unconditional love, he says, which is also an aspect of the sacred feminine lived naturally through women.

> Unconditional love is shown through a mother's love for a child, and offers a sacred lesson. Unconditional love of a mother can be built up till there is unconditional love for self, others, and creation... If that's built up, that's an entry point to the womb at the center of the universe. Another way in is

through experiencing the power of giving life. Women experience it directly, but men can have this lesson through witnessing childbirth – through staying aware energetically during this process. Birth-giving has a power of the unknown. When one incorporates this into one's own being it's transformative. When one experiences the act of birth through witnessing, one has an indescribable experience of the unknown, of the magical, mystical, sacred unknown.

But the man must be fully opened to receive what the cosmic womb provides. To receive you've got to surrender completely in trust and faith. Just as women surrender to the power of the body in giving birth. Men don't usually experience that kind of surrender. Women do, all the time.

Centuries of Imbalance

While enlightened sexuality can activate this energy field in women, and offer men a way into it, Larry explains that the likelihood of working with this energy field through sexuality is unlikely.

This is a challenge today, as many women are injured by the imbalanced male energy, and thus defended emotionally and bodily. Men who don't know better are only 'takers' for their own needs and desires. When men are on this level of consciousness, they emit the energy of 'take,' which is subliminally and energetically picked up by women, causing a closing off, and a false surrender.

This dynamic described by Larry is the result of centuries of power dynamics between the masculine and feminine, between imbalanced men and imbalanced women. He suggests that at the heart of men's fear and violence against women is a primal fear arising from just this encounter with the formless during lovemaking.

The primal fear of man was probably activated first when a man was inside a woman sexually and began to dissolve. In that sacred space inside a woman a man can actually experience being dissolved into nothingness. This is a great power. The ego starts to dissolve but it freaks out – it says, 'I'm disappearing!' That's where the first fear came from in man.

The male ego is about form and structure in the outer world. The ego is afraid that if it dissolves during sex, it will die from the physical world completely and stop existing. So the ego is thrown into fear. The primal fear is that women can kill me. The response is then, 'Not only do I need to get away from this, but I need to kill it before it kills me.'

Larry explains that men's fear of women's power – the power of the void, or the formless space – and violence against women are part of a long story of masculine and feminine imbalances that has left men and women afraid of and angry at each other and closed to some of the greatest spiritual mysteries in creation, including this process of death and rebirth through sexuality. Indigenous traditions of many kinds, including the Aleut, describe a historical process of imbalance through which a pendulum has been swinging between the masculine and patriarchy and the feminine and matriarchy. It is clear where we are today. Larry explains this long-term battle between the male and female shadow and power dynamics:

We are in a time of great masculine imbalance, reflected through the patriarchal world all around us. This time is marked by control, disconnection, separation, and the dissociation from life by science and technology, and the primal fear manifesting in the unconscious need to control.

But this masculine imbalance is a reaction to the feminine imbalance that came before. What are the marks of the feminine imbalance? Manipulation through the use of sexuality and sensuality.

Through time, each collective consciousness – both male and female – reacted to the other. The shadow reacted to the shadow. The manipulation by women either destroyed or enraged men. How did it destroy? Women can go right to the heart of the man and shatter it in a few words. Men shatter through the physical or the use of vocal violence. With men, the language is more harmful than the energy. With women, it is the energy that harms. Women perceive and understand connection, and this perception and understanding is misused in order to manipulate and shatter the men. The men push back – and they have pushed back through physicality and destruction. That creates rage in women, and we go back and forth between these shattering forces.

Now we are at a time of masculine imbalance that has affected our souls. We have suffered thousands of years of violence against all things feminine.

This violence has created a collective conscious energy field of women that contains great rage. It is compounded by the fact that our mothers have downloaded their rage into fetuses all the way back through the female line. You're born a female in a masculine imbalanced world. And you start to experience your own soul wounding and then access the collective consciousness of this greater wounding. There are multiple levels of the shadow reinforcing each other.

The consequences of the decimation of the feminine extends into our spiritual lives in ways we don't acknowledge or understand, says Larry. As we live out this imbalance in an outer way, through violence against one another, we also internalize this violence in ways that fracture ourselves and inhibit inner balance. Men, afraid of women's power, cut themselves off from a deep honoring of their own personal feminine nature, which is the entryway to the sacred feminine. Women, fearful of and angry at men, deny themselves their own masculine power. This creates inner barriers to spiritual power. He continues:

> There is a spiritual purpose to masculine and feminine energies mirrored by our bodies and the way bodies come together for transformation. There is a profound spiritual aspect to the woman opening and receiving, and a spiritual aspect to the man expressing and penetrating outward. This has relevance in terms of how effective our prayers can be.
>
> For example, when a woman smashes the masculine side because of all the rage and says, 'No way am I going to trust men or masculine,' she puts up many defenses and shields. But what happens then when we pray?
>
> The consequences of smashing the masculine on our capacity to pray are not often looked at. The source of prayer should be from the heart. But if I am smashing the masculine energetically and spiritually, then the masculine principle, which is an outward movement, will also be smashed. The prayer is not going to have enough power; it will come out in a stunted way.
>
> And if the female aspect is damaged, my ability to receive and be receptive, the answer to my prayer is equally stunted. If my masculine is strong, then prayer can go out, but my ability to receive is stunted by feminine wounding.
>
> We don't understand how the power of prayer is so diminished... We have stunted ourselves unbelievably in being able to evoke prayer.

Healing

The spiritual journey we are on as individuals and as a planetary community includes and requires restoring the sacred feminine, and healing the wounds that dominate our consciousness, our unconsciousness, and our habitual behaviors to each other, ourselves, and the earth. For women, this means disconnecting from the numbing and deadening patterns that keep us unaware of how we are participating in our own oppression and power-lessness, and acknowledging both what our ongoing patriarchal world does to us and others, and how we are complicit. There will be tremendous grief and rage as we come to see more and more clearly the damage that has been done, but without acknowledging it we will stay on the surface and likely continue living through our shadows.

According to Larry, part of the healing process for women includes reclaiming our sensuality and sexuality, and our special connection to the body and the body of the earth.

Because of the masculine imbalance, when women do get into their bodies and use their sensuality there is a fear that men will just take this as sexuality and not know it as sacred. And this is true since men are stuck in their first and second chakras, where this sense of the sacred isn't awake.

Women have to release this fear and look at how they can live in a world where they are so sexualized.

We can't offer Mother Earth anything helpful if we are stuck in the same consciousness of duality. If women are really sincere about wanting to restore the sacred feminine or heal the earth with their energetic field, they cannot do it if they live unconsciously from their rage against men.

Because of the thousand of years of disconnection from self, because of the wounds created by this time of masculine imbalance, women have split within themselves. Many have smashed the feminine within themselves. It is internalized oppression. The consequences of this have never really been examined.

If the woman has not done the work to release all that which is ingrained in the cellular unconscious level it shows up in the woman as a closing off of the womb. You can physically know when that has happened if you are in touch with your body.

We must bring ourselves back to health and parity. Men and women are equal but different. And we have to understand how the masculine and feminine are both part of our spiritual life, like how we say our prayers. We have to bring balance back to our inner life – to develop a relationship to self, to the inner world, which is the feminine.

We have an external god because of a masculine imbalance. Because of that we are separated from our own sacredness. We are born into a universe with duality as a basic structure. We've taken duality and gone further into polarization. How do we regain a relationship to self? To our own sacredness?

The prophecies say there is a high potential for the imbalances to stop, for the pendulum to stop in the center during this time of great change. How do we do that? What's required for it to stop in the center? We need to remember and honor the sacred feminine in a way that does not try to destroy the masculine. We have – as a spiritual journey – we have to figure out what we need to do and how to do it.

Women and Ceremony

In many indigenous spiritual traditions, including the Aleut, ceremony is used to restore balance and health, and to activate and align individuals and community with spiritual power. And for women in ceremony, there is a unique possibility not to just heal individually, but to birth something new into the world through activating the energy matrix of the sacred feminine and projecting it outwards so it can be present in a trans-personal context.

For Larry, this understanding of how to activate the sacred feminine was an integrated aspect of his community. Women would gather in ceremony and participate in the creative process through activating the womb 'on the outside,' he says. It was also acknowledged in his tradition that this activation is primarily women's work, as it is women's energy systems that include the womb matrix, the creative power to birth something new into the world.

This collective need to birth something new is evident as we examine the destruction and degradation of our world and world systems. He says:

> If we don't create something new, we will just reproduce the same system we have now, and nothing new can be created in existence without coming from that sacred container that women create. Nothing new. In other words, everything else we do outside of that will perpetuate the old paradigms.

How do women approach this challenge and responsibility to use our power in service to collective transformation? Are women today capable of coming together in this way? Are we powerful enough, healed enough as individuals? Larry explains that while women do need individual healing, this should not keep us from working together for collective rebirth:

> In terms of women and ceremony and the larger evolutionary healing, we can't go through to the larger picture without honoring and being aware of our own sacredness and center. Through ceremony women bring their sacred power outward. But for many women, their sacred power is muffled by feelings, emotions, past wounding, past experiences transferred by the mother to the daughter in the womb. Women carry the entire lineage of feminine wounding along with their own individual wounding. A woman's full power comes when one heals, when a woman becomes and embodies love in every cell of the body.

Women must do their own healing work, but women do

not have to wait for perfection before being in ceremony for this greater transformation. For most women, the greatest power is achieved in groups. This is why women must come together even as they do their own healing work.

The threshold of when a woman is powerful enough to engage this other level of work is a mystery. Women should do the ceremony at the same time as their healing because nobody knows what the threshold is. And ceremony will be a healing experience. The healing can happen instantaneously in a properly constructed ceremony. A person can be healed in a microsecond. Ceremony is like a muscle – the more women are in ceremony, the more they will be in touch with their sacred self and the more powerful they will become.

The power of people with open hearts with no judgments is so great. We need to suspend judgment as part of the preparation of going into the circle. The field might get created in five minutes or never. Might take days and might not ever happen. You cannot judge and you cannot know.

There are women who understand how ceremony works – and one piece is the intention. They come with an intention. The intention is set out at a cellular level of the body. The body knows. The heart knows at a cellular level. It's an energetic expression that comes from every ounce of who we are. It comes from knowing, feeling, sensing – the inherent intelligence in the body all working and synthesizing at the same time. And the transformer that provides direction is the heart.

This is far more profound that most people realize. The women who know don't just carry knowledge. They know that the most important aspect of the work is invisible. Knowing comes from a place of great mystery, that is vibrationally expressed through our bodies.

This does not mean ordinary women can't do it. Because it's formless, there is no reason it can or can't happen…

Part of the work to get to that point is that we understand we can all do it. This is who you are! If we assume a wounded person cannot access the power of the sacred feminine, we preclude it from happening.

The formless is about expression that happens in the moment from the heart with trust in the process. That is why it's new! Everything else is created in this world by those indoctrinated into the patriarchy, created from a disconnected consciousness, which repeats itself over and over again, and gets worse over time. Even the most brilliant people can't solve these problems in the world because they aren't accessing the sacred womb. Only from this sacred womb can something new come because it comes from this ultimate consciousness.

This is why every single woman who has this in her body is going to lead the way.

Elements of Ceremony

Ceremony is not a thing of the past or restricted to those initiated into indigenous spiritual systems. Women across the globe can remember this ancient way to come together for individual and collective rebirth. This is a remembering more than a need to learn through the mind. And as Larry says, ceremony is a muscle that develops as we practice it.

But there are some guidelines and some suggestions that can inspire and enhance the space of ceremony as we engage with it. There are attitudes that we can cultivate and there are elements both deep within and beyond ourselves that can be trusted. The first thing to keep in mind, especially as we hope for and work toward our own healing, is that our wounds themselves will be part of the circle, says Larry:

What happens when women come into ceremony and they want the healing of the feminine? Whatever wounds are carried by the women into the circle become part of the ceremony whether we want or know it or not. To become aware of that is really important.

We create our own reality. So, in the healing process no matter what ceremony is coming forward the question becomes – what are we doing? Are we doing ceremony because of what we want to move away from? Or what we want to move towards? That creates the reality.

If we focus on the healing of the masculine imbalance then we will contribute to it. But if we construct ceremony around creating something new, then we will create something new. This means constructing ceremony around the authentic process of our own hearts.

Constructing ceremony around the authentic processes of the heart includes the power of trust, says Larry:

There is so much energy out there to help, but we need the space. And the space is trust. Trust in your own authentic being. But to trust it you have to access it – access and trust in our body and being. Trusting in the body is so simple, and it is feminine. The body is feminine. It is mother earth. Trust in the body internally, then you can trust externally – Mother Earth, people, men, all these have to come into play.

That trust gives power to everything we do. It is power in who we are and connected to all that is. If I do not trust some aspect of myself I will not trust that in others. If I do not trust my intuition, I cannot trust what is coming through. The power of that trust comes only from the heart in the present moment.

It does not occur in any other place.

For many modern women, the idea of women in ceremony might not make intuitive sense. And yet, more and more women are gathering together in various groups and circles, not quite knowing why or what they are doing, but responding to a deep call from within themselves.

Constructing a ceremonial circle does not require education or even a sense that we know what we are doing. In fact, not knowing is very important. We cannot think our way through ceremony. Ultimately ceremony is a vehicle for mystery, a way for human beings to align with spirit in a creative space. But as Larry says, there are traditionally proven ways to protect this formless space and guide us as we create with it.

> You have to be able to be in the space. The original instructions tell us how to cleanse and purify, how to ask for help and trust that help will come. Before the ceremony you have to purify, cleanse and set an intention that is aligned with spirit. How do you know it's aligned with spirit? It's not always easy, but if you purify and meditate and pray then something will come.
>
> Cleansing, purifying, asking for help are so important now. We don't have the wisdom in our minds to know what to do! That's part of the sacred power of women – being able to draw upon that mystery with much greater ease than men can, if you just clear the surface stuff that's muffling it. It really does require trust and faith and it's not intellectual. A deep feeling inside of one's heart is the ultimate guide.
>
> Ceremony traditionally includes this preparation and cleansing, setting the intention aligned with spirit, purifying and cleansing the sacred space, preparing offerings for the altar next to a sacred fire. If you don't have fire, even a candle will do. The items and offerings anchor the intention and help the members focus.
>
> The purification, the cleansing, and the setting of intention put you into a receptive state. Then you know what to say, offer, and pray for. It is a mystery. It comes. When it comes in

this way, it is in alignment with spirit.

Then create the sacred womb through intention and prayer before ceremony begins. Start the ceremony in song and chants and prayer. Last, give thanks and prayer in closing.

These are guidelines. They will protect the space of ceremony so that what is done and experienced is in alignment with spirit. Ceremony is a totally, utterly and completely creative act.

Purification, preparation, setting intention, offering, and prayer are traditional aspects of ceremony, and will likely be present in any powerful ceremonial space. But Larry explains that we also must be open to new ways of being in ceremony:

Remember, we are in transition to another level of consciousness. We are blazing the trail to the new. Gradually what's not useful to the new is put aside. The ceremonies will be created new and different to what has been done. The original instructions can help us construct ceremony to create something new.

At the core of ceremony, beyond the forms or the structures, is the heart and its powers to trust the ceremonial space and to keep the space clear of judgments about others.

'Intention, trust, and open heart' help to create the sacred space of ceremony, says Larry. So does the listening that comes from not dialoging with people in the circle. Ceremony is not a place for 'cross-talk' during which people talk back and forth, analyze, give advice, or impose ideas instead of only listening and holding what is said. There is no authority in ceremony, he says. 'Everyone is equally valuable and has an equally important contribution. There is no one answer, but everyone grows and heals in their own way.'

Across the world, more and more women are coming together in circle, led by a longing to be part of this ancient and creative process Larry describes. Even though they are not necessarily from indigenous cultures, women from many backgrounds are responding to a need to participate in individual and collective healing *as women*, learning to project their feminine power outward to create a womb on the outside. One woman from New Zealand explains how it is in the first ceremonial circle she's participated in. This circle meets monthly, and there is sharing and listening but no cross-talk, and a silent meditation and time for prayer:

I am not a group or workshop person and easily get overwhelmed, confused and uncomfortable around many words or prescribed rituals. I also too easily slip into being a 'good girl' trying to please (or rebel!) if there is an authority around who 'knows' and very obviously leads. I've committed to this particular women's circle because it is rooted in silence and unknowing and is totally non-hierarchical. Together with other women in what feels like a very empty space I feel freed up to really listen, both within my own being and to what arises from within the other women. In this deeply respectful and receptive listening space a trust arises that invites me to patiently wait on, and remember, qualities and powers that I know lie within my female being, even if they've been buried for a long time.

Another woman from a circle in northern California says:

The coming together with other women, just sitting and listening or sharing about my experience without getting advice or being analyzed, helps me to gain a more conscious understanding of how the more hidden feminine works in myself and in life. I can then recognize and honor it when it comes, giving it more space and life to be.

Being in ceremony for the sake of personal and community healing, honoring of the sacred, and the regeneration of the earth is a spiritual gift and also a responsibility that most women have forgotten. And yet this is a work we must remember not just for our own selves but to serve the times we are in, times that so clearly suffer from women's forgetfulness and our unconscious absorption into a patriarchal culture.

And while men must also find their way of participating in all that needs to be attended to in this time of great global transition, women have a particular responsibility that needs ceremony as a vehicle. It is for women to work together with the power of the sacred feminine, through our own energy systems, in a way that will energize and heal all levels of life including all creation. Men cannot do this particular work, says Larry:

Women have that sacred space of creation and creativity inside them. Energetically the womb is identical to the womb in the universe. So, everything new that is in harmony with the universe was always created by women. Women help create the energetic field of the womb on the outside. This is the purpose of ceremony. To access that place and put it in the physical world, outwardly. It has to be in ceremony. That's how it has always worked.

Always a 'Thank You'

One of the most important things to remember when we approach the issue of working in ceremony for healing or transformation is that we cannot be rooted, as Larry says, in past wounds or the past paradigm that created the wounds. We need to find ways to be in the space of mystery, a space where spirit can be present, through which something truly new can come. And we have to do this not by denying our wounds, but by holding them with us, but not at the center. Through an open and empty center – not clouded by desires or quick fixes – the power of creative space does its work. Sandra Ingerman explains:

> Look at the planetary changes. All the floods, cyclones, fires, and earthquakes are leveling huge parts of the planet – not just in isolated areas. We're seeing dismemberment on a massive level. Can we allow for the visions, dreams, deep intuitive knowing, and time to move into the new creation without rushing the process?

Sandra suggests not rushing anything, and Larry emphasizes trust. Patience and trust protect the space for something to happen. Working with the power of creative space always means including attitudes that keep us open and receptive. If we approach a problem with a predetermined idea about how to fix it, we are already closed. Attitudes like receptivity, trust, humility, awe, and gratitude act as continual forces creating passages and vehicles for the new.

Larry tells a story of how Native Americans allow gratitude and complete trust to bring about change:

> I was in the desert in the southwest at a time when there had been great drought – years of drought. I came across a medicine man in ceremony. He was saying prayers. I watched him for a number of hours, and then it started to rain. I asked him, were you praying for rain? He answered, 'No, I was being thankful for the rain.'
>
> The original Native Americans prayers follow the original instructions that were given to humanity. The prayers are always prayers of gratitude. 'I thank you for the healing.' 'I thank you for the blessings.' It is always a 'thank you.'
>
> There is always trust in the prayer, an embodied faith at the cellular level. There is not one thread of doubt – physical,

spiritual, or emotional doubt. That's when the prayer has its ultimate power.

How do we trust when we fear the worst? How can we be grateful when we are struck by loss and deficiency? How do we allow a great need for things to be different without determining that things must change? These are the paradoxes of transformation that are held together in such a way that the paradox itself keeps us open to the mystery of change. Sandra Ingerman describes a very simple example of how, in her own life, she struggled to leave a place of doubt and fear and live an alternative:

> We all have that egoic part that can move into fear about the world and the coming times. Many years ago I watched a public television special about drought in the southwest. I moved into this unbelievable fear state. I work with shamanic journeying, which is a way to connect with the earth and to receive visions. During one shamanic experience, I brought the drought issue up with my helping spirit, and she said to me, 'If you really believe that there won't be water then that's what will be created.' She shared with me that basically what we put our energy into is what we are creating. This was an important lesson. I could relax this terrible fear and allow a very different alternative.

It is not easy to feel the chaos and incredible uncertainty of the times and not be doubtful or afraid, but instead to connect to energies that are essentially creative, like gratitude and trust. This is perhaps especially true for women who have been so disconnected from our hearts and our bodies, where our trust is alive and present. But we can touch back into this trust. Larry says:

The less we analyze, the more we trust. It's a muscle. The more we practice, the stronger it gets. Ceremony is all about moving energy, and the heart is the ultimate transformer. We each have a heart. We are the gurus. We are the ones.

Everything is intensifying – it's a special opportunity in our lives. The Hopis are saying – let go of the sides of the riverbank. Move to the center and find those who have done the same, and celebrate.

Can we celebrate in a time of great unrest? Can we step aside from our fears, our anger, our rage at what has gone wrong and leave open a space for the joy of something new?

In women, we find this capacity – like so many others in this book – naturally lived through giving birth. Despite our personal hopes for our children, our expectations, and our own needs, we always give birth to something entirely unique to itself. And if we are lucky, our unconditional love keeps us attuned to this new being that grows by its own needs, encouraging and supporting us as we sacrifice and nourish, give to and serve this form of new life.

This template for the renewal of life is in our bodies and in our hearts, and it is our responsibility to engage it. It is a lost power, a great treasure we have allowed to disappear behind less powerful ideas and images of healing and change. Can we return to what is alive and unformed in us, return to the sacred? Can we put aside our intellect and trust something so much more wonderful and mysterious? Can we live as we really long to do – free from the filler of our lives, free in the space of creation that is birthing itself anew, calling us to be a part of something so unknowable and so grand that we are forever grateful to be given even a taste of it? Can we come back to ceremony and to the circle of life that we honor in ceremony?

In Larry's words:

Don't worry about what direction or how it's going to be done. The river knows where it is going. Be present, be in your heart, suspend everything from your mind, and trust. This will lead back to the circle...

Chapter 10

The Sacredness of Life

Sweet Medicine's earth is good.
Sweet Medicine's earth is completed.
Sweet Medicine's earth follows the eternal ways.
Sweet Medicine's earth is washed and flows.
Cheyenne Song[34]

Something important happens when we recognize life's sacredness. That which is sacred in us starts a conversation with that which is sacred in life. Whether it is a plant, a rock, another human being, or a bird – when we recognize the sacredness in another being, our eternal light reaches out and sets its hidden light aflame in another.

Knowing life's sacredness changes everything. It changes how you treat others, yourself, and everything on the earth. It changes what you want from life and how you give to life. It changes what you see and how you see. It changes your consciousness and your body too. It changes everything about how you live in the world.

Its power to transform is vast. The awareness of how divine life is threatens every man-made power structure that exists, and it threatens every conditioned belief one holds. It can render competition pointless and reveal the absurdity of self-interest. It decays preferences for good over bad or any this over any that and brings you into the one heart of life that belongs to everything.

Recognizing the sacredness of life is like the skeleton key for all the powers discussed in this book. Without this fundamental awareness that life is sacred the other powers can be diminished or rendered altogether meaningless, and with it, all the other powers work to their greatest potential.

For example, we can allow our longing to draw us into relationships and life situations but if we fail to take those situations deep into the heart where their lessons have relevance to the soul, we go round and round in our superficial desires. If we create community and reject the genuine contribution of even one individual, we are just forming a clique. If we work with the energy and resources of the earth in a way that does not serve its living holiness, we are just perpetuating its objectification. We can create many things, but if we are not giving space for the sacred to create with us, we are just adding to the objects of life. Beauty and the sacredness of life are so intertwined that as we see something or someone's beauty, we know its divine nature. And of course when we nourish others or feel nourished ourselves, it is just passing appeasement if it is not the sacred itself feeding us.

Experiencing life's sacredness happens in and through the heart, where we are free of prejudice and our personal desires lose their central place in our world, where the wisdom of our true nature can digest experience and know it for what it is. In this process of the heart we find meaning in experiences that might seem random or worse – painful or unnecessary. Recognizing the sacredness of life doesn't do away with difficulty, but reveals meaning and brings light to what is hard to bear. Life's holiness is whole, after all; when we activate this power we both accept how things are and attune to how things can change – the great paradox of holiness.

This fundamental power brings us into right relationship to what is and what has been in preparation for creating what will be. It is our way to know and represent the eternal in a moment of time.

The vision of life as sacred is one of the most powerful experiences you can have and it is unique to human consciousness. Dogs, plants, clouds, grass are all sacred, but do not have self-reflective consciousness to know their sacredness. It is a gift of humanity for the purpose of knowing and serving what is Real, right here with us. It is how we become, as every living spiritual tradition directs us to, a vehicle for the divine, because we see and feel and know and reflect back the truth that all is holy.

But recognizing the presence of the divine in a patriarchal world that either ignores the divine altogether or locates it in a heaven beyond earth is not easy. And to live this vision after catching a glimpse of it – to stay true to it and honor it – demands so much courage and perseverance that few really want to know it. It asks us to be ourselves in a world that constantly distracts us from this one simple but critical challenge. It asks that we live in accord with something mysterious in a world that rewards those who bring a predetermined agenda to every task. It asks that we love in a world that seems to make hatred and violence so much easier. It asks that we divest from competition and territoriality and all the structures of society that undermine our lived understanding that all beings command respect by the simple truth that they are divine.

The sacredness of life is the domain of the Divine Feminine. It is the experience of God *in creation*, the knowing of life's holiness. Without experience of this aspect of the divine, we are always looking away, and in our looking away we do not see, we cannot honor, and we fundamentally deny what is present and possible here on earth.

This avoidance and denial are so prevalent that all life has suffered tremendously from it. And while we all have a responsibility to turn to what we have ignored and remember what we have forgotten, when it comes to the divine presence on earth, the sacredness of life right here with us, women have a special responsibility. It is the *feminine* dimension of God, after all.

Women have a power in our bodies and energy systems described in different ways by the different people in this book that *creates* life and allows spiritual light to come into creation for something new to be born. It happens every day to millions of women as the soul of a child enters the womb; it can happen – as the Aleuts say – for women in ceremony as they put their womb on the outside to birth the new; and it can happen as women consciously relate to life on earth with an awareness of sacredness. This is a special gift of women that serves a unique purpose in the revelation of the divine through creation.

Sacredness and Spiritual Seeking

As represented by most spiritual paths, the awareness of life's sacredness becomes available to 'awakened' individuals often after years of seeking. Recall the Buddha eating a simple orange in bliss, after years of ascetic denial. After years of practice, Zen eventually brings us right into oneness, as in the final stages of the ox-herding pictures, which show a rider finally in harmony with his instinctual nature, imaged by the ox. Or consider the poem 'No More Leaving,' by Hafiz, the 14th-century Sufi poet:

At
Some point
Your relationship
With God
Will
Become like this:

Next time you meet Him in the forest
Or on a crowded city street
There won't be anymore
'Leaving.'

That is,

God will climb into
Your pocket.
You will simply just take

Yourself
Along![35]

This traditional model of spiritual awakening takes time. 'At some point...' says Hafiz. This common model, so familiar to us, is nonetheless not as universal as we think. It is a male model, expressed and lived throughout centuries primarily by men who leave behind ordinary life, transmute their sexuality, and 'slay the mythic dragon' of instinctual power before returning to the radiant beauty of the everyday with reverence and awe.

But as this book has emphasized, as the *only model* it is dangerous for humanity and especially for women, who do not need to deny or master sexuality, nor can they afford to remove themselves from ordinary life and those – children and community – who depend on their love and nourishment. In fact, through sexuality what is sacred in our energy systems can become available to others, as Larry Merculieff and Llewellyn Vaughan-Lee discussed in previous chapters.

For many women, it will be helpful to remember that the power and impacts of knowing life's sacredness are often simply part of how we live. It wouldn't naturally occur to most mothers that birth is not a miracle, that her newborn child is *not* divine. It wouldn't naturally occur to many women that their lovers and partnerships are *not* sacred, that their sexual nature is not sacred, or that their home, and the earth, need not be respected as a ground of love and transformation.

Women know these things, even as we keep them hidden like a dangerous secret.

The power of knowing life's sacredness is how women have endured lives of hardship and sacrifice for family and children. We live it through unconditional love, which might acknowledge one child as smarter or more attractive but certainly not more holy than another, and which grows as we open our hearts through difficulty and devotion.

Recently a mother from California had to move her young son into a new school system, and this move left her family without the network of friends and connections they had had in the previous neighborhood. Despondent and somewhat weary, she had a dream that she was told, 'Take out your needle!' She understood this to mean she had to do the work of threading love from her heart into life around her to create a new container that will support and hold nourishment for her family. So often we think this kind of 'sewing' happens naturally, and sometimes it does. But we also always have the capacity to do this work consciously and creatively, to take what we know as sacred within and thread it outward for the purpose of nourishment and transformation.

The task for most women is to redeem what is natural and bring it out of the solely intimate and personal sphere and use its power beyond the family. Wherever we go in life, if we are not including the wisdom that knows and works with life's sacredness, then we are a slim shadow of ourselves. We do not find meaning, we cannot be nourished, and we do not nourish others. We do not really participate.

Visions of Women's Sacred Power

This book offers descriptions of how women's sacredness is alive in our bodies and at work in our capacity to give and care for life. The Grandmothers, emanations of the Divine Mother, speak of women's bodies as *home* – not just physical home, but spiritual home, so much a part of us that the Grandmothers emphasize our power as carried in our blood. Larry Merculieff, from the far north, emphasizes women's womb as the same 'womb at the center of the universe' that can transform and rebirth. From across the world in China, Dr. Sun has said women's uterus works with her breasts in a 'powerful assembly of energies' for purification, nourishment, and transformation. From the distant land of Africa, Sobonfu Somé also emphasizes our womb as 'a gift that has been bestowed on us':

The womb is not just a place for babies; it is a very charged magnetic center for a lot of energy that comes from many different dimensions. We need to take better care of it and value it more, and know that this is a very delicate and powerful tool that we have been given.

And Sufi Llewellyn Vaughan-Lee makes a clear distinction between women's and men's spiritual nature and how women have a sacred substance that men do not have.

This substance in women's spiritual being can directly interact with the sacred substance, or light, in creation. This substance is like the catalyst of life – the sacred connection between humanity and life and the earth. When women honor this in themselves – this sacred essence that connects them to life – they can feel how it nourishes them and nourishes life directly. They are connected to creation and can nourish creation in a way men can't. It is that simple.

This connection between women's sacred substance and that in creation affects the way women's consciousness functions as much as how their body functions. So the energy flows through their bodies into the earth in a different way – actually this is not really the correct image because it suggests separation from the earth, as if it were not part of essential feminine consciousness. Women are just naturally part of the web of life, the energy flow of creation, the pattern of life... If you look at the energy of the earth, how it flows, then women are just part of it... while masculine consciousness has this quality of being separate.

The connection between women's sacred spiritual nature and the sacred spiritual nature within life means women have a different spiritual unfolding, unique challenges and gifts.

In a woman's spiritual unfolding, the power of recognizing

life's sacredness is one of our greatest allies. How does this work? The recognition of life's sacredness is a perception that connects to the essence of life beyond the appearance of good or bad, or what we want and don't want. This power is a great equalizer. As we see and know life's sacredness, we enter a consciousness of oneness, which encourages the flow of love and nourishment without prejudice. As we recognize life's fundamental sacredness, we honor *all life*.

There are great ramifications to this perception. When we see life's sacredness, we are called to honor life and respect all beings. When we look into the eyes of another's child, and we see the beauty and sacredness of that child, can we deny to that child what we would give to our own? As we look into the eyes of a homeless person and see their essential humanity, we are then forced to reckon with the inequities of the world and our own choices. Seeing life's sacredness does not mean we bring the homeless man back to our house, but it means our consciousness must come to terms with our choices and how we live. It requires expansion and wisdom and sometimes change.

Recognizing the sacredness within life almost always compels us to expand our capacity for unconditional love. As an awareness of the heart – not the mind – it pushes us to develop wisdom and to trust our instincts and intuition. It calls into question intellectual constructs and conditioned power structures. It asks questions about where our responsibilities rest and pushes us to develop our capacity to discriminate and discern.

This is the real detachment, which is not separation but openness – the neutrality of the heart mentioned by Elizabeth Frediani – that reveals the holiness of everything when we accept without judgment. This neutrality in the heart is the seat of discrimination and the home of wisdom. In this freedom we respond to need, not preference; we discriminate and serve, rather than limit what is possible by our own agenda. This is not a detachment that denies life its beauty or its power, but allows the knowledge of all life's beauty and power as the ground for decisions and choices.

This does not mean we lump life together in a jumble as if there were no distinction between this and that, but it means we see beyond personal desires as the reason to value one thing over another and instead use the discrimination of the heart that sees what is needed.

We use our natural wholeness not to absorb everything into sameness, but to expand our capacity to love everything as it is.

This is a path women know and live in normal daily challenges; we just don't understand or value how powerful this path is.

For many women, a tragedy of modern spirituality is that even as we struggle to honor the cultural shift toward seeing and living in accord with a new feminine spirituality that emphasizes earth traditions and the ecstasy within ordinary life, we are doing so largely without real awareness of how deep our prejudices are against this exact orientation. Just as we long to know life's holiness, we work continuously to veil ourselves from it, because so many of us are still ignorant, fearful, and incapable of living in the mysterious juncture of spirit and body where this consciousness rests. The sacredness of life is part of life after all, and life includes the body.

But we still don't really want to include the body in the spiritual journey or in our lives. Too often it is still a place of entrapment, still an object, just as all earthly things are. We don't really want to accept ordinary life because we have been told for so long it is a lesser way.

How can women surrender into ordinary life after centuries of believing it is a life of no spiritual relevance? It isn't easy but we have the tools to do it right here with us. Because as much as we have been told they have lesser or little value, we know our lives as women are sacred. Somewhere we have not truly forgotten. We need only to remember and reignite this sacred understanding.

Sanctifying

As we become conscious of our sacredness, we sanctify life. Life needs sanctifying. It is losing something that humanity can return to it, and women have a role in this returning.

This recognition of life's sacredness is a conversation of our sacred substance with the sacred substance of creation. Even a moment of knowing how holy life is, one instant of our light touching the light within life, is enough nourish and serve the whole. In the moment that we honor what is sacred, the infinite pours through. It is the power of recognition, of seeing and being seen, of being one with the divine, *here*.

It is a dialog that has been largely unheard and unspoken for centuries. And life around us has suffered from its absence. Llewellyn describes this devastation and women's roles in transforming it:

Men have made a real mess of the world. We've treated the world so badly that we've actually damaged the light cells of the earth. People see ecological devastation, but most people can't see the spiritual desecration that has been done. It is horrible. Like the pristine Mt. Everest littered with trash. In the inner worlds, temples have been totally destroyed. The light in the inner worlds is receding, becoming less accessible.

A certain spiritual work needs to be done by women because women are the matrix of creation. They carry the spiritual seeds of creation. This work has to do with healing and transmuting the earth so we can once again function as a living spiritual organism. Women's instinctual selves – their bodies, their sexuality – are sacred in a way that is not the case for men. Which means a higher energy can come down through a woman's spiritual vehicles into her body and through her body into the physical body of the world. When it comes into the world, it brings with it a sacred substance that a woman has which is always pure.

The world is dying because of the lack of a certain spiritual nourishment. A certain sacred substance – the Sufis call it the secret of the word 'Kun!' – 'Be!' It is actually like liquid gold – it is a very beautiful substance. You could say it is light of God made manifest in the world. And every woman carries it in the light of the cells of her body. If she honors it, then that substance begins to flow back into life, healing the damage that has been done to the spiritual body of the world. Women can re-energize the world.

The human being is very powerful. A human being can be like a catalyst – helping change come about at an accelerated rate. In this case, women can help change something much more quickly than if it is left to its natural cycle. If women don't give themselves to this process, the world could regress. Then the magic in the world would not be accessible to humanity; the wisdom, the light in the world would not be accessible. Through the spiritual work of women, what could take a thousand years if allowed to happen naturally could take two, thirty, or forty years.

How do women do this work? Llewellyn emphasizes engaging in the simple rituals of life with love and sacred awareness:

Women can give their sacred substance back to life, for the sake of life. This substance used to be given to life by women through the simple rituals of everyday life, grinding corn, baking, weaving. There used to be particular feminine mysteries associated with grain, and how it went into the earth as seeds.

Nowadays, although there can be the simple rituals, for example of cooking in a sacred manner, I think that what is needed is first for women to honor the sacred within themselves and within the earth. Then there can be a conscious relationship that can be brought into all aspects of life – not necessarily in the form of rituals, but a conscious offering to life, to the earth. In a way it is for each woman to make her own individual relationship/offering to life, to the earth. Of course it can be directly with working with the earth, gardening, but it can also be through making a relationship with a tree, with water, or with the earth itself. It can be through sexuality, though mostly this has been forgotten.

There is a way for women to *be* in life that naturally restores life and the light of the earth. But she must trust herself and give of herself. She must value her own being-ness, her own capacity – as the Grandmothers say – to represent, in flesh and blood, the lineage of the Divine Mother. She must know herself as sacred. Without this fundamental knowledge and conscious honoring of ourselves as sacred, women will not be capable of restoring the sacredness of life.

To know oneself as sacred is not easy. This book aims to help wipe away the conditioning and the dust that cover our understanding and direct experience of who we really are – how beautiful and how powerful – while we reclaim what is natural and see it in a new light.

But as we remember ourselves as sacred, as we shine light into what has been forgotten, we will naturally become more aware of the extent of the damage that has been done, and the degree of complicity for which we are responsible. As women come to wake up not only to what has happened to us but to *how we have participated in* our own disempowerment and neglect, we will experience tremendous amounts of rage and grief. We cannot avoid it. As we acknowledge the violence that has been rendered against women and against everything dear and natural to us, we will inevitably have to face both what has been lost and what we have given away. We will know what has been violated and we will know the patterns in ourselves that have allowed and contributed to this violation.

Without a way to sanctify this historical and deeply personal violence and destruction, we cannot live our greatest power, which knows that *all things are sacred* and that even the darkest times have the potential to serve life.

If we do not sanctify our own experiences as women, we cannot step into our power as women. And if we don't take this step, we cannot help bring about a future that is balanced and whole, that brings the pendulum of imbalance between the masculine and feminine, as Larry Merculieff has called it, to its central resting point.

Sanctifying Rage and Grief

According to Llewellyn, women's closeness to life, the unique connection between women's own sacredness and the living sacredness of life, means we can help heal life. But there is a flip side to this closeness. It means that as we consciously begin to relate from our own nature to the nature of life, as we come to know and live as we are, consciously opening the channels between our own energy systems and the systems of the earth, we run the risk of allowing our darkness – our anger and violence – to enter the earth. This will do more harm than good he says:

> Before women can help heal the earth, a redemption will have to take place. No healing can be done without forgiveness. If women put their anger and resentment toward men and everything that men have done into the spiritual body of the world, who knows what will happen?

Larry Merculieff also addresses the importance of this step:

> If women are really sincere about wanting to restore the

sacred feminine or heal the earth with their energetic field, they must find a way to heal their rage. Women cannot offer Mother Earth anything that helps if they are stuck in the same polarized consciousness of the past.

This requires forgiveness. This has to be a forgiveness that is not demanded; rather it is a forgiveness because your heart is open to understanding. Forgiveness is the major first portal of the transformation of rage.

What's happened to men today is they've been emasculated unwittingly. So men today don't know what it means to be a man, how to live the sacred masculine principles. They are lost. The grandmothers – the elder women today – understand we can't leave the men behind; otherwise the pendulum would swing for another eon.

In the process of reckoning and redemption, we can employ the power of life's sacredness. For there is a way to see, acknowledge, take responsibility for, and forgive – all through a heart that knows how redemption happens, how life's darkness becomes sanctified through honest acceptance, through a deep awareness of wholeness, and through the neutrality of non-judgment.

And herein lies another paradox of healing and transformation. Women need to access the sacred place within – which has never been harmed – in order to heal what is broken. We need our wholeness to relate to life as whole. We need our natural purity to purify what has taken place. We need our magic in order to know the world as magical. We need our capacity to hold all life as sacred in order to sanctify the past and create the future.

Every woman will have her own opportunities to become more conscious of how we have been part of a great forgetting, and forgive both ourselves and others. We will live this out through our partnerships and at work, in community and alone. It will be part of therapy and part of our prayers. This is psychological work with great spiritual implications, and spiritual work that will transform our psyches, our bodies and the world.

The Need of the Time

There aren't rules for this work – for a work we can acknowledge as one of the greatest contributions women can make to the evolution of life throughout time. But regardless of what we do in the outer world, surely the constant need is to thread the awareness of the sacred into every moment. Mother Teresa understood this work when she advised all of us to 'do little things with big love.' There is a way to bring the infinite into each simple moment and explode it with sacredness.

But this process implies we know 'big love' in the first place. And so many women feel disconnected from love, and unsure of how to bring it into life.

To this impasse, we need to bring our trust – the trust alive in the cells of our body, as Larry Merculieff says. If working with love were something we could not do, did not know how to do, how would we raise our children? How would we make love? How would we maintain friendships? How would we care for a garden? How would we respond to beauty? How would we long for change? We can remind ourselves that we know and we have access, because it is how we live; it is our nature.

Every chapter in this book is simply a reminder of what is natural to us. We can trust our longing to help draw love to us, and trust our capacity to nourish to guide that love back where it is needed through the web of life. We can trust our sense of what is beautiful and ask others to see this beauty. We can trust that life's wholeness is alive with its own power, just as our instincts guide us if we let them. We can trust that as we allow our power to emerge, it works with power that is dormant and waiting for us. We can trust that just as power takes us over as we give birth to physical children, power is present to help give birth to the child of the future.

Our longing and our dreams will show us how to live as

ourselves. And we will need each other for support – in ways that our individualized society and communities do not readily allow. So we will have to find ways to come together. We will need to honor what emerges from within, what touches the heart, what speaks to each of us. We might feel too tired to do what we need to do, too afraid, and we will have to open our hearts further and put more trust into our longing and our wisdom to move past the fears and the hesitation.

And we must always come back to the body and the body of the earth as our ground. It is the great mystery we have denied for centuries, the magic under the sea. It is the forgotten world of our longings that history has tried to erase from our books and our memories.

But our bodies know.

Our bodies have not forgotten. We still birth and feed our children, we stroke our lovers, we cry with our friends, we feed the birds, we lift our face to the sun, we throw our longing and prayers to the wind as we hang the laundry on the line, we rest in the bath, we drink from the stream and we raise the water from the well for the community.

And our bodies remind us that we are our most powerful when we are serving life as it includes and expands beyond ourselves. We come into our own when we are consciously part of life creating life, life nourishing life, life loving and renewing itself. For women's natural power is so much about connection through time and through dimensions. We live who we are as we receive new life from the realms of non-being and offer it into creation, as we continue to build communities that sustain life well beyond us, as we connect human consciousness and love with creatures of the earth, as we find ways for beauty to reach out and transform, as we link the infinite realms of space with solid life-forms, just as our bodies do in the womb.

Women nourish and receive. We connect and relate. Which means we cannot live as ourselves until we come to terms with the utterly simple fact that the extreme self-interest and self-focus which mark our modern world is contrary to our nature, and that our power expands when we give ourselves permission to relate, care and give – to life, God, earth, humanity. The norms of extreme individualism and the social structures supporting self-interest undermine what is natural and real for us. Which is why when women live as ourselves, the world will change so dramatically.

Sobonfu Somé describes a traditional practice in her village of women welcoming men home from war with breasts exposed:

> The breast is a sacred source of energy that enables life to continue. In our tradition the breast is used to welcome people and restore balance. Women in our tribe go topless, not as an invitation to intimacy, but to help the psyche receive what is life-giving.
>
> Men go off to war and when they return women will present their breasts as a way to say: 'This is a sacred place that values life. You can release your negativity and live peacefully here.'

In our bodies we find powers that are direly needed around us. Isn't it time to live peacefully? Haven't we all been at war for too long? Our bodies, so attuned to sacredness, to the natural ways life supports and renews life, are living sources of peace and nourishment.

In our bodies of great wisdom, women will find what is needed to renew the war-damaged world we live in. To bring nourishment and peace, to restore and recreate. Let's use our power to sanctify what has been neglected, and make more vital our beautiful earth. Let us use our wisdom to make life stronger, just as all things that are healed are stronger than before, brought into an expanded wholeness, known as they have never been known, loved as they have never been loved.

Exercises

What powers need your attention? The first set of exercises has to do with sensing into which of the following powers need your attention at this time. There are a number of ways to discover where your attention is needed. Here are just a few:

Ask yourself what you long for

Often the information is right here. Just ask yourself, 'What do I long for?' Is it community? A deeper relationship to the earth? To know yourself as beautiful? To connect to life's sacredness? What makes your heart beat a bit faster? What brings a tear to your eye? Ask yourself and write down some answers, and the power you need to connect with just might be right in front of you.

Ask in meditation

Sit quietly, knowing that you will not be disturbed for at least fifteen minutes. Turn your attention inward. Ask yourself which powers need your attention. Go through the list of powers (you might need a cheat sheet to look at!) and sense how your body or energy system reacts to each. Is there resistance? A sense of excitement or longing? An inner knowing?

Ask for a dream

For many women, dreams play a key role in helping us understand what our soul wants us to attend to. Before going to bed, lie quietly awake for a few moments, asking yourself to reveal where your attention is needed. Make sure to have a pen and paper near your bedside in case you wake up with a dream.

Ask life

Life is alive! It wants more of a conscious relationship to you. Life will show you where your attention is needed. You can help this process by consciously intending to learn from life. In the morning, in a quiet space, ask life to help you understand which power needs to be strengthened. This is similar to asking for a dream. Understand and trust that life will reveal to you what is needed. During your day, continue to nurture your sense of curiosity and commitment to reading the signs of life. Did you run into someone who wants to start a garden or become healthier? Does a magazine story about community catch your eye? Do you overhear conversation about the beauty of a new art opening or new wilderness trail? Pay attention to the information that comes to you during the day, and you will find which powers are calling to you.

Nourishment

Bring attention to your food habits – to everything from what food you eat and how it got to your table to how you prepare it and who you share it with

The point of this exercise is to help you develop a more conscious relationship with food, which is an essential source of nourishment and an essential way to connect to – and thus nourish – life around you.

Becoming more aware of how you eat should not be an 'exercise' but usually it is, as most of us have lost awareness of and appreciation for how food connects us to our own bodies and spirit, to others, and to the earth. But please don't let this exercise become a form of self-punishment. We are not suggesting you become vegetarian or eat only organic food or cut out sugar or alcohol. This is not a diet. It is an exercise in becoming more conscious of the multidimensionality of food.

Food is a key way of connecting to a great nourishing system we call life. And there are no fixed rules around this connection. Rather, there is only the need to know that this connection is present, it is flexible, it is a source of tremendous power. This exercise is about bringing attention to this aspect of your life and sensing what is needed *for and from you*.

For this exercise, you will need to keep a journal. Writing helps you become more conscious as it heightens self-reflection. Set aside a specific amount of time – a week or a month, for example – and keep a daily record of what you experience through this exercise.

Make sure to try at least half of the following. Pick the exercises you want to do and do them every day. Do not skip.

* Read ingredients on the food you want to buy.
* Hold food in your hands before you buy it. Practice sensing whether or not your body wants or needs it.
* Be grateful and appreciative throughout the growing, buying, cooking, and eating process. When food passes through you, can you also be grateful?
* At every meal, take a small bit of food and offer it to nature – to the birds or to the spirits of the animals in your area. Even if you live in a city, there are likely birds that can enjoy a crumb on your windowsill.
* Start even the smallest garden – a few herbs on a windowsill is enough – and record how it feels to grow what you eat.
* Eat slowly.
* Allow the story of your food – where it came from, who grew it, how it got to the table, how it was prepared and by whom – to be part of the eating process.
* Every night, before bed, ask for a dream or some form of guidance to help you uncover the power of nourishment through food.

Understand that there are no rules here. This is an exercise in becoming more conscious of how you relate to food – an essential source of nourishment. For some, it might feel OK to buy some prepared or pre-packaged food as long as they also eat fresh organic greens every day. It might seem fine to buy pre-packaged food as long as it is prayed over and asked to serve the body and spirit. Others will find that they can no longer buy food that comes in plastic. This is a highly individual process, just as every relationship is highly individual, based on the specific needs of the relationship.

Self-nurturing meditation

This exercise comes from Elizabeth Frediani's book, *Where Body Meets Soul: Subtle Energy Healing Practices for Physical and Spiritual Self-Care*.[36]

The energy system serves your body, mind, and soul by receiving, conducting, transmitting, and conserving life-force energy. Receptivity in this context is vital to maintaining physical health as well as emotional and spiritual wellbeing. Receptivity can be understood as the ability to *take in* – take in life experience, support, love, energy, and self. To be receptive is to be self-nurturing.

Meditation:

Close your eyes and take two or three gentle cleansing breaths, inhaling very slowly through your nose and exhaling very gently and slowly out of your mouth.

Now, focus your attention in the physical center of your heart chakra. This chakra is located approximately one to two finger-widths above the bottom of your sternum. Focus inward from this point and as close to the core of your body as is comfortable for you.

In your own words, speaking internally to yourself:

Affirm your intention and commitment to love and support yourself.

Affirm your responsibility as a creative force in your own life.

Forgive yourself for any pain and difficulty you have created for yourself.

Now, just as you would love and support a dear friend who

needed healing, be willing to love yourself in the same way.

Hold yourself in your heart chakra and call the love and compassion that you would give outwardly back into your own heart chakra.

Continue to hold yourself and receive your love. *Hold this receiving focus for as long as you wish.*

When you are ready, ask yourself what you need and listen in your heart for the answer. When you hear your response, make a commitment to meet this need.

Gently release your focus when you are ready and open your eyes.

Questions to answer in a journal:

1) What did you feel emotionally during the meditation?
2) Did you have any trouble affirming the statements in your heart?
3) Did you feel love and/or energy flow back into you?
4) What was your need? Do you have any resistance to meeting that need?
5) Write down any feelings and experiences you had during the meditation.

Tonglen – A Tibetan Buddhist meditation of 'sending and taking'

Tonglen is an ancient meditation practice in the Tibetan Buddhist tradition. There are a number of websites and books that describe variations on this practice. The version below is simple and informal.

This practice is extremely powerful as it undermines the human tendency to exclude or push away painful or negative experiences and want only good things for ourselves. It reveals the great power within us to nourish others through working inwardly with energy that is always available to us. *Tonglen* can help us become more aware of an inner space where we are all connected, where the usual boundaries of 'us and them' do not exist, or are understood as irrelevant. This opens us to tremendous powers of nourishment, as it is from within in this boundary-less space that we can nourish others and feel most nourished.

1) Sit quietly and rest in your body. Bring to mind someone you know who is suffering. This might be a personal friend or family member, or an individual you saw on the news whose suffering touched you.
2) As you imagine this person, imagine that you can absorb his or her suffering into your energy system. Understand that, as connected to a vast wholeness, you are empowered to work with this suffering.
3) As you breathe in, take that suffering into you. Visualize the suffering as thick smoke. Inhale it into your being. Imagine absorbing it into your heart center, which is at the same time the center of the entire universe. In this heart center, you rest in infinity.
4) As you breathe out, breathe out from this very center, this heart center, that has just taken in the suffering. As you breathe out, you can breathe out that same suffering but now it is in the form of a stream of light and peace, compassion, and anything else that is needed by this individual.
5) Continue this 'taking and receiving' with each breath for as long as you feel is needed. Feel the peace and the compassion that come from your heart. Consciously recognize that your heart has the power to digest and transform what comes into it.
6) When you have finished the taking and receiving, sit quietly and relax.

Earth

As you try any or all of these exercises, remember that your energy system is highly connected and attuned to the earth. You do not have to do anything to make this connection. You are seeking to become more aware of it, and to heighten or strengthen this connection through your intention and attention.

Walk barefoot

Walking barefoot is a very simple way to facilitate the flow of earth energy into your energy system through the feet. As Dr. Sun explains, in women, energy generally flows from the earth up through the feet.

In my previous book, *The Unknown She*, Sobonfu Somé describes a situation in her tribe in Africa where women were given shoes: 'In my village we tried different things, including giving shoes to women. And they went crazy. Some women would not put shoes on. And if they do, then they are sure they have some time with earth under their feet.'

Try to find some part of the world – even if it is just standing on a blanket in a city park – where you do not need to have shoes on. Trust that you are allowing your body to absorb and exchange energy with the earth this way. Even if you do not feel anything happening energetically, simply allow yourself to physically feel the earth under your feet.

Lie on the ground

Spend some time simply lying on the earth. Relax. Receive. Clear your mind and feel the earth. Elizabeth Frediani advises to lie face up. She writes:

Earth herself is part of the Great Mystery and the dark. Despite the efforts of some to control her, she moves in her own cycles and draws from her own matrix of energy. Our link to the Earth is primal and spiritual. Our bodies, souls, and consciousness are nourished and informed by her. It is our birthright to receive from her and our responsibility to honor her – as home, healer, and living being.

Go to the Earth knowing that she nourishes your spirit and your consciousness. Place your body on the ground. Lie there without thought, fully extended on your back and receive the Earth's energy, allowing it to move and re-align your energy.

In the quiet of your receptivity, you are brought into resonance with stillness and with the mystery of the dark. From the deep rhythmic life force of Earth, you will find gentle and, sometimes, dramatic renewal. Your thoughts will change, your emotions will balance, and your body and energy system will come into coherence.[37]

Grow your food: Create your own garden or contribute to a community garden

For this exercise, you need to experience growing food and eating food anew.

* Create a garden: Gardening can take a lot of time, but it does not have to. If you do not have space for a garden, you can still grow an herb garden on your windowsill. Find some way to plant and participate in the growing of food that you ingest. Even a small herb garden is a place of magic and revelation.
* Participate in a community garden: Even if it is only volunteering a bit of time at a community garden or co-op in exchange for fresh vegetables. You can do this with your family and children.
* Volunteer at a local farm for farm produce: These days many local farms have programs that exchange food for work. Bring your family and participate in a local farm, and enjoy the healthy produce you help grow. These last two suggestions are also excellent ways to honor and

generate the power of community!

These suggestions above will likely mean re-arranging your priorities of how you spend time and money. But a conscious connection to the earth can be a priority in your life. It is imperative both to the earth and to your own physical and spiritual health.

Consciously connecting with your food is critical to consciously connecting with the earth. Food becomes your own body, which is the most intimate arena where consciousness and earth meet. If you harm your body through poor food choices, you impede your potential to create deep and nourishing relationship with earth. If you do not eat well, or if you eat unconsciously, changing your food habits will likely create reverberations through your emotional body as well. This is a sign of just how powerful food is and can be.

Love your body

This exercise is a way of life. Women are prone to inflicting harm on ourselves. We will hurt ourselves often through violating our bodies, as it is our bodies – and the body we share with others, the earth – that are subjects of so much widespread physical and psychic violence. We might unconsciously feel that if we control and harm our own bodies we are keeping our bodies from being harmed by others. This reasoning is of course problematic. The antidote is to love our bodies so that they are powerful enough to sustain and possibly transform any violence that should ever come our way.

We might not be able to feel love or its partner – gratitude – right away through all our negative thoughts or beliefs, but we can practice working with love. And we can direct this love to our physical nature as a way of connecting and honoring the body of earth. As we love the body, we bring love – an essentially spiritual power – into the material world. We can do this for ourselves and of course for others. We do this naturally through touching a lover, a child, a friend, or a pet. We often don't know how alive love is, how our longing to be whole and healthy can draw to us the love we need in order to heal ourselves or others. We don't know how we can guide and direct love, and we don't understand that we must do it to ourselves.

How do we love our bodies? Here are some basic suggestions:

* Sit quietly and scan your body with your attention, from the inside out. Does one part of your body need special care? Ask it what it needs. If you get a clear answer, try to respond to the need appropriately. It's fine if you do not get a clear answer. Remember, your body is a living being: it is a form of consciousness. It will know you are relating to it just as a flower or any other part of the earth knows when it is being related to. That knowing is a strong foundation of deepening your relationship.

* Eat well. We will suggest this again and again. Food is a vehicle, a way energy – including love – is transmitted through the entire web of life of which we are a part.

* Be grateful to your body. Find a quiet time and space, like while taking a bath or a shower, or lying in bed alone. Make sure you can see or touch or otherwise recognize and acknowledge your body. Bring yourself into a mental space of wonder and awe that you are alive. Generate gratitude for the parts of your body that keep you alive – your heart and your organs – and for the parts of your body that serve you continually in so many ways. As you move your consciousness around your body, touch or look at or sense from inside each part.

* Consciously touch your body with love. Women know how to use love as we touch others. Consider how we stroke a pet, or brush the hair of our children, or rub the back of our partner. We know – intuitively – the difference between

when we are doing this unconsciously and when we do it with love. Turning on the love is often a conscious decision, requiring willingness and a special attention. Turn this attention to your own body.

This suggestion is to help you make a direct, loving connection to your body. *It does not translate as 'go get a massage from someone else!'* Getting a massage from someone else can be rejuvenating, but it can also be a way of reinforcing the idea that it is someone else's job to love us, or that others have more capacity or responsibility to love us than we do. Love is available all the time – learn to offer it for yourself as well as others.

Use your longing to connect with the earth and your body

This exercise uses the power of longing to awaken and deepen your conscious connection to the earth.

Lie or sit down in a quiet place. Consider being a human being who is naturally in touch with her body, naturally aware of the wisdom of her body, and naturally attuned to the earth and earth spirits. What would it feel like to go outside into nature and hear – and know – what the birds are saying? Did you ever want to be like Dr. Doolittle and know what the animals were thinking, and what they need? Do you have a longing to live in the way we know some indigenous peoples lived and still live – in a state of conscious communion with the earth, its needs, its cycles? Do you know someone who seems confident in her or his own skin in a way that you envy? Are you tired of imposing dietary restrictions onto your own body in a search of fitting in or feeling better about yourself?

Allow yourself to want, need, and long for a more harmonious and wholesome relationship with the earth and your own body. Let the longing for wholeness and the power of connecting with your earthly self grow. If it brings tears or anger, that is just fine. Let your longing release itself from your heart, reminding you of what you truly need.

Let yourself need what you need. And as you come out of this deep state of need, don't make any promises or commitments to change; just make a commitment to honor this need, to acknowledge it and to let it be present in your life.

Pray for the earth

Let any of your contemplative practices – meditation, prayer, offerings – include the earth. Even if you are attempting a formal meditation practice with its own guidelines, before you begin add a few moments to offer your practice to the earth. As you begin prayer – to God, Jesus, Allah, a Goddess, Oneness, etc. – include a moment to pray for the wellbeing of the earth. Remind yourself that the earth is a living system with consciousness. You might consider that just as your own body has a soul embedded in it, the earth is the body for a soul that can evolve like your own soul. Your own soul can give and receive from the earth's soul. With that in mind, consider the impact that your contemplative spiritual practices can have on the soul of the earth.

The following is an excerpt from an article by Llewellyn Vaughan-Lee about including the earth in your prayers.

The earth needs our prayers more that we know. It needs us to acknowledge its sacred nature, that it is not just something to use and dispose. Many of us know the effectiveness of prayers for others, how healing and help is given, even in the most unexpected ways. There are many ways to pray for the earth. It can be helpful first to acknowledge that it is not 'unfeeling matter' but a living being that has given us life. And then we can sense its suffering: the physical suffering we see in the dying species and polluted waters – the deeper suffering of our collective disregard for its sacred nature. Would we like to be treated just as a physical object to be used and abused? Would we like our sacred nature, our soul, to be denied?

For centuries it was understood that the world was a living being with a soul, and that we are a part of this being. Once we remember this in our minds and in our hearts, once we hear the cry of our suffering, dying world, our prayers will flow more easily and naturally. We will be drawn to pray in our own way. There is the simple prayer of placing the world as a living being within our hearts when we inwardly offer our self to the Divine. We remember the sorrow and suffering of the world in our hearts, and ask that the world be remembered, that divine love and mercy flow where it is needed. That even though we continue to treat the world so badly, divine grace will help us and help the world – help to bring the earth back into balance. We need to remember that the power of the Divine is more than that of all the global corporations that continue to make the world a wasteland, even more than the global forces of consumerism that demand the life-blood of the planet. We pray that the Divine of which we are all a part can redeem and heal this beautiful and suffering world.

Sometimes it is easier to pray when we feel the earth in our hands, when we work in the garden tending our flowers or vegetables. Or when we cook, preparing the vegetables that the earth has given us, mixing in the herbs and spices that give us pleasure. Or making love, as we share our body and bliss with our lover, we may feel the tenderness and power of creation, how a single spark can give birth. Then our lovemaking can be an offering to life itself, a fully-felt remembrance of the ecstasy of creation.

The divine oneness of life is within and all around us. Sometimes walking alone in nature we can feel its heartbeat and its wonder, and our steps become steps of remembrance. The simple practice of 'walking in a sacred manner' in which with every step we take we feel the connection with the sacred earth is one way to reconnect with the living spirit of the earth.

There are so many ways to pray for and with creation, to listen within and include the earth in our spiritual practice. Watching the simple wonder of a dawn can be a prayer in itself. Or when we hear the chorus of birds in the morning we may sense that deeper joy of life and awake to its divine nature. While at night the stars can remind us of what is infinite and eternal within us and within the world. Whatever way we are drawn to wonder or pray, what matters is always the attitude we bring to this intimate exchange: whether our prayers are heartfelt rather than just a mental repetition. It is always through the heart that our prayers are heard, even if we first make the connection in our feet or hands. Do we really feel the suffering of the earth, sense its need? Do we feel this connection with creation, how we are a part of this beautiful and suffering being? Then our prayers are alive, a living stream that flows from our heart. Then every step, every touch, will be a prayer for the earth, a remembrance of what is sacred. We are a part of the earth calling to its Creator, crying in its time of need.[38]

Purification
Honor your menses

The next time you have your period, follow Dr. Sun's suggestions to become aware of how your physical cramps and emotional discomfort could be related to your own stress or difficulties and those of others. Here are some other specific ideas:

* If you use tampons, make sure they are not synthetic materials or bleached with chlorine.
* If possible, for some time of your period, do not block the flow of blood. Wear a pad or other form of blood-catching. Stopping the flow of blood can exacerbate a plugging or halting of energy flow from your body.

* Consider catching blood and using it for some conscious purpose. Offer it to the moon, bury it in the earth, say a prayer for another person or use it as a symbolic offering.
* Do something to honor this time of month. For example, take a day off from work to rest or go inward, and do not be afraid of telling your employer why you are taking time.

Offer your power to someone in need

It is important that women understand that we have the power to purify within our own bodies and energy systems and we can use this power in service to life. Have you just heard of a river that is polluted, a species that is dying off from disease, or a friend who is ill or distressed? While on your period, when you feel strong and intuit that you are capable of this exercise, sit in meditation and consciously offer your power to purify to someone or something in need. You can keep in mind the individual who is suffering, or just ask life to take the power and use it where needed. Do not do this if you have strong psychological patterns of 'helping' or 'saving' others. If your spiritual power gets co-opted by self-destructive psychological patterning you will harm yourself.

As you do this exercise, understand that just as you have the power to purify and can help others, so too does the vaster earth-based web of life have the power to help purify you. After you offer your power to someone in need, ask the earth's purifying system to help you. Or, if you can hold both these intentions at once, all the better. You might lie on the earth after completing this exercise.

Women's menstruation ceremony

Women's power to purify is amplified when we come together with other women. One of the most potent ways for women to use their power to purify is by gathering with other women and consciously directing this power where it is needed.

This is not just a celebration or recognition of this power and how it works in our own lives, but also a way of using this power to heal – individuals, community, and the environment. This is a step most women do not currently take. Our spiritual milieu is quite focused on how we can use our own power for our own healing and transformation. Of course this is important, and our power is available for us, but when women come together to serve life itself, the scope of our power expands way beyond the individual. And in that process we are included, as we are part of that bigger picture.

The formation of women's ceremonial menstrual circles does not follow a rulebook. Find a group of women and establish some intentions and get together! Some ideas for intentions:

1) We intend to use our power to purify what is needed.
2) We intend to come together and offer our power to life.
3) We intend to serve life; we trust our power will go where it is needed.
4) We trust life will help replenish us as we need.

Before your menstrual circle meets, be especially attentive to information from life about where purification or transformation might be needed. You might hear of a colleague who is ill with cancer. You might hear a story on the news of a polluted lake in a distant country. You might have a dream about a dark cloud somewhere in your own body. When you gather with women for the purpose of purification, you might take turns going around the circle giving voice to what you sense needs healing. Follow that offering with a few minutes of silence, during which you trust your energy and power will go where they are needed.

Be a vehicle for your wisdom

Your wisdom will heal and purify, and wisdom resides in your intimacy with your own body. Your willingness to respect, protect, and stand up for the dignity of your own body – like the woman from chapter 4 who refused to have her body scarred unnecessarily during cancer treatment – is a vehicle for transformation. Imagine what could happen in our world if every woman suddenly was willing to honor her own body and refused to participate in the degradation of her own body by others and society.

The key is your own awareness of what feels right and what feels wrong, and your courage to stand by this awareness. You might find that you can no longer allow people around you to ridicule others for how they look, or to gossip negatively about others. You might feel drawn to dress in a new way, to celebrate or care for your body in a new way. Your own inner compass of what is good and right points the way to purification. *Listen to your body and follow your instincts.*

Enlightened sexuality

Please consider the mystery of sharing your energy system with life itself and another human being while you make love. Understand and feel how open you become when you are sexually aroused; become more conscious of the power of this openness, how your energy system can absorb and transmit energy during this particular moment. Sense into what is happening when you make love and are particularly vulnerable and present. Feel what is given and what is received. Listen to your partner before, during, and after to note what has been given or what has changed. Feel in yourself what has changed.

There are no specific rules to activating your power while making love. Be attentive, sense what is happening, give yourself, and understand that sexuality is sacred. Be very intentional about who you share yourself with. Understand that making love is sacred.

Mother/Daughter ceremonies

It is important that women come together to ensure that today's young girls grow up honoring the power of their menstrual time and the power of women gathering. Bringing mothers and daughters together to honor the power of womenhood and specifically to honor the menses will have a significant effect on how these girls come to appreciate and respect their bodies and the experience of being women.

You can develop a structure that works for you and your community. But here is one example provided by a circle developed by a group of women near Seattle, consisting of four basic elements: Share, Celebrate, Eat, and Create.

Gather a group of women and their daughters together. The daughters should be around the age of their first menstruation. Sit in a circle. You might want to smudge or otherwise purify the participants as they enter the circle.

1) Share: Go around the room, asking three basic questions. Do not discuss. There should be no cross-talking here. Rather, listen and share:
   What power animal or plant spirit or other helping being do you want to invite into the circle and why?
   What does it mean to you to be a woman?
   What does menstruation mean to you?
   You might be amazed at how the girls answer these questions and you will be moved at how they listen to the women sharing their experiences. This sharing between mothers and daughters in a larger community can be extremely powerful.
2) Celebration: When the sharing is complete, let there be drumming, dancing, or singing of some kind. This group in Seattle had a four-person drum, and the girls and their mothers drummed together.
3) Eat: Share food that has been brought by everyone, or

offered by a mother whose daughter has just started menstruating.

4) Create. This group from Seattle beaded necklaces that mothers and daughters could wear during their period. As one young girl said, 'When my mom wears her necklace, I know to be more helpful and understanding.' As a mother said, 'When she wears her necklace, I can make sure to give her more space and not make her do the chores she would usually be responsible for.' These secret signs between mother and daughter to respect this important time of the month are a form of intimacy and understanding, a way to honor what is between all women.

Beauty

One of the most important ways to activate this power is to give yourself space to feel and know beauty, to trust it, to share it, regardless of what anyone around you says or does. This process includes time and space when you can sense for yourself what is beautiful both inside you and out. While this sounds simple, most of us just don't do it. It's easier to buy into what the general collective finds 'attractive' and conform. It's a safer route, and for women who have collectively been terrorized by a patriarchal culture, safety is important. But the safest place for any woman is knowledge about and trust in herself. To this end, please take time for the following:

Find the beauty

Everything that is alive is a vehicle for beauty. Can you find it? For this exercise, you will develop your trust that beauty exists already. You do not have to create beauty, but rather you will locate and honor the beauty that is present. This is true for people and all aspects of nature especially. Is it true for objects as well? Is there beauty in your ragged couch or your dirty windowsill? What is the beauty there? Where does it come from?

Use a journal to write down what is beautiful about what you see. Challenge yourself. Go to a city street and sit on a bench and notice the first thing that catches your eye. Write down the object or the person and describe what is beautiful. Do not give up, even if you are looking at something that disturbs you or seems unattractive.

Find your beauty

This is the same exercise as above, but now turn your attention to yourself. Look at your body and write down what is beautiful. Every aspect of your body is an expression of beauty – leave nothing out. Make sure to give attention to a part of your body that you do not find attractive and open yourself to asking, 'Where is the beauty here?', trusting and knowing that it is there.

Now, consider your character traits. Consider your more attractive qualities, like kindness or generosity, and describe why they are beautiful. Consider your less attractive qualities, like your anger or pettiness, and find how they too contain beauty. Do not give up until you have found and described why these aspects of yourself are expressions of beauty.

Create beauty

If you are an artist or enjoy creating things this is still a great exercise, as it requires that you create beauty with what you can find. This is not about buying something to create beauty – don't go out and buy new yarn in order to knit a beautiful sweater, or new shoes to look beautiful. Find ways – big or small – to create beauty around you. Understand that your own energy and consciousness can work with the power of beauty. Beauty exists, and it can be heightened. Engage with nature's beauty by bringing inside a flower or plant and find just the right place for it in your house or apartment. Why and how does this new arrangement between nature and your home bring forth the beauty of both?

*Allow your imagination and intuition to be guides. Beautify – inside or outside of your home – with the following:

A rock or rocks
Plants or flowers
A stick or sticks

* Rearrange papers or books so they are more beautiful to you.
* Open your cupboard and make beauty out of your stored food or pots and pans.
* Rearrange your furniture to find a new way of expressing its beauty.
* Open your dresser drawer and be creative with how your clothes are stored there.

Don't stop here... every day, consciously create beauty from found objects in and around your home.

Offer beauty

Take the above experience of creating beauty outside of your home, into areas that are public. Understand that beauty has power in the moment, and even if you are not present to see other people's reactions to what you create, beauty still has power. Create beauty in a city park, in an office building, on a sidewalk or restaurant. Place stones in a certain pattern on a trail or at a friend's driveway. Rearrange a tray of coffee/tea on an office counter before a meeting. Put a flower on a park bench with a poem attached. Create beauty and walk away, knowing that beauty is not for you to own or control. Offer beauty to life itself.

Acknowledge beauty

Something tremendously powerful happens when beauty is

made conscious, and when it is recognized. The next time you go outside, find something and acknowledge its beauty. Let an aspect of nature – a tree or a rock – catch your attention. Tell it how beautiful it is. You don't necessarily need words, though if you want to speak to it, that's just fine. Or you can express your acknowledgment mentally, or through touch. Touch a rock with love, stroke a tree with love, thank a flower for moving you with its beauty.

Do the same to your furniture and your home – find its beauty and acknowledge it somehow, maybe even through cleaning, repair, or care.

Now, try this same exercise with people. The next time you are with someone, share how you find something about them beautiful. Be honest. Do not take this lightly. You must be moved by something – an attitude in the other person, a way they are in the world, a way they have acted or something they have said, or even the way their hair is done or the clothes they have chosen. Find what is beautiful and acknowledge it. See what happens between you and this other person when this beauty is made conscious.

Walk with beauty

Re-read the final Navajo chant at the end of the Beauty chapter and consider how you can walk with beauty. Can you be with beauty in such a way that you restore and harmonize your own environment? Can you feel beauty inside you and thread it outward into the world? Work with love to do this. Open your heart, feel the beauty inside you and use love and attention to bring it out, through touch, movement, breath, or words. How does the beauty inside influence life outside you? Can you reverse the process and breathe beauty into you? How does this restore something within?

Community

Many of the exercises above help create community, as they encourage the conscious connecting between you and all the living beings in the environment. But here are some more.

Create new connections

Say hello or be helpful to someone in your community – your neighborhood or your workplace – that you don't know well. Create and navigate the needs of a relationship with someone you will not be deeply intimate with, but with whom you share resources, like the space you live or work in. This might develop into a friendship, but consider that you can create community without it being deeply personal. Don't be afraid to nurture connections with others when you don't know what you can get out of it. Just connect and sustain...

Women Within Walking Distance

This exercise comes from a group of women living in a rural area in western Washington. A few of these women had the feeling they wanted to get to know their neighbors better. So they invited a group of their neighbors and created Women Within Walking Distance (WWWD), a monthly potluck that took place at each other's houses. Every month, the women would walk over to the hosting house with food or drinks and enjoy an evening of getting to know their neighbors. You can of course do this with men too, but women alone will create a different atmosphere and perhaps strengthen community ties more than if husbands and partners are present. For this group of women, the meetings lasted more than two years. Friendships were developed, but so were simple, less personal experiences – like a feeling of safety and dependability in the neighborhood, an ease with each other, and a sense of not being isolated.

Mentor a child in need; become a foster parent; be a big sister

These are excellent ways to expand your sense of community and empower the community of girls and women. Don't hesitate just because you already have children. In the West, and especially the United States, the nuclear family can isolate us from a wider sense of community. We keep our resources – financial and emotional – for our children and their future, which is of course important, but at the same time this can be a limitation that restricts resources from flowing outward into a wider community. Bring a child in need into your own life. Expand your responsibilities to include others beyond your family. There are so many ways to do this.

Join an international project

Expand your community to include an individual from across the globe. There are many programs where for just a few dollars a month you can support a child or a woman or an entrepreneur from another country. Help your city become a sister city to a distant community, if it isn't already. Start a letter-writing relationship and offer financial support to a woman in a war-torn country. Support a young child through a children's aid group. Find another way to create relationship to someone in a distant land and share your financial and emotional resources with that person.

Join a community garden

We suggested this in the 'Earth' exercises and it's an excellent way to create community with people and with nature both.

Longing

Activating the power of longing depends upon our willingness to recognize and stay true to what we really want and need. And while this sounds simple, the vulnerability it can call forth can feel disturbing. Which is why we often cover over our real need with more superficial needs that we can control and satisfy. To work with longing means looking closely at this tendency and being honest about what is deep and true within.

What do you really want?

This exercise requires a quiet contemplative space and could take place over a few weeks or a few months. Don't stop till you feel certain you have arrived at the deepest answer you can find. This requires writing, so have a pad or journal with you.

Find a quiet space with at least 20 minutes of protected time.

Ask yourself, 'What do I really want?' Write down the answers. Try to be succinct. (After all, how many things could you *really* want?)

With each answer that you come up with, ask yourself: 'Why do I want this?'

Consider the reasons behind the answers. Then, ask yourself, 'Is this what I really want?'

If the answer is 'Yes' ask yourself, 'Why?' again. If it is 'No' return to the initial question – 'What do I really want?'

When you determine the essence of why you want what you want, go back to examine your first answer. Ask yourself: 'Is my initial answer the best way to get what I want?' Are there other ways that might be easier, more direct, more available, less culturally prescribed, more original to your own path in life?

For example: A woman might answer the question 'What do I really want?' with 'A partner.' Then, in answer to 'Why?' she might write: 'So I feel safe,' 'So I feel loved,' 'So I can love someone' etc…

Each of these answers needs to be examined. Is 'finding a partner' the only or the best way to feel 'loved'? Is it the only or best way to feel 'safe'? What other ways can this need be satisfied? Are you willing to honor this need by trying other things?

Consider where you spend your money

When you buy something, you extend energy out and draw something in to your life. Adjusting your consumer choices is one of the most potent ways to change the dynamics of energy exchange and align your deep longing with how you live day-to-day. Ask yourself why you buy what you buy and if you really need what you buy. Don't take this as a self-punishing chore resulting in self-denial. Just take this as an opportunity to gain insight into how you express your longing through commerce. If you become aware that you are spending money on things that you do not really need, please consider stopping. Align your consumer choices with your deep values. In other words, put your money where your mouth is! (And your heart!)

Ask life what it longs for from you

Is your longing really your own? Take some time to look at how your desires have taken you into certain situations. What do these situations want from you? What is life longing to find through you?

To answer this question, you might also ask for dreams, or ask life directly. Instead of focusing on what YOU want, ask what life wants for and from you. Can you give yourself to the answer that comes? Look for answers to this question all around you, in your heart, and through your dreams.

Receiving
Listen

1) The next time you disagree with someone, just listen. Do not argue. Take in what the other person is saying. Notice how this listening affects you and the other person both – how does it feel in your body, how is the other person's physical stature changing as you listen?

2) The next time someone compliments you, don't explain away the compliment. (You know when you do this! For

example, when someone says, 'What a beautiful skirt you're wearing,' and you respond, 'Oh, it was on sale!') Try not to even say 'Thank you.' You might just smile, or just listen and take it in. See how this space created by not responding verbally affects you and the other person both.

3) Listen to life. For an entire month, assume life is talking to you. Life is alive after all, and you are in a relationship with it. Your consciousness has a role in how life speaks and relates to itself through you. Wake up in the morning and set an intention to listen to life. Practice listening all day. Listen through your mind, through your eyes, ears, and bodily senses, and through your heart. What is life telling you? If you practice this for a month, it can start to become a habit. It should become a way of life.

5) Listen to yourself. Take time to turn your attention inward and sense what you are telling yourself. What messages are you getting from deep within? Listen to yourself through dreams, through sensations in your body, past your mind and its chatter in your head. What are you telling yourself about who you are, how you should be in the world, the friends you have, your job, where you live? What does your inner world want you to hear?

Inflow exercise

This exercise comes from Elizabeth Frediani's book, *Where Body Meets Soul: Subtle Energy Practices for Physical and Spiritual Self-Care*.[39]

In the course of your daily activity and work you likely exert a great deal of energy. You focus on the job at hand. You complete your to-do lists and fulfill your external commitments to your children, your spouse, extended family, career, and community. Energetically speaking, you are exhaling. You are in outflow. An emphasis on expending energy, rather than receiving and conserving it, depletes you physically, mentally, emotionally, and spiritually. The antidote for energy depletion is retrieval and inflow.

Close your eyes and focus attention in your body.

Take time to notice and be aware of the energy that you give out. Give yourself time to review your day, your week. Notice what in your life has recently required a great deal of your energy.

Now, in your heart, ask your outflowing energy to gently flow back into you. If the energy flow seems uncomfortable or too strong, place your hands over your heart and that will help regulate the flow of energy.

From time to time, notice how your body feels. If your body is tense, soften your stomach area and take one or two slow, deep breaths. This will support your body in receiving the inflowing energy.

Continue this process until you feel complete (3–10 minutes).

Gently release your focus and intention. Open your eyes.

Questions to answer in your journal:

1) How do you feel physically, energetically, and emotionally?

2) Were you able to feel the inflow of your energy? If so, did it feel good, comfortable? If you were not comfortable, did placing your hands over your heart help you?

3) If you were unable to inflow your energy, were you consciously aware of any concern about doing so?

4) Write about all other feelings or experiences that you had during this practice.

Energy gain and body feedback: After completing this exercise, wait approximately 20 minutes and notice how you are feeling. If you feel a little 'top-heavy' or headachy, it means that you are not absorbing all of the energy you have gained. If this is the case, please close your eyes and ask that *excess energy* release out your tailbone into the

Earth. It is important that you say and intend that *only* excess energy release, then all the energy that you can easily utilize will remain.

2nd chakra containment

This exercise also comes from Elizabeth's book, *Where Body Meets Soul: Subtle Energy Practices for Physical and Spiritual Self-Care*.[40]

As Elizabeth explained in chapter 8, receiving energy is only helpful if we can contain this energy and use it. It does not help to take in energy and release it immediately. The 2nd chakra is critical in containing energy. Elizabeth offers an exercise for 2nd chakra containment:

The second chakra concerns itself primarily with issues of power, self-containment, nurturing, and deep connection with others. Students of both sexes can find their second chakras chronically stressed. However, women often embody one consistent conflict.

Many women will describe how much of their energy and efforts go to caring for their families and securing a relationship with their partner. These same women say that they feel weak-willed, unfulfilled, and lacking in personal power.

The second chakra activities of caring for family and focus on relationships emphasize merging and nurturing. Energetically these activities can create an outflow of energy, which can lead to minor or extreme depletion. Self-containment is also governed by the second chakra. Containment refers to the ability to hold and conserve one's energy as a source of personal power and strength. Containment requires clear boundaries and balances outflow.

If you find that you outflow too much energy and lose balance in the second chakra, I recommend that you try the following exercise:

1) Close your eyes and focus your attention in your second chakra.
2) Internally direct your energy to flow from the center of the second chakra upward to your heart chakra.
3) Hold this focus for 5–10 minutes.
4) When you are ready, release your focus and open your eyes.

During this exercise did you feel a physical sense of inner strength and containment? If you did, keep practicing this exercise. If you did not feel it, keep practicing this exercise. This exercise, along with thoughtful self-examination, will help you correct second chakra imbalances.

It is important to remember that the second chakra governs a set of complex issues – many that involve sexual roles and identities. Therefore, expression of second chakra issues varies in context from culture to culture, religion to religion., and family to family. It will be helpful for you to consider these external influences as you work with your second chakra.

Creative Space
Create space

Whether alone or with another person, look at how you fill silence or space with words, thoughts, or activity. At a time when you usually would feel crowded and busy with no space, like when you start the day first thing in the morning, or in the midst of a busy work-day, pay attention to your breath or to the silence that is present. Space is always available! You can find and enhance it through listening or sensing your body or breath. Give yourself these 'Ahhh…' moments all day long. Space is critical in receiving, so notice how you fill space as a way of not being open or receptive.

1) Sit quietly at home with no entertainment. Intend to create space. Listen, feel, sense the nature of space and what can enter and be in it.

2) In conversation with another person, notice how you use words to avoid uncomfortable spaces. Practice listening and silence to create space. When you are actively creating space, how does it change the flow of conversation?

Clean your house

Physical space and energetic space are highly interconnected. This exercise is the simple process of clearing out and cleaning up your home, office, and even car space. If you are surrounded by clutter outwardly, you will be impeded by inner clutter – thoughts, emotions, feelings. The simple act of cleaning – with awareness that you are clearing out un-useful or extra physical and energetic material – will go a long way in creating space for... (not new stuff!).

Practice silence

Silence and space are so close to each other. Space is silent and silence is spacious. Listen to the silence that exists throughout life. Even a moment of attuning your attention to silence activates the power of creative space. Silence is like a beautiful flower growing amongst high grass at the corner of the garden. It has to catch your eye, but once you notice it, all the powers of the book come together – you are connected and maybe entranced; you feel a sacredness that is present but unnoticed in all life; you know how beauty is the breath of the formless coming into the world, how we are so touched by something in life that has no explanation, and how this is what we long for.

Notice the silence. Let it talk to you. Let it create a space for life to reveal itself anew.

Women's ceremony

In chapter 9 we learned from Larry Merculieff that women have the power to create a space outside ourselves that can birth something new into the world. He has provided some key elements regarding how to do this in ceremony. Women's circles and ceremonies have been sprouting up around the world, seemingly to answer this global need for something truly new to be born into the world. Be a part of this experience!

There do not need to be firm rules to ceremony, but the intention of the ceremony does need to be present along with other elements.

1) Set the intention for the ceremony. This might be a ceremony to heal an individual, a community, or the earth. It might be a mother/daughter menstruation ceremony. It might be a celebration of the solstice or the harvest. Find a group of women and set the intention.

2) Purify and cleanse for the ceremony. Before the ceremony begins, make sure to prepare in your own individual way. This could include bathing or smudging oneself. It might include saying prayers before arriving at the ceremony. It might include asking for a dream to share at the ceremony. This is a private time of preparation, to attune to the deep intention and power of the ceremony. As the ceremony begins, smudge the participants with sage to enhance the purity of participants and ensure that nothing un-needed is brought into the ceremonial space.

3) Sit in circle at the ceremony and begin the ceremony consciously through a song, through lighting a candle, or through a group prayer. Make sure that the prayers are about giving thanks, as Larry Merculieff advised – 'Prayer is always a thank you!'

4) No cross-talk. Make sure that when the sharing takes place it is in tune with the purpose of the ceremony and that

nobody is interrupted or even responded to. There should be no cross-talk. There is no analysis or dialog. This is ceremonial sharing into the space of the circle.

5) Close the ceremony with an offering or a prayer. This might include putting something in the circle for another person or for the group itself, or it might include individual or group prayer.

6) Do not return home to television or too much activity. Allow the ceremony to infuse your evening and following days. Be open to dreams or symbols from life. Be especially attuned to life and what it brings you.

The Sacredness of Life

An important element in recognizing the sacredness of life is to understand that life's sacredness wants to be known. Just as we each travel through life wanting to be known for who we really are, sharing ourselves with others so they can know us, and expressing ourselves so that we will be seen and acknowledged, life needs to be known and seen and related to as itself. All around us life is asking us to see and relate to its sacred essence, which is expressed through so many million facets – including each one of us.

The exercises in this section depend upon seeing with fresh eyes, opening to what is present in you and around you, and being willing to leave behind what is not sacred and to make space for what is.

Clear the clutter (yes, again!)

For an entire month, commit yourself to clearing out what is not sacred in your life. Late at night and early in the day are ideal times to examine your life with the hard questions – 'How much time, energy, money, effort do I spend on things that are not sacred to me?' Examine your material world – the things you spend money on, the stuff you collect in your house – as well as your psychic world – the people you give your energy to, the work you spend most of your time at. Determine what aspects of your life have not borne fruit, what aspects seem dry of meaning, what aspects have outworn their welcome.

If possible, let them go – people, stuff, ways you spend time that really do not affirm life's sacredness. If you are in a job that is meaningless to you but you need the money, hold the situation in full consciousness. Allow your longing for something deeper and more meaningful to burn in your heart and your gut. Watch for opportunities to change. If you feel stuck in any situation that seems to have grown meaningless but you are yet unable to leave it, hold the situation in full consciousness, pray for an opportunity to move on, watch and wait for the a change to present itself.

Find the sacred in your life

Like beauty, life's sacredness is all around and within us. We can activate the power of knowing life's sacredness by acknowledging it, just as acknowledging beauty empowers and transforms. Let this exercise follow the one above; let the understanding that results from this exercise enter into the empty space you've created by the previous one.

Set aside some protected time and space to look into the nature of the things, events, and people of your life. Ask yourself and journal about:

1) What are these situations teaching me?
2) How does my heart connect with the heart of the people and situations of my life?
3) Where is the beauty in the people and situations I give myself to?
4) What makes this person or situation sacred? Can I focus on this sacred aspect and relate to it?

Exercises

Acknowledge the sacredness of food, water, air, and earth
During your day, take time to acknowledge the holiness of the elements around you.

1) When you eat, recognize that food keeps you alive, and that this is a great gift.
2) When you drink water, acknowledge how the water comes into every cell of your body and enlivens and activates your life-force.
3) When it rains outside, acknowledge the sacredness of rain – how it makes grass green and provides you drinking water, and how it nurtures the cells of the earth and cleans and purifies earth.
4) When the winds blow, ask the winds, 'What are you blowing away?' 'What are you clearing out?'
5) When a bird flies by, ask it if it needs anything from you.
6) Do not kill spiders or flies without acknowledging that they are gifts of life. If you do kill them, do so with full consciousness of what you are doing. Say a prayer as you do what you need to do.

Working with omens

Recognizing life's sacredness includes listening to life and communicating with life on an ongoing basis. What is life telling you? How do you need to respond? Only when we are intimately engaged with life will we deepen our experience of its sacredness. A way to step into this dimension is to look to life for signs and omens. This following commentary about reading the signs of life and working with omens comes from Sandra Ingerman:[41]

In indigenous traditions it is believed that everything that exists in nature is alive and interacts with us. Nature is always communicating with us and often this occurs by showing us

287

omens and signs.

Working with omens and signs shows us that we are in harmony with the flow of life. Physics uses the term 'a unified field' to describe a state of oneness. In indigenous cultures the term used is the web of life.

We are connected to one universal force and we are part of nature. When we flow with 'the river of life' the universe shows us signposts that lead us to making healthy and wise decisions. We get these signposts as we walk through both nature and an urban environment as we raise our awareness to the daily messages we are being given.

As you hold questions about what your next step in life should be if you pay attention the universe is always giving you a sign. And in spiritual traditions these signs are also called omens. This can feel like the universe is laying down breadcrumbs for us to follow.

We are being led to receive guidance in ways that are beyond our logical understanding.

As you walk in nature or even travel to work you might see the appearance of an animal whose qualities might give an answer to your question. You might notice the forms appearing in the clouds in the sky that present a metaphorical response.

You also might find yourself meeting a complete stranger and in the conversation you find yourself receiving an answer to a question or problem you have been dealing with.

Sometimes signs come in a song being sung on the radio while you are pondering a question. You might be focusing on an issue in life and a bus drives by with an advertisement posted on the side with words that hold a solution or some kind of inspiration. You might be flipping through a book and you come upon a perfect sentence or paragraph that provides you with the inspiration you need.

You might wonder if the omens you receive are an answer

to a question or a coincidence. Albert Einstein reminds us that coincidence is God's way of remaining anonymous.

In the 1980s I found myself going through a challenging time. One day I called out a prayer to the universe. I said, 'Please show me obvious signs that I can follow.'

From that day forth I have found that as long as I pay attention life gives me all the omens and signs I need to make healthy choices. Of course the key is I have to be aware and listen.

We have all had times in our lives when we reflect on a past event we realize we ignored signs we were given. We might have decided to ignore the information we were receiving or we just were not aware of the guidance given. Many of us go through life asleep and living in a trance created by so much outer stimulation in our lives.

We don't always realize that the help and guidance we need is being shown to us. We are not awake to the signs we are being given. Our minds are often too busy and distracted to notice what the universe is revealing to us for our highest good.

A good way to start your practice of watching for omens and signs is to take a walk in nature. Before your walk think about a question you have that you need guidance with. You might be considering making a choice that will impact your life. Think about this and hold the intention that you wish to be shown a sign.

As you walk allow the beauty of nature to quiet your mind. Just be observant. Take some deep breaths. Notice if you are aware of cloud formations in the sky that might provide insight for you. You might see an animal, bird, insect, etc. that has certain qualities that act as a sign. Use your imagination and just stay aware.

When you come to a decision about a change you are going to make in your life take a walk and ask for a sign of confirmation. As you focus on your new decision a breeze might come out of nowhere which feels like it is whispering 'yes' to you. A beautiful butterfly might come along and land on your hand as you imagine bringing a change into your life. You might notice that the sky is thick with clouds and when you think about a new life choice the clouds part and the sun shines. As you pass a tree while thinking about a life change all the leaves might shake in a way that feels like an affirmation. With this way of working you must trust your intuition as nature responds to you.

Be persistent and be willing to practice. You might not find yourself feeling your connection with the natural world on your first try. Keep holding your intention and taking walks.

At home, work, or school let your intuition lead you to a book on a bookshelf. Simply open to a page. Read the page and see if you were led to an important message.

Notice if you end up having synchronistic meetings with old friends or strangers where what seems like a random conversation holds great wisdom that inspires and assists you in some way.

As you do this more and more you will notice that your path ahead is being lit to show you the way. When we open our awareness to how the universe participates in our healing, growth, and evolution life takes on a deeper meaning.

Notes From and about Contributors

From Dorothy Atalla

My conviction is that the very qualities of caring that women have so long practiced in the private sphere are needed in the larger world. That kind of attention, love, and nourishment are what our earth needs as she undergoes the tremendous changes we are now witnessing.

In 1981 I entered a dialog with a beneficent feminine Presence who spoke of the re-emergence of the Feminine to restore balance on earth. That dialog is now between the covers of my recently published book, *Conversations with the Goddess: Encounter at Petra, Place of Power*. The Presence said that women would become agents of planetary transformation. In the early 1980s her words seemed radical, but today we can see evidence of the death of old ways of being all around us, and we sense that something new is trying to be born, just as she predicted. Here are her words for the future:

> Women will be given visions for building the new world. Certain women who become leaders will attain stature as visionaries equal to that of a Leonardo da Vinci. These women will be enabled to see the outlines, and even the details, of what the new collective will be. Yes, the picture of the new society will be perceived through visionary powers, just as the outlines of new societies arising throughout the history of the planet have always been perceived, though usually not described as such.
>
> These women will be in challenging positions of authority. They will hold high political offices, run corporations, establish businesses with a new ethos. In fact, in *all* of the arenas of the public sphere in which men have predominated, these key individuals will seed the possibilities of the future.
>
> There will also be those women visionaries in the various

fields which comprise the humanities in academia who will create a picture of possibilities that enliven a society. I refer to the arts and the social sciences in particular. Some of these women will hold posts of distinction in the world of higher education.

There will also be visionaries who will teach the very young. They will work with future generations to seed the possibilities of a new way of life, and these youth will set forth with these visions in their hearts and minds, to carry them forth and bring them into manifestation.

All of these changes will happen rather quickly in terms of the length of earth's history, for within the space of the next two hundred years all of which I have spoken will transpire, and the beginnings of the new world will be in place.

In the process of publicizing and promoting her book, Dorothy ('Chickee') Atalla has written online articles, been a guest on a number of radio shows, and has created several tele-seminars in which she collaborated with women leaders talking about topics important to women. She has a website, www.conversationswiththegoddess.net, as well as a Facebook page, 'Conversations with the Goddess,' where she engages in dialog with visitors.

Chickee lives with her husband, Rajai, in a country suburb on the outskirts of Madison, Wisconsin. She is the mother of two sons and grandmother to two girls.

From Elizabeth Frediani

Power can be defined, simply and purely, as the life-force that comes through living according to one's true nature. Power is the result of authenticity. It is without pretense or external condition. Power comes directly from *soul*.

Embodying our power generates a vital resonance that extends forward to our daughters and their daughters, to our sons and their sons, and reaches into the past to inform and heal our ancestors. Living our power benefits all our relations – human, animal, green, spirit, and elemental – and our beautiful earth.

Elizabeth Frediani is the author of Where Body Meets Soul: Subtle Energy Healing Practices for Physical and Spiritual Self-Care, *which explores the interrelationship between subtle energy and health, consciousness, and spirituality. Elizabeth's work in this field spans over 30 years. She lives on Whidbey Island in Washington and works in private practice and facilitates group mentorship programs. Her recent teaching projects include 'Shadows, Wisdom and Wholeness: Reclaiming Selves from the Dark' and 'Cultivating the Resources of the Heart Chakra.' Elizabeth can be reached by email: Elizabeth@elizabethfrediani.com or mail: PO Box 1634, Langley, WA 98260.*

From Sandra Ingerman

Change and creation flow from within us. An idea is planted within and then as the seed is nurtured it is born at the right time. As women we understand that life is birthed from within.

In the western mind we want outer change in the world to just appear. We forget that change and creation is part of a natural process of birth.

In spiritual traditions it is taught that all creation starts in the invisible world – the world of spirit – before manifesting in the physical realm. Our thoughts, the words we speak, imaginal dreams are all what create our outer world.

Being the dreamers of a world filled with peace, love, harmony, respect, and honor is what is needed right now. The spiritual practices we engage in are where we have power to be positive changemakers. And when we gather our spiritual energies together and join our hearts as one community dedicated to bringing universal love and divine light into our planet, the healing power is exponential. What we can do as one is greatly magnified as we work together.

We are already seeing great change and power as women join together to speak about injustices. This is wonderful to see! It is important to add to this a joined effort in holding space, anchoring the energies, and dreaming together. Let us dream a dream of beauty and equality for all of life.

Sandra Ingerman MA is the author of eight books including Soul Retrieval, Medicine for the Earth, Shamanic Journeying: A Beginner's Guide, How to Heal Toxic Thoughts, How to Thrive in Changing Times, *and* Awakening to the Spirit World: The Shamanic Path of Direct Revelation. *She also recorded five audio programs produced by Sounds True.*

Sandra teaches workshops internationally on shamanic journeying, healing, and reversing environmental pollution using spiritual methods. She has trained and founded an international alliance of Medicine for the Earth Teachers and shamanic teachers. Sandra is recognized for bridging ancient cross-cultural healing methods into our modern culture addressing the needs of our times.

Sandra is devoted to teaching people how we can work together as a global community to bring about positive change for the planet.

Sandra is a licensed Marriage and Family Therapist and Professional Mental Health Counselor. She is also a board certified expert on traumatic stress as well as certified in acute traumatic stress management. She was awarded the 2007 Peace Award from the Global Foundation for Integrative Medicine.

To read articles written by Sandra, to listen to interviews, and to get more information on Sandra's work, you can visit her website at www.sandraingerman.com. This is also the site to read Sandra's monthly column 'The Transmutation News.' The Transmutation News is now translated into thirteen languages.

To find a local shamanic practitioner or teacher in your area please visit www.shamanicteachers.com.

From Larry (Ilarion) Merculieff

Perhaps the most salient issue of our time is the restoration of women as the 'original healers'. As many indigenous prophecies indicate, 'movement into the World of the Fifth Hoop' shall be led by women. As women collectively reconnect with their own sacred power and return to ceremony, masculine imbalance will be corrected. This imbalance is at the root of thousands of years of destruction, exploitation, oppression, and violation of all that is feminine, including Mother Earth based cultures, women, and Mother Earth herself. During our lifetime we shall see the world remember why women are sacred and come to understand why women are absolutely essential to birthing something from a place of higher consciousness.

Indigenous peoples who have intimate and sustained contact with their lands and waters and who have maintained the spiritual basis for relating to everything in their environment have a profound understanding of what 'sustainability' really means. Rooted in an understanding of the sacred feminine principle, these lifeways are an important balance to western concepts of sustainability, which are generally used outside of meaningful context, limiting the depth to which we can go collectively in restoring harmony in our relationship with Mother Earth and thus the Sacred Feminine. As Earth's life-supporting systems are being pushed to the edge of viability, restoring this balance becomes ever more urgent. As an Aleut (Unungan) Traditional Messenger, Ilarion Merculieff is charged with the cultural task of carrying ancient wisdom into modern times, to sharing Indigenous elder wisdom and the messages from Indigenous spiritual leaders with the world.

From Sobonfu Somé

Sobonfu Somé is a respected lecturer, activist and author. She is the founder of Wisdom Spring, Inc., an organization dedicated to the preservation and sharing of indigenous wisdom which fundraises for wells, schools and health projects in Africa. She is one of the foremost voices of African spirituality to come to the West, bringing insights and healing gifts from her West African culture to this one. Sobonfu often tours the United States and Europe teaching workshops. Her books include The Spirit of Intimacy: Ancient Teachings in the Ways of Relationships, Welcoming Spirit Home: Ancient Teachings to Celebrate Children and Community *and* Falling out of Grace: Meditations on Loss, Healing and Wisdom. *She is also the author of* Women's Wisdom from the Heart of Africa, *a set of six CDs. For more information about Sobonfu's projects and teaching schedule please visit: www.Sobonfu.com, www.walkingforwater.org or www.wisdomspring.org. Sobonfu Somé can be reached at: Sobonfu@aol.com.*

From Dr. Guan-Cheng Sun

Creativity, vital energy and new life are outcomes of the interactions of yin and yang. Yin has its root in yang. Without yin, yang cannot arise. Yang alone cannot grow. The balance and harmony of yin and yang are the key for personal health and growth and collective wellbeing. Women not only possess the nature of yin, the power of the feminine, but also the source of nourishment, caring, and the wisdom of intuition. Women also have natural cleansing ability and healing power within. To recognize, encourage, and support the development of the unique nature of women will greatly nourish the spirit of women and benefit the betterment and transformation of humanity. Respecting, honoring, and appreciating women's nature and wisdom are essential to developing a healthy, happy and vital society.

Guan-Cheng Sun PhD is the founder of the Institute of Qigong & Integrative Medicine (http://www.iqim.org/). Dr. Sun earned his PhD in molecular genetics from the Graduate University for Advanced Studies in Japan in 1993 and was awarded a fellowship from the Japan Society for the Promotion of Science. From 1994 to 1997 Dr. Sun conducted postdoctoral research in molecular endocrinology at the University of Washington. This research enriched his theory and practice of Chi Gong. His understanding of modern molecular genetics and scientific principles, as well as his experience with internal culti-

vation, allowed him to create a unique bridge between cultures. Dr. Sun has spent over 30 years refining his skills and has developed a new system of Chi Gong called 'Yi Ren® Qigong.' The way of Yi Ren Qigong practice is to refine internal qi/energy, promote health; increase awareness of consciousness, understand the Way of Xuan; realize the authentic self, accumulate virtues; and contribute to the betterment of humanity. He is currently engaged in medical qigong, mind-body medicine, and energy medicine research at Bastyr University, Kenmore, Washington (http://www.bastyr.edu/).

From Llewellyn Vaughan-Lee

Women are the matrix of creation and hold the seeds for the healing and transformation of the world that is so desperately needed at this time. We need to regain the wisdom and power of the feminine, her deep knowledge and understanding of the rhythms of creation and its sacred nature. Without her presence and participation nothing new can be born, and we will be left with the soulless wasteland of our present global materialistic culture. If women can regain their own sacred power and deep knowing, we can begin the vital work of healing and transformation, the work of redeeming the soul of the world.

Llewellyn Vaughan-Lee PhD is a Sufi Teacher in the Naqshbandiyya-Mujadidiyya Sufi Order. Born in London in 1953, he has followed the Naqshbandi Sufi path since he was 19. In 1991 he moved to Northern California and became the successor of Irina Tweedie, author of Daughter of Fire. *He has specialized in the area of dreamwork, integrating the ancient Sufi approach to dreams with the insights of modern psychology. In recent years the focus of his writing and teaching has been on spiritual responsibility in our present time of transition, and the emerging global consciousness of oneness (www.workingwithoneness.org). He has also written about the feminine, the Anima Mundi (world soul) and spiritual ecology. Llewellyn is married with two children and is the founder of The Golden Sufi Center (www.goldnesufi.org) and author of several books, including* Sufism: The Transformation of the Heart, The Return of the Feminine and the World Soul, *the autobiographical* Fragments of a Love Story: Reflections on the Life of a Mystic, *and the inter-spiritual book*, Prayer of the Heart in Christian and Sufi Mysticism. *He lectures throughout the United States and Europe.*

From Pamela Wilson

Women are all Heart! Resilience, Giving and Compassion itself. Gathering together, we invite each other to bloom out of the known and habitual into our deepest strength and clarity, so we may offer the world balance, discernment and true rest.

Pamela's website is www.pamelasatsang.com.

Endnotes

1. Lady Nijo, *The Confessions of Lady Nijo*, trans. Karen Brazell (Stanford, CA: Stanford University Press, 1973), 221.

2. Mata Amritanandamayi Devi, 'The Awakening of Universal Motherhood' (address given at the Global Peace Initiative of Women Religious and Spiritual Leaders conference, Palais des Nations, UN, Geneva, 7 October 2002).

3. Taittiriya Upanishad 3.10.5–6, quoted in John Mabry, *People of Faith: A Companion to the Revised Common Lectionary* (Hants, UK: O-Books, 2009), 120.

4. Hildegard of Bingen, quoted in Heinrich Schipperges, *Hildegard of Bingen: Healing and the Nature of the Cosmos* (Princeton, NJ: Markus Wiener Publishers, 1997), 81.

5. Hildegard of Bingen, *Meditations with Hildegard of Bingen*, edited by Gabriele Uhlein (Santa Fe, NM: Bear & Co., 1983), 59.

6. Mother Teresa quoted by Edward W. Desmond in 'Interview with Mother Teresa: A Pencil in the Hand of God,' *Time Magazine*, 4 December1989.

7. M.K. Ghandi, *From Yeravda Mandir* (Ashram Observances), trans. Vaiji Gofindjii Desai (Ahemadabad – 380014 India: Jitendra T. Desai, Navajivan Mudranalaya, copyright Navajivan Trust, 1932) 'Ahimsa or Love,' http://www.mkgandhi.org/yeravda/chap02.htm.

8. Mirabai, 'Mira the Barterer,' from *Mirabai Ecstatic Poems*, trans. Robert Bly and Jane Hirshfield (Boston: Beacon Press, 2004), 58.

9. Bhai Sahib, quoted in Irina Tweedie, *Daughter of Fire* (Inverness, CA: The Golden Sufi Center Publishing 1986), 497.

10. Camille Paglia, *Sexual Personae: Art and Decadence from Nefertiti to Emily Dickinson*, First Edition (New York: Vintage Books, 1991), 11.

11. Bhai Sahib, quoted in Irina Tweedie, *Daughter of Fire* (Inverness, CA: The Golden Sufi Center Publishing, 1986), 634–635.

12. Ibid, 497.

13. Gyalwa Dendun Drub, first Dalai Lama, 'A Gem to Increase Life and Wisdom Praise of White Tara,' trans. Glenn Mullen from *Selected Works of the Dalai Lama 1: Bridging the Sutras and Tantras* (Ithaca, NY: Snow Lion Publications, 1985), 194–197.

14. Rachel Carson and Nick Kelsh, *The Sense of Wonder* (New York: HarperCollins, 1956), 100.

15. Gioia Timpanelli, *Sometimes the Soul: Two Novellas of Sicily* (New York: WW Norton & Co. Inc., 1998), 150.

16. Peire Vidal, *Plus que l. paubres quan jaia el ric ostal*, trans. and selected by A.S. Kline, 'From Dawn to Dawn – Troubadour Poetry,' http://www.poetryintranslation.com/PITBR/French/FromDawnToDawn.htm.

17. Arnaut Daniel de Riberac, *En c'est sonnet coind'e leri*, trans. and selected by A.S. Kline, 'From Dawn to Dawn – Troubadour Poetry,' http://www.poetryintranslation.com/PITBR/French/FromDawntoDawn.htm.

18. 'Beautiful You Are, Our Lady' Part II, a talk by Medjugorje Visionary Marija, 10 August 2009, http://www. medjug orje.com/medjugorje-today/medjugorje-witness/678-beautiful-you-are-our-lady-part-2.html.

19. Ibn Arabi quoted in Laleh Bakhtiar, *Sufi Expressions of the Mystic Quest* (London: Thames & Hudson, 2004), 21.

20. Hafiz, quoted by J. Nurbakhsh, *Sufi Symbolism Volume 1* (London: Khaniqahi-Nimatullah Publications, 1984), 23.

21. Jalalludin Rumi, *Rumi, Fragments, Ecstasies*, trans. Daniel Liebert (Santa Fe: Source Books, 1981), 14.

22. Shaykh Muhammand Hisham Kabbani, *Angels Unveiled: A Sufi Perspective* (Chicago: Kazi Publications, 1995) 99-100.

23. Ibid, 100–101.

24. 'The Night Chant' in Neil Philip's *In a Sacred Manner I Live:*

Native American Wisdom (New York: Houghton Mifflin Company 1997), 19.

25. Mother Teresa, *Where There is Love, There is God* (New York: Doubleday Religion, an imprint of Crown Publishing, 2010), 86.

26. Quoted by Kristian Hvidt in *Von Reck's Voyage: Drawings and Journal of Philip Georg Friedrich von Reck* (Savannah: Beehive Press, 1990), 47.

27. Roger L. Nichols, *The American Indian: Past and Present* (New York: Alfred A. Knopf, 1986), 201.

28. Rainer Maria Rilke, *Letters to a Young Poet*, trans. Mark Harman (Cambridge, MA: Harvard University Press, 2011), 38.

29. Mechtilde of Magdeburg, edited by Sue Woodruff in *Meditations with Mechtilde of Magdeburg* (Santa Fe: Bear & Co. Inc., 1982), 59.

30. From Emmylou Harris's 'Prayer in Open D' from her album *Cowgirl's Prayer*, Elektra, 1993.

31. Attar in *The Ocean of the Soul: Man, the World, and God in the Stories of Farid al-Din Attar*, trans. Hellmut Ritter (Leuden, the Netherlands, Konikklijke Brill NV, 2003), 262.

32. Sylvia Plath, *The Bell Jar* (New York: Harper & Row Publishers, Inc.), 97.

33. Encyclopedia of Religion and Ethics, vol. VIII, 'Life and Death – Mulla,' ed. James Hastings (New York: Charles Scribner's Sons, 1916), 849.

34. Cheyenne song, quoted in T.C. McLuhan, *Way of the Earth* (New York: Touchstone, 1995), 465.

35. Hafiz, 'No More Leaving' in *The Gift: Poems by Hafiz the Great Sufi Master*, trans. Daniel Ladinsky (Middlesex, UK: Penguin, 1999), 258.

36. Elizabeth Frediani, *Where Body Meets Soul: Subtle Energy Healing Practices for Physical and Spiritual Self-Care* (Langley, WA: Spring Mountain Publishing Alliance, 2008), 41–43.

37. From Elizabeth Frediani's 'Transmutation Points Newsletter,' April 2012.

38. © 2011 The Golden Sufi Center. See: http://www.huffingtonpost.com/llewellyn-vaughanlee/prayer-and-nature_b_921007.html or: http://www.workingwithoneness.org/articles/praying-earth.

39. Elizabeth Frediani, *Where Body Meets Soul: Subtle Energy Healing Practices for Physical and Spiritual Self-Care* (Langley, WA: Spring Mountain Publishing Alliance, 2008), 45–46.

40. Ibid, 107–108.

41. See Sandra Ingerman's April 2012 blog, *How to Work with Omens*: http://redroom.com/member/sandra-f-ingerman/blog/how-to-work-with-omens.

Acknowledgments

I express my sincere gratitude to the following individuals and organizations for granting permission to use their work in this book.

A.S. Kline for the use of his translations of Troubadour poetry by Peire Vidal and Arnaut Daniel de Riberac available at: http://www.poetryintranslation.com/PITBR/French/FromDawnT oDawn.htm.

Daniel Ladinsky for the use of his translation of Hafiz's poem, 'No More Leaving,' from the Penguin publication of *The Gift: Poems by Hafiz the Great Sufi Master* © 1999 Daniel Ladinsky and used with his permission.

Shaykh Hisham Muhammad Kabbani and the Islamic Supreme Council of America for the use of excerpts from *Angels Unveiled: A Sufi Perspective* (Kazi Publications), 1995.

Glenn Mullin for the use of his translation of the first Dalai Lama's 'Praise to White Tara: A Gem to Increase Life and Wisdom' from Snow Lion's publication of *Selected Works of the Dalai Lama 1: Bridging the Sutras and Tantras*, 1981.

The Golden Sufi Center for use of excerpts from the writings of Llewellyn Vaughan-Lee and excerpts from *Daughter of Fire* by Irina Tweedie, 1986.

Bear & Company, for use of excerpts from *Meditations with Hildegard of Bingen* edited by Gabrielle Uhlein, published by Bear & Company, a division of Inner Traditions International (1983). All rights reserved www.Innertraditions.com. Reprinted with permission of publisher.

For use of the poem 'Mira the Barterer' from *Mirabai: Ecstatic Poems* © Robert Bly and Jane Hirshfield, reprinted by permission of Beacon Press, Boston.

About the Author

Hilary Hart is a writer and teacher focusing on women's spirituality and its role in collective evolution. Her previous books include *The Unknown She: Eight Faces of an Emerging Consciousness* (Golden Sufi Center Publishing 2003) and *Pearlie of Great Price: Following a Dog into the Presence of God* (O-Books 2007). In 2010, she founded *Women's Power Wheel*, a network of women's circles designed to help women uncover and use their power for global change. Originally from New England, Hilary studied Philosophy at Yale University and the University of Colorado before turning her attention to the traditional spiritual search. She has extensive experience in Tibetan Buddhism and Sufism, and currently works as a children's advocate in Taos, New Mexico. For more information, please visit: www.hilaryhart.org and www.womenspowerwheel.com. To contact Hilary, email hh@hilaryhart.org.

BOOKS

O is a symbol of the world, of oneness and unity. In different cultures it also means the "eye," symbolizing knowledge and insight. We aim to publish books that are accessible, constructive and that challenge accepted opinion, both that of academia and the "moral majority."

Our books are available in all good English language bookstores worldwide. If you don't see the book on the shelves ask the bookstore to order it for you, quoting the ISBN number and title. Alternatively you can order online (all major online retail sites carry our titles) or contact the distributor in the relevant country, listed on the copyright page.

See our website **www.o-books.net** for a full list of over 500 titles, growing by 100 a year.

And tune in to myspiritradio.com for our book review radio show, hosted by June-Elleni Laine, where you can listen to the authors discussing their books.

MySpiritRadio